PRAISE FC

"The latest queen of erotic literature."

—The Sunday Times

"Malpas's writing is spot-on with emotions."

—RT Book Reviews

"A brave, cutting-edge romance."

—Library Journal on *The Forbidden*

"Unpredictable and addictive."

—Booklist on *The Forbidden*

"Super steamy and emotionally intense."

—Library Journal on *With This Man*

"Jodi Ellen Malpas delivers a new heart-wrenching, addicting read."

—RT Book Reviews on *With This Man*

"Malpas's sexy love scenes scorch the page, and her sensitive, multilayered hero and heroine will easily capture readers' hearts. A taut plot and a first-rate lineup of supporting characters make this a keeper."

—Publishers Weekly on *Gentleman Sinner*

"A magnetic mutual attraction, a superalpha, and long-buried scars that are healed by love. Theo is irresistible."

—Booklist on *Gentleman Sinner*

The
Surrender

OTHER TITLES BY JODI ELLEN MALPAS

The This Man Series

This Man
Beneath This Man
This Man Confessed
All I Am—Drew's Story (A This Man Novella)
With This Man

The One Night Series

One Night—Promised
One Night—Denied
One Night—Unveiled

Stand-Alone Novels

The Protector
The Forbidden
Gentleman Sinner
Perfect Chaos
Leave Me Breathless
For You

The
Surrender

JODI ELLEN
MALPAS

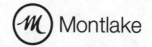

Text copyright © 2025 by Jodi Ellen Malpas Ltd
All rights reserved.

Published by Montlake, Seattle

www.apub.com

Amazon, the Amazon logo, and Montlake are trademarks of Amazon.com, Inc., or its affiliates.

EU product safety contact:
Amazon Media EU S. à r.l.
38, avenue John F. Kennedy, L-1855 Luxembourg
amazonpublishing-gpsr@amazon.com

ISBN-13: 9781662530180 (paperback)
ISBN-13: 9781662530197 (digital)

Cover design by Hang Le
Cover image: © pot_pixel, © janniwet / Shutterstock

Printed in the United States of America

For Valeria Sykes, the woman who single-handedly sparked the idea for Arlington Hall. Thank you.

Chapter 1

It's the perfect day for a wedding—fierce sunshine, a light breeze, the temperature on the warmer side of cool. The balcony off the ballroom at Café Royal is set up beautifully, flowers spilling over the sides of tall vases dotted between the outdoor furniture and pyramid patio heaters. Regent Street is bustling down below, this little canopied secret spot secluded and out of the way.

Which is why I'm here now.

I just needed to escape the chaos of Clark and Rachel's wedding day for a moment. Various members of the bridal party are stressing out over flowers, dresses, hair, and makeup. And the fact they're running a few minutes behind schedule. I feel like an empty vessel of a woman standing in the middle of the madness. Lost. Not hearing. Not seeing.

But feeling.

My heart turns in my chest again, as it has constantly this past week, my eyes closing briefly to blink away the relentless reminders of him. Reminders of us.

On a deep breath, I approach the edge of the balcony, looking down onto the crowds of London. Scooters weave around red double-decker buses and black cabs, horns honk, bells on bicycles ding. It's chaos. A lot like my thoughts.

Lowering to a nearby rattan couch, I turn my phone in my hand as it notifies me of another message. I shouldn't read it. And yet my eyes drop to the screen.

Amelia, I'm begging you. Please, I need to see you.

I swallow down the lump in my throat and delete it, sending his worthless words to the trash along with every other message and email he's sent. I try so hard to find the fixed smile I've worn this past week before I return to the celebrations, but my shattered heart is far from done hurting. Everything is an effort. My only saving grace is that everyone is so wrapped up in the day, my distraction isn't being noticed.

My phone clutched tightly in my hand, I get up and step back into the ballroom, gazing around. It's stunning when it's an empty room. Now, with rows of gold chairs lined up, two enormous vases at the end of the aisle bursting with blush roses, and candles lighting the way, it's beyond that.

"Oh, thank God, I've found you."

I whirl around and find Clark pacing towards me. "Hey." I smile and motion to the masterpiece of a ballroom. "Doesn't it look incredible?"

"Wonderful." He frowns and gives the space way less admiration than it deserves. "I've lost the cake. My one job was to get the cake here, and it's missing." He takes my hand and squeezes, crushing my phone in my grasp. "Please help me find the cake."

"The cake is safe and sound." I flex my hand, encouraging him to release me. "The wedding planner had the kitchen staff move it to the fridge to keep it cool."

Clark deflates before my eyes. "Christ." His cheeks puff out, the back of his hand wiping his brow. Then he smiles. "You look lovely." He steps back and takes me in. "This colour suits you."

I gaze down my front to the floor-length chiffon skirt and matching bandeau top, just an inch of my midriff exposed. "Thanks."

"Teal."

I freeze, jarred, my eyes still cast down. "What?"

"It's teal," he says. "The colour of your dress."

"Sure. It's teal."

"Actually, it's more muted. Like the sea. You know, when you're not sure if it's blue or green."

Jude's eyes.

"Seafoam," I murmur.

"Yes, that's it!" Clark sings, as if the colour of my dress is something to celebrate. I suddenly want to rip it off my body. And since when has my brother been so observant? "Fuck, I'm nervous." He starts twiddling his thumbs and looking around the ballroom before checking his watch. "Fuck, fuck, fuck."

His anxiety is the distraction I need, to be able to focus on someone else's worries. "Hey," I say, trying to get my head on straight. "You've got this." I link my arm through his and start to lead him out of the ballroom. "We need to vacate; your guests will be directed in from the bar shortly."

"Why haven't I had a drink?" he asks. "I need a drink."

"Let's get you a drink." I could do with one myself too, so I take Clark to the bar on the bottom floor rather than the bar where all the guests are congregating and drinking cocktails. I order two dirty martinis and sit my beloved little brother on a stool, putting a drink in his hand when the barman slides them across to me. Clark frowns at my choice but doesn't question it, knocking the olive aside and tipping the drink back. "Jesus, Clark, you're supposed to sip."

He gasps and sets the glass down. "I feel better already." He pops the olive in his mouth and sighs. "Is she nervous?" he asks. "Even a bit?"

I smile, *sipping* my martini. This is what I should be consumed by. My brother's wedding day. "She has butterflies, her words."

"Rachel doesn't get nervous."

He's right, come to think of it. In the seven years they've been together, I've never seen her flustered or awkward. She just gets on with things. It was a novelty to see her a little apprehensive.

"Can I tell you a secret?" Clark checks the vicinity before leaning in closer. "You can't tell a soul."

My eyebrows rise over my glass. "What?"

3

His lips press together briefly. "We're pregnant."

I cough over my sip. "Fuck."

"I know!"

"Oh my God, Clark, that's amazing." My glass lands on the bar with a loud clink, and I haul him in for a hug. "Congratulations." Then I quickly push him away, scowling. "I knew there was something afoot when I walked into the bathroom and Rachel pulled a hand towel off the rack to cover herself. How far gone is she?"

He chuckles. "Only a few weeks. She's not even showing. She's just paranoid she won't get into her dress. And you know Dad. She's worried he'll think less of her."

I snort. "She doesn't need to worry about that when I'm around to continuously disappoint him."

My brother's face softens, and he takes my hands, squeezing. "How are you doing?"

"You mean because you're a total shitbag and neglected to tell my ex he's been uninvited to your wedding?"

He winces. "I couldn't do it."

I can't be too pissy with Clark. I couldn't do it either. Or, more like, I just didn't have the energy to spare. So I will be spending my day avoiding Nick. "Don't worry," I say over a tired exhale. "It's not like you didn't have other things on your mind."

"Correct. As do you, obviously, and it isn't the fact that Nick's here today. You're not alright."

"Okay, let's not do this today."

"No, we *will* do this today, and you have to listen to me because it's *my* day."

"You look very handsome."

"Thanks." Clark peeks down his front and grins. Then scowls, returning his attention to me when he's figured out my strategy. "Jude turned up at our flat again this morning."

I shrink, feeling the walls closing in. "On your wedding day?"

"He didn't know it was my wedding day until he saw my suit hanging on the hook in the hallway and I explained."

"So now he knows."

"Yes."

"Therefore he'll back off and let me be with my family." Stop texting? Stop calling? Stop trying to reach me through my friends and loved ones? No, he won't, as demonstrated with his latest message. I don't know what he intends to say if I give him the grace of my time. Regardless, I don't want to hear it.

"Amelia, I—"

"Not today." I stand, releasing myself from his hold. Not *any* day. Clark doesn't know the circumstances of my and Jude's demise. Charley and Abbie do, but that's only because I turned up at Abbie's soaked to the bone, barefoot, and crying rivers. She was straight on the phone to Charley. Not to FaceTime, but to tell her to get her arse there immediately, which she did. I then sobbed my way through the whole hideous, embarrassing story while they fed me wine and gasped their disgust. I can't tell my family. I feel like a big enough fool without them knowing I was taken for a complete mug. "Today is about you."

Clark sighs. "I just don't get how you went from seriously besotted to . . . nothing."

"I never said I was besotted."

His expression is full of impatience. "You were seeing a lot of him, Amelia. You told Mum and Dad you were seeing him too. Then the next day you're suddenly not? What happened? Did he do something? Because the crap you fed Mum and Dad about him being a bit too keen was utter bullshit, and you know it. You were keen too. I saw it in you, and now it's like you hate him."

I do.

I stare at my brother, at a loss. *Let's get deeper.* "In other news, I've found an apartment. And Dad starts his golf lessons next week."

Clark sighs louder and harder as my phone rings in my hand. I reject the call, irritated, and his eyebrows shoot up. "Him?"

"No." I slap on a smile. "I've got to get back to the suite."

"There you are!" Abbie hurries in, holding up the bottom of her blush gown. "The guests are being shown into the ballroom."

"Fuck." Clark becomes all nervous again, scanning the top shelf behind the bar.

"No," I say, linking arms with him. "You'll be swaying as your bride glides to you."

Abbie chuckles and takes Clark's other arm, and we start to walk him out of the bar. She peeks across my brother to me, her dark hair piled high, loose locks cascading down sporadically here and there. She looks lovely. I put my hair up too, until I saw the disappointment on Rachel's face. It's now free and wavy, spilling over my shoulders, a small gold jewelled clip keeping one side back.

"That colour looks lovely on you," Abbie muses.

My smile is tight. "Thank you."

"Teal," Clark mumbles, distracted by his nerves.

"It's slightly paler than teal," Abbie declares. "Like—"

"Seafoam," Clark adds.

"Yes, seafoam!"

Jesus Christ. "I better get back to Rachel." I hand my brother over to Abbie. "Can you make sure he gets to the ballroom?"

"Just give me a minute," Abbie says to Clark. Then she claims me and pulls me to one side. Clark eyes us suspiciously. I shrug. "Jude showed up at my flat as I was leaving."

I breathe out my exasperation. "Was that before or after he showed up at Clark's?"

"Oh?"

I want to ask what was said, but I won't. I can guarantee it involved the cold shoulder from Abbie.

"I know everything," Clark says as he moves in, playfully shoulder-barging Abbie.

I laugh under my breath. How wrong he is. "Look, guys, I'm sorry he's bothering y—"

"There you all are!" Charley hurries in, her wild strawberry-blond curls looking like a bouncing cape fanned out behind her. I dread to think how long it took her to do her hair. It's incredible, though, and her sickeningly tight body—post two children—encased in a silver satin wrap dress is seriously banging. "The minister is asking for you, Clark. And Rachel is stressing about where *you* are." Charley nods at me. "That colour on you!"

Someone get this fucking dress off me. "I'm going," I say, leaving them to get Clark where he needs to be.

"Wait." Charley chases at my heels, stopping me at the door. "Lloyd said Jude stopped by."

"Oh my God," I yell, stressed, frustrated, angry, and every emotion in between. I give each of them a moment of my eyes. "It's Rachel and Clark's wedding day, so can we get on with it?"

All looking wary, they retreat, and I nod, happy, hitching up my skirt and leaving them, wishing I could take my own advice and get on with it.

Get on with my life.

Chapter 2

It was such a beautiful service. A stunning meal. Wonderful speeches. Alcohol on tap, although I've been very cautious with what passes my lips. Alcohol makes me weak, and as I've found another five missed calls and two more texts since I last checked my phone, I can't be weak.

If medals for avoiding eye contact were a thing, I'd get the gold. I've managed to evade Nick's gaze all day, and that's an achievement since he sat directly opposite me throughout dinner. As soon as coffee and petits fours were served after dessert, I was up and out of there, heading onto the balcony to get some air, along with a dozen or so smokers.

Abbie and Charley join me, both with reluctant smiles. "That was beautiful," Abbie says, dropping down on the rattan couch next to me. "I'm full to the brim!"

"Me too," Charley moans, rubbing her tummy. "Lloyd's taken the kids to your parents' room for a nap. I might join them."

I chuckle and reach for the same glass of wine I've been sipping throughout dinner. "Did you see the cake?"

"Yeah." Abbie frowns. "Why does it look like the Leaning Tower of Pisa?"

"The chef's mislaid the cake stand. I don't think anyone's noticed."

"How long before Rachel starts popping out babies?" Charley asks, making my glass falter on its way to my lips.

"I don't think it'll be long."

Mum and Dad wander out onto the balcony, throwing smiles everywhere as they head our way. Mum's eyes are still puffy. She's spent most of the day weeping, along with Grandma. "You two okay?" I ask.

"Yes, darling, Grandma and Grandpa have gone to lie down for a while. It's the noise, you see, and the band are about to start."

"Oh, the band." Charley hops up, suddenly full of beans. "I haven't had a good dance since we got shamelessly drunk in Amazonico and forgot to pay our bill." She chuckles, I wince, and Abbie hisses her disapproval. "Fuck," Charley blurts. "I'm sorry, that was insensitive."

"It's fine," I assure her.

"What was insensitive?" Dad asks, reminding all three of us that we're not alone.

"Nothing," I sing, jumping up and kissing his cheek. "You look very dapper today, Dad."

"Doesn't he?" Mum gushes. "Come, come, it's the first dance." She shoves Dad back into the ballroom, and we all follow to watch the happy couple take to the floor.

I spot Grandma with Grandpa and hurry over. "You two oldies are supposed to be having nanna naps."

Grandma expresses nothing but sheer disgust. "I'll smack that arse of yours, Grand Girl," she warns. "You think I'd miss the first dance?" She grabs my arm, pulling me close. "You've lost your sparkle," she says, making my smile fall. "Where's it gone, Grand Girl?"

I soften in her hold. "I've just misplaced it for a while, Grandma."

"What happened?"

"It just didn't work out." The lump in my throat I've managed to keep under control starts rising.

"Love hurts, Amelia Gracie Lazenby." She takes me in a squishy hug.

"I don't love him," I whisper.

"Oh, you silly, *silly* girl." Breaking away, she takes my cheeks, getting her nose close to mine. Her old eyes shine knowingly. "The best kind of love hurts the most."

"Clark and Rachel are on the floor," I whisper, my voice noticeably broken. I can't talk about him.

"So they are," she murmurs, hooking her arm through mine and turning us to face the floor, just as Mazzy Star's "Fade Into You" starts and Clark swoops Rachel into his hold. My bottom lip wobbles. He looks so happy, and no one can deny Rachel is perfect for him. She catches my eye as Clark twirls her, and I smile through my emotions as she puts a finger discreetly to her lips. Clark's told her I know about the baby. My mum will be on cloud nine when they decide to break the news.

I find Grandpa on my right and pull him close, replacing my arm through Grandma's with his. "I just need to use the ladies'," I say, leaving them, but I don't go to the ladies'. I take a fresh drink off the bar and head outside, hoping the cooling air will clear the glaze in my eyes.

Avoiding the gathering of smokers at the far corner, I take a moment before I'm undoubtedly discovered hiding. I underestimated how hard today would be. Keeping my game face on, trying not to let my heartbreak show. How I wish my family had never found out about Jude.

I sigh, glancing over my shoulder.

And freeze when I see Nick through the smattering of guests who've stepped out onto the balcony too. "Shit," I whisper, moving myself between one of the tall pyramid lanterns and the edge of the balcony so he can't see me.

My position gives me direct sight down onto Regent Street, and I nearly stop breathing when I see a man standing on the pavement across the road, his head tilted back to see up to the balcony, people dodging his static form. My stomach drops into my gold heels as I take him in, unable to look away. Messages and calls are easy to ignore. But when he's within sight? He's tired, I can see it even from up here. But despite that, he's still too stunning for words. And I hate him for that too. His white shirt is tucked into grey trousers, his sleeves folded neatly to his elbows, the knot of his tie perfect.

I meet his eyes, and once they lock, I can't tear them away, no matter how hard I try. No matter how much I know I should. He lifts his phone to his ear, and mine starts ringing from the satin purse dangling from my wrist. On autopilot, I knock back the drink in my hand, parched, and set the glass on the ledge before getting my mobile out. I know I shouldn't take this call. Everything is screaming at me to reject it. Reject *him*. And yet I still swipe the green icon and press my mobile to my ear.

The sound of the street below becomes amplified down the line. "Come to me, Amelia," he says, his voice strong. Commanding. It's the kind of tone I should scoff at. The kind of demand I should rebuff with a plain *fuck off.* "Don't make me come up there."

I take a breath, feeling every muscle engaging. Tightening. To keep me here, or to take me to him? Jude hangs up first, leaving that threat hanging.

Stop.

Don't go.

But that's the power of Jude Harrison.

I tuck my phone away and dip out from behind the lantern, and the second I do, Nick spots me. He smiles mildly, coming my way, and I start to shake my head, warning him off. I take no pleasure from the hurt that dilutes his expression as he halts. "Your dad said you're not seeing that guy anymore."

I pick up my feet. "I can't, Nick." I pass him, trying to keep my cool. Today is not the day to lose it, not with Nick *or* my father.

"Amelia, please."

Skirting around the edge of the room, I follow my feet to the stairs that'll get me to the lobby. Or am I following my heart? *No.* I stop at the top of the stairs, taking the rail. Then turn around and take a few steps back towards the wedding. My teeth grit. I feel like I'm being pulled in two directions, but I need answers. *Deserve* some answers.

"God damn it," I say, a little too loudly, pivoting and taking the stairs down to the lobby, my feet fast. My heart is out of control, pumping hard, but it's leading me to him.

You were a bet.

I stop abruptly, trying to catch my breath, feeling panicked. My head and my heart are at war; I'm cursing constantly, fighting to ignore my heart and listen to my head.

"Are you okay there, madam?"

A suited man appears beside me. The concierge. "Yes, thank you." I divert to the elevator and press the button. I need to go to my room and regroup. Find some strength and resistance. The elevator dings, the doors open, and I stare at the empty cart. *Just get in. Get in and let it carry me away.*

As I look back over my shoulder to the revolving doors that lead out onto the street, my lip begins to wobble. But I still turn away from the elevator. The elevator doors start to close without me in it, and my feet move without me telling them to, carrying me towards the source of my distress and heartache.

Pushing my way round the ornate revolving door, I find Jude waiting for me immediately outside. He was coming to find me.

My heart turns, my throat closes. His chest visibly deflates from his exhale of relief, his eyes dull, and I wait for his words while we stand in the middle of the pavement, in everyone's way. Except he doesn't speak. He just holds my eyes, his face expressionless.

A car pulls up to the kerb. A Rolls-Royce. Jude steps towards it and opens the door, then stands back, waiting. I look at him. See his jaw tighten and his Adam's apple protrude from his swallow. "Get in," he orders, his tone flat but radiating authority.

I shouldn't even be here on the street. I definitely shouldn't put myself in his car.

But against my better judgment, I step forward and hitch up my skirt, climbing in. Humphrey's in the driver's seat, and I catch his eye in the rearview mirror. He nods mildly as I settle in the soft leather seat, Jude climbing in behind me. The armrest isn't down, so I fix that, putting a pathetic barrier between us as Jude watches out the corner of his eye.

As soon as the door closes, Humphrey pulls away and Jude reaches for the button that raises the panel, giving us privacy.

What am I doing?

Even now, with half a metre between us and a ton of hurt and anger, I can feel the chemistry sizzling. And it fucks me off. My unstoppable reaction to him *really* fucks me off. Braving facing him, I take in his stunning profile. "I'm only here for some answers." I sound confident but feel far from it.

"Sure you are," he replies, not even looking at me.

"Don't be an arsehole, Jude. You used me in a sick game you play with the married woman you're fucking."

His jaw rolls, and his nostrils flare.

"Were you still fucking her?" *Is he still fucking her now?*

"No, Amelia, I was *not* fucking her."

Whether I believe him isn't something I can devote any time to right now. "If I was a bet, why didn't you just try to pick me up that night?"

Sad truth is, I was so intoxicated, fresh off the back of a breakup, I probably would have done something reckless like sleep with a stranger.

Jude remains quiet, and my patience continues to fray.

"Katherine was right. You like the thrill of the chase. The game." He likes dazzling women and stretching out the seduction, bending them, making them fold under his power until they beg him to blow their world apart.

"At first, yes." He finally faces me. Faces the mess he's made of me, because make no mistake, I'm a fucking mess, and no amount of makeup, hair spray, and a fancy outfit can disguise that. His jaw tics, a sign of his temper flaring. He's glaring at me like this is all somehow my fault. "Yes, you were a bet, but then I got an unhealthy dose of obsession, and the game wasn't so much fun anymore."

"You poor thing," I say tightly, making his eyes darken to the shade I know so well. Teal. Not muted or soft, but dark, the perfect blend of green and blue. The perfect shade of angry. "So the voucher for the spa day—you had that sent to Abbie?" His brother's reaction comes back to me. How surprised he was that Arlington Hall was offering discount spa days.

"I did," he confirms.

"And the conference?"

He inhales. "Anouska's boyfriend manages the Hilton on Park Lane."

"Jesus," I breathe over a laugh, breaking our eye contact. "What about the partners' gathering I was invited to at Evelyn's?"

"I had nothing to do with that."

"Oh, how good of you." I jump in my seat when he smashes his balled fist down onto the armrest between us. Why the hell is he so angry? Stalking me, finally getting me where he wants me, and now he's all het up and aggressive? This was a waste of my time. I've got my answers.

He's a whore, and I'm an idiot.

"If being a first-class wanker was a sport, you'd be the fucking champion, Jude Harrison."

"And if denial was, you'd win that one, Amelia." He turns his eyes my way, and I withdraw, hurt, as his gaze falls to my lips.

Just as Enigma's "Sadeness" filters through all the speakers.

I laugh in disbelief under my breath, outraged, but the swirling fury immediately starts mixing with something else entirely different. Desire.

I stare at Jude as he stares at me, and I'm ambushed by the memory of his hands working my muscles. Right before he turned me onto my back on the massage table and brought me to climax for the first time with his mouth. I can't say it was the start of his seduction. Because the start was the second I looked into his eyes. But that moment in the Library Bar wasn't the first time *he* saw *me*.

"No." I whisper the word, feeling my body tightening.

"Yes," he retorts, unapologetic.

"No, Jude. I'm not doing this again." Humphrey stops at some lights, and I open the door to get out. To escape. I've had enough of this shit, and I'm terrified I'll fold under his power and our unmistakable, maddening chemistry. Why the hell did I get in this car?

"Wait." Jude grabs my arm, and I still, my worst fears realised. My skin burns under his touch, my heart beats faster, and my stomach twists and turns, the connection electric and irresistible. "We can have angry sex now," he virtually grates, "you can take everything out on me, or we—"

I slam the door and launch myself across the seat, crashing my mouth onto his and kissing him like I hate him. I need to be rid of this building, burning pressure inside. Pressure that's a mix of desire and frustration. The desire is self-explanatory. The frustration is a result of my fucked-up desire for him.

Jude pulls me onto his lap. I fist his hair at his temples, straddling his waist, and he's with me in an instant, his tongue battling with mine as he yanks his trousers open, shoves my skirt up my legs, and wrenches my knickers aside. I feel the hard, wet head of his arousal push at my opening, and inhale as I slam myself down, crying out into his mouth as he repeatedly mutters "Fuck" into mine. The burning ache subsides. The music seems to get louder.

We still, both of our bodies rolling, both of us panting, our mouths touching.

"Are you going to argue with that?" he asks, nipping at my tongue. "I dare you, Amelia. I fucking dare you to argue with how good that feels. How *right*." He thrusts up, pushing himself deeper inside, and I moan my despair, rolling onto his invasion, yanking at his hair. "Fuck!" he yells, reaching for my top and pulling it down. My breasts fall out, and his hands cup them harshly, squeezing. "God, I've missed this body. Come on, baby. Fuck me like you hate me." He lifts me and slams me back down. "Give me all you've got." His mouth resumes attacking mine, and we go at each other like two people possessed, our kisses messy and wild, our bodies pounding into each other as I ride his lap, forcing his head back to the seat. His hands squeeze my boobs harder, and his cock seems to grow inside me, swelling, throbbing, filling me lusciously to the brim.

With every powerful pound, I feel a little bit more stress leave me. With every lash of his tongue around mine, I feel the anger dissolve. It shouldn't. I should still be raging with him.

On that thought, I lift and smash down onto his lap.

"Fuck," he barks, moving his hands to my head and grabbing my hair.

I go again, whimpering at the pain I'm causing myself. It's a better pain. A pain I know will fuck off when I'm done.

"Amelia!"

I lift, hover, groan, relishing his matching moan. And smash back down, grunting, biting at his bottom lip like a savage.

"Jesus," he yells as I go at his mouth like it's a meal I've been starving for. His hips buck, his grip of my hair meeting the ferocity of mine on his, my temples throbbing with the force of his hold. "I'm going to come," he blurts out in a panicked gasp, sitting up straight. "Shit, Amelia, I can't hold it."

My pace increases, my own release on the horizon, my urgency fierce.

"Amelia!"

"Shut up," I bite back, rocking the moving car with my momentum. "Just shut the fuck up."

He hisses and yanks his mouth off mine, pushing into my chest so he forces me back. I don't let it upset my flow, my hand reaching for the window and splattering against the misty glass. Our eyes lock. And they remain that way as I ride him, chasing my release, his eyes wild, his breathing shot.

The moment my orgasm hits, every internal muscle tightens and holds on for dear life as lightning bolts shoot through me, my body rigid, my hand moving from the window to the ceiling of the car. I come so fucking hard, my scream suppressed when Jude slaps his hand over my mouth, taking my other hand and putting it over his to prevent his own bellow.

Eyes glued.

We come together.

Hard.

Long.

Intense.

The sensations of his dick inside pulsating, pushing against my walls, extends my pleasure, my body rolling to cope with the intensity as I reach for his hand over my mouth and knock it away, needing air, heaving. The way he's looking at me now, his eyes on the greener side of what I know and love . . . I can't take it.

He slips a hand around my nape and tries to encourage me forward, but I remain steadfast in my position, not allowing him to pull me close for what I know will be a tender kiss.

And only when he relents and releases me, his frown fixed, do I move in, getting my face close to his for a brief few moments before taking my mouth to his ear. I breathe into it, feeling his body roll in anticipation. "I dare you to try and contact me again," I whisper. "I fucking dare you, Jude."

"What the fuck?"

I ease off his lap on a held breath and get my skirt into place before lifting my top up. And as soon as the car stops, I get out.

"Amelia!" he yells, lunging across the seat to stop me.

I slam the door in his face.

Take a breath.

And immediately hate myself for caving in to the power of Jude Harrison. I see an opening into Hyde Park and hurry through the crowds, glancing back over my shoulder when I hear him bellowing my name. He's scanning the masses of people, his hands working to fasten the fly of his trousers.

I disappear into the park and fall against a wall, breathless, sore, and angry again. "Fuck!" I yell, burying my face in my hands, hating myself for surrendering. For lowering myself to his fucked-up level. Tears pinch the backs of my eyes, and I roughly and angrily wipe them away.

I need a drink.

I need to regroup.

I need to forget I ever met Jude Harrison.

Trying to figure out where I am exactly, I soon conclude it's too far to walk back to the hotel, especially in these heels. So I walk until I reach the other side of the park and flag down a cab.

Chapter 3

After cleaning myself up in the bathroom, I arrive at the ballroom, and I have to stop on the threshold and take a moment to listen, wondering if I'm hearing what I think I'm hearing. It takes only a few seconds—and beats of the track—to confirm it.

The band is performing "Hey Jude," and everyone is on the dance floor.

I do an about-turn, planning to get straight back out of there.

"Amelia!"

Clark intercepts me, his bow tie now unravelled, the top few buttons of his shirt undone.

"Hey," I say, clocking Nick across the room at the bar nursing a drink. He looks a bit worse for wear.

"Where have you been?" Clark asks. "And where are you going?"

"I had to freshen up." I squirm, patting down my hair and wishing I'd reapplied my lipstick. Nick spots me, and his whole stance changes, his body standing taller. "And I was just going to use the ladies'." Lie. I was going to find a bar and beat myself up about what I've just done over a glass of really expensive wine.

"Oh, come dance," Clark says, taking my hands and backing up, encouraging me into the room. "Please, I've hardly seen you today." He performs a perfectly executed adorable pout.

And that effectively makes it impossible to refuse my little brother. Even with my ex across the room ready to move in.

"Let your hair down, Amelia."

"It is down." It went against all my instincts. How tragic. But as I stand here in front of my brother on his wedding day, his face wearing a familiar expression of boyish charm that he's depended on since he was a kid, I realise that the only tragedy is me. Because I'm making myself one. Over a man. A man who doesn't deserve my emotions. A man I definitely should not have gotten in the car with. A man who will be a distant memory very soon.

I wince, praying that's true.

"Fine," I relent, letting him lead me to the floor, where everyone is forming a huge circle, arms around each other as they sing at the tops of their voices with the lead singer. I work hard to block the music out and focus on the faces of my friends and family. All except Nick, who, unbelievably, is dead opposite me again. I can feel him staring at me. Willing me to look at him, give him a chance, let him win me back. For a split second, perhaps because of my turmoil, I forget why I left Nick. He was stable. I knew where I stood with him. I could depend on—

I pull up, rewinding. I *thought* I knew where I stood with him. Until he announced he wanted to move to the next step. *My* next step was career driven, moving up the ladder. *His* involved knocking me down it. Our conversation about kids happened mere weeks after I finally told Nick I was shooting for partner.

A coincidence?

I blink and look across the circle of people to him. *Mistake.* Our eyes meet briefly, and I flinch on the inside, quickly breaking our eye contact, grateful when Rachel puts a glass in my hand and nods. "Your dad keeps getting me wine. I can't tell him I'm not drinking, or he might cotton on."

"Congratulations," I say, accepting.

"You're not yourself, Amelia," she replies. "Clark's worried."

"I'm okay."

"I'm sorry about Nick. I tried to push that situation along."

"Hey, please, don't apologise. You had enough to deal with. I'm coping."

"And the other guy?"

"He's history," I say, feeling my thighs brush, my insides still throbbing in the aftermath of a reckless encounter. Rachel gives me a look I'm not sure I like, letting Clark pull her away from me. They both get on the stage, and the lead singer hands them each a microphone. The Killers' "Mr. Brightside" kicks in, and they start belting out the lyrics together, as everyone cheers them on. I peek at the glass of wine in my hand and knock it back. It's not like I could be any more stupid. I just fucked Jude in the back of his car.

My eyes closed, I let the happy, drunken vibes take me off to a place far nicer than where Jude Harrison resides. I don't need to be in his world. Don't want to be.

"Amelia Gracie Lazenby, move aside." Grandpa breaks out of the circle and shimmies his way into the middle, arms up high, beckoning Grandma to him.

"Oh God, I think I'm gonna cry," I choke out, watching as he serenades her in the middle, both their old faces alive with joy.

"They're the cutest," Mum says, as I dig into my purse and find my phone, snapping a picture of them.

"And lucky for you, I get my moves from him," Dad declares, sweeping Mum off to join them, twirling her all the way. I look at Clark and Rachel on the stage. Grandpa and Grandma cheering them on. Mum and Dad on the floor laughing.

This is what matters.

Their presence. Everyone's presence.

Especially mine.

◆ ◆ ◆

My feet are throbbing by one a.m., my voice hoarse from singing with everyone. I certainly let my hair down. Speaking of which . . .

I feel for the jewelled clip in my blond waves, frowning when I don't find it. I wouldn't be surprised if it shot across the room with the force of me jumping to "Mr. Brightside."

Abbie, Charley, and I all sway out of the ballroom after saying our slurry goodbyes, our heels dangling from our fingers. "God, I'm going to pay for this in about"—Charley squints down at her watch—"five hours." Her head drops back, her wild curls skimming her arse. "Ohhhhhh Goooodddddd."

"Come stay in my room," Abbie suggests. "Lloyd can't make you get up if you're not there."

Charley gasps. "That's the best idea you've ever had." Her arms go up over her head, a half-stretched yawn and a half-celebratory cheer. "I'll tell him I didn't want to wake the kids, so I stayed with you." She starts skipping towards the elevator. "I'm taking the right side."

"You'll take whatever side I give you," Abbie retorts.

"I'd sleep in the fucking bathtub if it means I don't have to get up at six."

I laugh and herd them into the cart, pressing the button for floor three. "What a lovely day," I muse, falling back against the wall. Aside from my interlude with Jude, it turned out better than I expected. Thank you, Chablis, and some good old party tracks.

"It was!" Abbie sings.

"So who's next?" Charley asks, looking between us. Abbie and I snort. Not happening. Maybe ever.

"Depends if I ever find the hot bastard that took me to bed in France."

"You'd marry him?" I ask. "You don't even know his name."

"I'd do anything that man demanded." She frowns at Charley. "Except put my finger up his bum."

I laugh hard as Charley gasps her indignance, and when the doors open, I stumble out, still chuckling. "Sleep tight, you two," I say, letting myself into my room. I can hear Abbie still winding Charley up as they zigzag down the corridor.

I drop my heels and purse and fall to my back on the bed with a sigh. "Water," I blurt out, immediately pulling myself up again. I glug back an entire bottle, hoping to hydrate my brain so it doesn't shrivel to the size of a nut, then grab my phone and prop myself against the headboard. I flick through the pictures I captured on the dance floor, smiling from ear to ear, particularly at the one of Grandpa and Grandma headbanging.

So precious.

But my smile drops when a text invades the screen. I breathe in.

I fucking dare, Amelia.

I jump when someone starts banging on my door, my heart going from zero to a hundred in one beat. "Shit," I whisper, scooting to the edge of the bed and creeping across the room. I hold my breath, shaking like a leaf, and peek through the tiny peephole. I don't know whether to be relieved when I see Nick on the other side. "Fuck." I move back, just as he starts banging again.

"Come on, Amelia, just answer the door. I know you're in there." A few more thuds sound as I lower to the mattress, still and quiet, praying he goes away. "Please."

My eyes move to the clock under the TV, and I watch as the minutes tick by, Nick constantly calling and knocking, me unmoving and mute. Twelve minutes pass before I hear another voice. Security? They exchange a few heated words, loud at first, and then the voices start to drift away. I get up slowly and carefully, padding to the door and peeking through. My exhale is loud and long when I see Nick and a suited man disappear from view. Rolling onto my back, I lean against the door, my face in my hands.

I fucking dare, Amelia.

The phone by the bed starts ringing, and I move my hands from my face, staring at it for an age, scared to answer. It takes everything in me and more to find the courage, my breath held when I eventually pick up the receiver. "Hello?"

"Miss Lazenby, forgive the late-night interruption; it's security here."

"Yes, I'm sorry about the disturbance."

"Indeed. We have *another* gentleman trying to get up to your room."

My stomach churns so much, I fear I might throw up all over the carpet. "Who?"

"Mr. Harrison."

Jesus Christ. "I don't know a Mr. Harrison." It falls out unexpectedly and quickly. Instinct. I hang up and move away from the phone, startling again when my mobile starts ringing. "Shit," I hiss, rejecting the call from Jude. I toss it across the bed before stripping and getting in the shower, washing the day away. Just standing there, ignoring the muffled sound of my mobile ringing persistently past the noise of the water pouring down on me.

Chapter 4

Sunday morning is a flurry of goodbyes and kisses, tears and laughs. I didn't sleep a wink, waiting for my door to be hammered down, and I was forced to put my mobile on silent after I finally braved getting out of the shower.

Everyone checks out and leaves, but I volunteer to hang around and wait for the chef to begin his shift so we can try to find out where he's hidden the cake stand. Clark's put a two-hundred-pound deposit on it, and he wants it back. Plus, I don't want to go to Abbie's just yet. I'm scared Jude will be there. Waiting to bend and break me again. Or maybe Nick will be there, ready to enhance this never-ending guilt.

Fucking hell.

In my Lululemon leggings, cropped sweater, and flip-flops—hair piled up, fuck you very much, Jude Harrison—I plonk myself in an armchair in the corner of Café Royal's vast reception area and relax back, happy to take the opportunity to be alone somewhere no one can find me. I reach for the paper on the table in front of me. The *Financial Times*. Perfect. It makes a change from reading it digitally.

Flipping it open, I start scanning the articles for ones of interest, settling on the hostile takeover of the international freight company XYZ. It doesn't feature in my portfolio, but I know it does Gary's. I check the date on the paper. Yesterday. Gary would have seen it, right? Just the mere fact I ask myself has me pulling my phone out and calling him. He's at Windermere this weekend, so chances are he hasn't.

It rings and rings before sending me to his voicemail. "Hey," I say, leaning forward and slipping the paper onto the rich wooden table. "I just read about the XYZ takeover and wanted to make sure you'd seen the article in the *Financial Times* yesterday. Call me." I hang up and stand when I see Rachel and Clark's wedding planner, Martina, appear across the lobby.

She spots me and smiles, floating towards me, only her legs seeming to move as she walks. "Amelia, I'm so sorry for keeping you waiting. We found the stand!"

"Oh, that's great."

She motions for me to follow. "Chef put it in the pantry cupboard out of the way and neglected to tell me before he went off shift. I feel awful. The sous-chef stacked the tiers directly on top of each other and they sank under the weight!"

"I'm sure they'll get over it," I assure her. "It's already been eaten anyway."

She laughs, loud and over the top. "Sure, sure."

We pass through the lobby, and Martina leads me up the first flight of marble steps. "It's this way."

"To the kitchen?" I ask.

"Yes." She flashes me a toothy smile and leads me down a corridor, stopping at a door. "Here." She opens it, and the very second I step inside and figure out we're in no kitchen, the door closes behind me, making me jump. And the wedding planner isn't in the room with me.

Jude is.

"I told you I dared," he says, relaxed in the leather club chair by the window that looks out over Piccadilly Circus. Waiting for me. His expression is cool. The giant illuminated billboard glows behind him.

I become a statue, my mind failing me. I don't leave, I don't speak. But I shake like a fucking leaf. He's in the same clothes, looks even more tired, but tranquil at the same time. As if he's at peace with where we're at.

"What are you doing here?" I ask like a fool, unlocking my eyes from his and scanning the room. It's a suite, a beautiful suite. Did he stay here last night?

"We need to talk." He slowly rises, cautiously, as if he's preparing for me to walk out.

"I've nothing to say to you."

"Your body did a lot of talking last night when you fucked me on the back seat of the Rolls-Royce."

My jaw clenches. "Fuck off, Jude."

Growling under his breath, he advances towards me. "Would love to." He slips a hand around my waist, his palm sliding across my bare midriff onto my lower back, and he hauls my body into his. Sheer contact makes my insides furl. Then his breath is on my face, his lashes tickling mine when he blinks. "But I can't."

"Try harder," I whisper.

He shakes his head mildly. "How sore are you after yesterday?"

My hands twitch by my sides, lifting and lowering, wanting to reach for his shoulders but not. "I'm not doing this."

"You said that last night too. Then you climbed onto my lap"—he moves his mouth to my ear—"sank onto my big, begging cock, and fucked me hard."

What the hell is he saying? I told him only days ago that I was falling for him, and now he's treating me like a bit of arse? And he expects my compliance? I wince at my thoughts. I've always found it hard to say no to him. Even now, when I hate him, I'm shaking with the effort to not kiss him. My move last night in the Rolls-Royce was pure frustration. Anger.

A revenge fuck.

"No." I push the word past my lips and pull away, fighting the magnet.

"Yes," he retorts, dragging me back.

"No." I shove his hands away from my body.

He hauls me into him again. "Yes."

"No!" Shaking him off, I move back, firm in my voice, if not my stance. "Don't think you can win me over with a bit of dirty talk and forcefulness. We're done, Jude. *I'm* done. Getting involved with you was the worst mistake I've ever made."

Anger is radiating from him quickly, flashing in his dark eyes, pulsing in his throat. "Why do you constantly fucking lie to yourself, Amelia? Talk yourself in circles, try to convince everyone you're some impenetrable ice queen whose best assets are her laser focus and drive?"

"I don't have to listen to this." I pivot, my fists balling. Jude Harrison is no good for me, just as I always suspected, and I fucking hate that I gave him the opportunity to prove me right. "We're done," I reiterate, full of grit, taking the handle and hauling the door open. "Have a nice life."

"Fuck, you're infuriating."

I feel his arm loop around my waist, and my feet are suddenly off the floor, the door shutting on a slam. "What are you doing?"

"You're not walking away from me."

"Wrong!" I wrestle my way out of his hold, my hair coming loose and falling all over my face. "I never want to see you again—what don't you understand about that?"

"What don't I understand?" he yells. "I don't understand *you*, Amelia!"

"You don't fucking need to, because we're—"

His lips are suddenly on mine, his tongue violently seeking entry, the backs of my legs pushed up against a cabinet. For a split second, when I feel the heat of his body touching mine, his mouth ravaging me, I forget myself, opening up, groaning. *Fuck, what am I doing?* "No!" I shove him away, reaching for the cabinet to steady myself, but I miss the edge, swiping my hand through a collection of neatly lined-up champagne flutes. "Shit." They scatter and smash across the wooden surface, the sound echoing around the suite, and my unstable form becomes a bit more unbalanced. My hand meets the wood, and a sharp pain has me hissing and retracting, the warm sensation of blood instantly trickling down my fingers, making me inhale.

"Fuck!" I curse, checking my hand, but I'm unable to see the damage through the blood.

"Amelia."

"Don't," I warn, grabbing a serviette from the cabinet and holding it to my palm. I grit my teeth. The temporary swab lasts a few seconds before it starts disintegrating, soaked. "God damn it."

Jude moves in. "Don't you dare fucking argue with me." He walks me to a chair and sits me down, bending his body over mine so I'm forced to sit back. "Don't move." He disappears for a few moments, then returns with a facecloth and removes his suit jacket, throwing it aside and pulling a chair closer. He lowers and takes my hand, checking the damage.

I'm helpless, bleeding all over the place, in pain, but that's not the reason tears start to form. Jude peeks up at me, and I look away, sniffing discreetly.

"Does it hurt?" he asks, pressing the towel to my palm.

"I'll be fine." I stand abruptly, holding the facecloth in place, and edge past him quickly, leaving the suite.

"Amelia, for the love of God."

I ignore him and make my way down to the lobby to get my bags, no hands free to wipe my eyes while I keep my makeshift swab in place.

"Come on, Amelia, you need medical attention," Jude says, chasing me down the sweeping marble stairs.

Looking at the facecloth, I wince when I see it's become sodden. "Shit." Fat drops of blood start to leak, hitting the marble floor and splashing. I hurry my pace through to the lobby, bleeding everywhere.

"Amelia, stop." Jude lands in front of me and grabs my hand, holding it up as he scans the lobby. "I need a first-aider over here," he yells, getting the attention of everyone floating around. Then he leads me to a chair and forces me to sit, perching on the coffee table before it. "If you move, you're in big trouble, do you hear me?"

He concentrates as he peels the soaked material away, and the moment he winces, I know he's right. I need medical attention. And maybe a mental assessment, because my guard is slowly lowering.

Jude glances up and meets my glazed eyes, and my heart softens when he breathes out and moves closer. "Don't," I whisper, begging him. "Please don't."

"Don't what?"

Hurt me. "Don't be worried and all sensitive."

"I *am* worried." Slipping his hand onto my nape, he directs my face into his chest, kissing the top of my head repeatedly as he holds me close. "I'm sorry," he whispers. "I'm so fucking sorry, Amelia." The feel of his chest expanding and retracting, warm and hard, eases me. It defies everything, but I relax. "It'll be okay. I've got you."

My throat is too tight to talk as my tears soak into his shirt. I don't know if I believe him. I don't know if I should expose my heart to him again. I don't know if I should let him take care of me now.

I just don't know.

I feel Jude's head turn, and he nods before slowly pulling me out of his chest and wiping my eyes. "First aid is here." A man appears, taking in the blood before sweeping a hand out in a gesture towards the back of reception. Of course they want to remove the bleeding, blubbering lady from the bustling lobby. "Come," Jude says, helping me up and tucking me into his side. He reaches for my face and pushes it into his chest as he walks me, following the first-aider. We're led into a room and Jude sits me down.

"And what have we here?" the man asks, pulling a chair over and taking my hand.

"She's cut herself," Jude answers. "It looks nasty."

The first-aider eases the material back and flinches. "Yes, a hospital visit for you, my dear. I'll get this covered for now."

I look away from the cut on the edge of my palm, which is still oozing. "Thank you."

Jude takes his phone to his ear. "I'll meet you in Air Street; I need to get Amelia to a hospital," he says, hanging up and facing me. His eyes tell me not to challenge him.

And I don't.

◆　◆　◆

We were only able to leave the hotel after completing an accident report, and the drive to the nearest hospital was bathed in an uncomfortable silence, as was the two-hour wait in the accident and emergency department, with Jude often standing and pacing, his impatience growing minute by minute. Because of my silence? Because of my distance? Because of the wait?

When a nurse eventually calls my name, Jude doesn't ask if I want him to accompany me, and instead slips an arm around my waist and walks me as we follow the nurse to a private room off the corridor. His attentiveness isn't helping my constant wavering, flimsy resolve to protect my heart.

The nurse checks my hand and concludes Dermabond won't be suitable due to the location of the wound on my palm. So stitches it is. Ten of them. "And how did you end up with a nasty cut like this?" she asks.

I clench my teeth as she starts to sew me up, her eyes moving to Jude every now and then. He's sitting in the corner with his head in his hands, and it hits me. She thinks he did this? I turn my gaze onto her, seeing the concern in her eyes. "No," I say quietly, shaking my head, but I'm very aware that her training has probably told her a victim might protect their partner. *Shit.* "It was my brother's wedding. It was a long day, too much to drink. I was a little fuzzy this morning. Clumsy." And now I'm lying, but I can hear myself trying to explain, and it doesn't sound good for Jude.

He looks up briefly from his place in the corner and shakes his head in despair before hiding again in his hands.

"Was it a lovely day?" the nurse asks.

"Stunning." I smile, and she gives me a forced one in return, telling me she's not convinced Jude didn't do this.

"Okay, do your best not to get it too wet. I'll get you some spare dressings to take home with you," she says, pulling off her latex gloves and dropping them in a bin. "Give me a moment." She casts her eyes over to Jude again, and I wilt. She's reluctant to leave me alone with him.

"I can't tell you how wrong you are." I'm perfectly safe with Jude. My heart, though?

She nods, still obviously torn, but she leaves the room.

I slip off the edge of the bed and assess my palm, thankful it's not my right one.

Jude comes out of his hiding place again and rakes both hands through his hair, standing. "She thinks I did that to you."

"It's her job to be vigilant." I pick up my bag and sling it across my body. "Thanks for bringing me. You don't have to wait around any longer."

"I'd wait forever."

I shoot my eyes to his, stilling where I stand, and he breathes out, moving in and sitting me back on the edge of the bed. Reaching for my thighs, he spreads them wide and puts himself between them, taking my uninjured hand gently and resting it on his hip before directing my face up to his. "Stop, Jude."

"Why?"

Because I'm not strong enough to stop myself.

"You've got to let me fix this, Amelia."

I haven't *got* to let him do anything. And if I do let him fix this, it can be broken again. "Why was she in your apartment?" I ask. "You cooked for her."

"I cooked for one. Katherine let herself in and helped herself to some pasta and wine."

"You had her lipstick on your collar, Jude." It's so fucking cliché. "So it looked like she helped herself to you as well."

"Nothing happened," he grates, his palms hardening on my cheeks. "She tried, I rejected her, and—"

"She stayed for pasta and wine."

He closes his eyes, gathering patience. "I took the opportunity, since I couldn't see you, to let Katherine know I wouldn't be continuing with our arrangement."

"That doesn't require a romantic dinner for two."

"Jesus Christ." His head drops back, and I remove my face from his palms and pull my hand from his waist. Jude puts it right back. "No," he says surely. I look away, frantically searching for the sensible part of my brain to help me out. "Stop." He forces my face back to his. "Just stop it." Moving in slowly, cautiously, he kisses me gently, holding his mouth still for a few moments to see if I withdraw.

I don't.

My body loosens, and I open up to him, letting his tongue slowly and softly explore my mouth as he moves in closer, forcing me to tilt my head back, his palms encasing my neck. It's such a delicate kiss and, like his attentiveness, not helping me. My uncertainties crumble under his devotion, and my heart hurts a little less. I don't understand it, and I wonder for the first time if I need to.

Dragging his mouth across mine, he kisses first one corner, then the other. "All better," he whispers, settling his lips on my forehead. I wish it were that easy. Breaking away, he gazes at me with imploring eyes. "Give me another chance."

"Are you asking or demanding?"

He squints, thinking. "Will you *please* give me another chance?" With big, green, imploring eyes, he waits, his beautiful face rough with stubble that's longer than I'm used to. "Please, Amelia, don't throw this away."

I chew on the inside of my cheek, mulling over everything I know about Jude Harrison. Stinking hot. Profoundly pained by his mother's death. Has been on antidepressants. Hot temper. Incredible in bed.

Passive-aggressive possessive.

But obviously deeply regretful. I can't be imagining that. I can't be *that* stupid.

Oh God, what am I doing? "We take it slowly," I say, leaning back a little, trying not to smile at his baulk.

"Slowly?"

I nod.

"Care to elaborate?"

I look away, trying to piece together what I want to say and how I should say it.

"I'm here." Jude takes my cheeks and steers my face back to him.

"I know." I pry his hands away. "You're hard to miss when you're crowding me."

Indignation swamps his face. "Slowly?" he prompts.

I take a breath and hit him with it. "Slowly," I say again. "You're in Oxfordshire, I'm here. It's too much going back and forth in the week, so perhaps we just do a day on the weekends for the time being."

"Not a fan."

I didn't think he would be, but he doesn't get to call the shots. I have to keep control. Set the pace. Resist the temptation to jump in feetfirst again. Listen to my head and not my heart, which is screaming my declaration of love for him, while my head is reminding me that I'm in the thick of a life-changing career opportunity *and* Jude's already let me down.

"Weekends," I repeat, pressing my lips together.

Jude narrows his eyes on me. "I'll think about it."

I laugh lightly, and Jude's nose wrinkles as I move him aside.

"Here we are," the nurse declares as she enters the room. She has hands full of dressings and a face that's quite alarmed when she sees Jude's so close to me.

"I didn't do that," he says, catching the nurse's expression too.

"Jude," I murmur.

"No, I need her to know I wouldn't hurt you."

"Jude, I—"

"I would never lay a finger on her. I lo—"

"Jude, for God's sake, shut up!" I snap, and he recoils, wounded, shrinking where he's standing. He's just making it worse. "He didn't do this," I affirm with grit as I take the bandages from the nurse. "He's an idiot, but he's not a monster."

Jude blinks, shrinking more, and the nurse bats her eyes between us before she eventually nods and backs out of the room. Whether that nod be acceptance or not, I don't know. I stuff the dressings in my bag and get down off the bed. "You can take me home."

"It's Sunday, so I believe you're on my time right now."

"You're taking me *home*," I say surely, ignoring my body's demand to let him at me. To fix this. To take us into that wonderful bubble of perfection. His body. My body. Connected.

"I said I'd think about your proposal, and you can't even give me the last few hours left of the weekend, when you just told me weekends are mine."

"I said one day on the weekend," I remind him as he takes my good hand and opens the door.

"Jesus Christ, Amelia, it gets worse."

"Jude, come on," I breathe. "I can't just run off to Arlington Hall with you like nothing's happened. Besides, I have to pack."

"Pack for what?"

"I'm moving out of Abbie's."

He recoils, looking down at me as we walk. "Moving out?"

"I finally found an apartment. I get the keys Friday."

"You have a new apartment? Where?"

"Plaistow."

"That means nothing to me. Is it on the right side of London?"

"For what?"

"Oxford."

I shake my head. "It's West London." And will add at least another half an hour onto the journey to Arlington Hall.

"Jesus, Amelia."

"It's what I can afford, where I can afford." And it's gorgeous, a cute little ground-floor flat in an old Victorian terrace with a courtyard garden, which is something I never imagined I'd get for my budget. "I need to finish packing and—"

"You said you'd let me fix this. How can I fix it when you're over an hour away from me?"

It's *how* he plans on fixing it that worries me. Falling into bed with him is not the answer. Building trust is. "Jude—"

"Please, Amelia." He stops us when we make it outside and cups the side of my face in his big palm. "I've missed you so fucking much. I just want to be with you."

I look at him, this tall, godly, stunning man, begging me, and my heart melts. And, really, I desperately want to be with him too. "Okay," I whisper, ignoring my head, seeing him fold with relief. *What am I doing?* "Fine."

"You're talking like you don't want to."

"You know I want to. I'm just not sure if I should."

"You should." I let him get me in the Rolls-Royce when it rolls to a slow stop. "Given you're incapacitated, I think it's wise for you to stay with me until you're better."

"Didn't you hear the conversation we just had?" I pull the armrest down. "We start slowly. Weekends."

Jude pushes it straight back up, reaching for me and tugging me close. "I heard, and I told you"—he kisses my hair—"I'm thinking about it."

"It's not a request." I put myself on the other side of the car, my back to the door, and look at him. His slight scowl is endearing. "How did you know where to have Anouska send your fake spa day special-deal email?"

His scowl deepens. "The night you left Amazonico without paying, I offered to settle the bill in exchange for the contact details on the reservation."

"Crafty. And what if Abbie didn't take your bait? Or maybe booked it for herself and didn't invite me?"

"Then I'd have found another way to get you to Arlington Hall."

"Like a work conference?"

"Maybe."

"And my wallet that was found in the changing rooms?"

"That was in case the work conference didn't"—he considers his words for a second—"work out."

"You stole my wallet?"

"I borrowed it."

"And how many women have you placed bets on with the married woman you were fucking?"

Jude winces, the conversation finally getting uncomfortable for him. "A few."

"Two, three? Ten? Twenty?"

"Why do you need specifics?" He throws his hands up, exasperated. "I'm not proud, Amelia. I'm a man who didn't have the time or energy to invest in a relationship. The arrangement with Katherine worked. I slept with other women. That's it."

"It doesn't seem like the new arrangement is working for Katherine."

He looks out the corner of his eye at me. "What do you mean?"

"Don't be a stupid man, Jude. She doesn't like you seeing me. I've taken away her shiny toy."

He leans over and hauls me to him, positioning me on his lap so I'm straddling him. "I don't want to spend the fraction of time you're allowing me talking about Katherine."

"You thought we'd fall back into whatever this is without it being mentioned?"

"What *is* this?" he asks, his eyes scanning mine.

"I don't know."

"Which is why you want to take it slowly?" he breathes, his words hot on my skin.

"Yes." My reply is a husky whisper, my body responding to his closeness. He must feel me throbbing on his thigh through the thin material of my leggings. "We have all the time in the world."

"Until we don't." He reaches for the button and raises the screen between us and Humphrey, before manipulating me down to my back on the seat, coming with me. I take in air deep in my lungs as he settles between my spread legs, raising a cheeky brow as he subtly flexes his hips. "Are you going to argue with me?"

"Let me think about it," I whisper, and he smiles. The sight blows not only my mind, but my ovaries too. "Tell me it'll be okay," I demand.

"*We'll* be okay." He pushes my hair back. "We have to be."

"Or else?"

"There is no *or else*." He grinds his hips, making me arch my back. "You're not going to argue with me, are you?"

I shake my head, and he swoops in and takes my mouth softly but with conviction, doing what Jude does best. Overwhelming me. "I'm sorry for hurting you," he murmurs around our kiss, not faltering with his pace, pecking his way across my lips. And then he says something like that and every shred of doubt vanishes.

Taking things slowly isn't going very well at all. *Shit.* "Wait." I use my good hand to push into his chest.

"Wait? For what?" He's dazed, confused.

"I said slowly."

Poor man. His eyes bug before a filthy look lands on his gorgeous face. "You're on my time."

"Does that mean we fall straight into bed again?"

"We're not in bed, and need I remind you that it was *you* who jumped *me* last night?"

"Don't you think we should, you know, do normal-style dating?"

"No, I don't."

"Jude," I breathe, forcing him back and sitting up. "You're the one who said you didn't want me to think you're nothing but a fuckboy."

"Right." His cheeks blow out. "And you'll get your reassurance by abstaining from me?"

"Don't devalue my concerns."

"I'm not. I'm just trying to figure out how to show you I'm mad for you without *showing* you."

"I want to get to know you."

"You know me."

I snap my mouth closed. That's not true. I know scraps of things, and what he's reluctantly shared. Or been forced to share. "I didn't know you were capable of doing something as low as sleeping with a woman for a bet and making her . . ." I drift off before I can finish. *Making her fall in love with you.*

"Making her what?"

"Nothing." I pull my handbag open when my phone rings, cringing when I see it's Abbie. I don't answer. I can't explain where I am; she'll yell at me.

"Okay," Jude says on a tired exhale. "We'll do things at your pace."

"Thank you."

"You're not welcome."

I roll my eyes and spin my phone, wondering what the hell I'm going to tell the girls. I'll reassure them I know what I'm doing. That I'm in control. I glance across the car to Jude. He's looking out the window, thoughtful, turning over the new approach to this thing between us. Am I in control? Truly? My body aches for him. And my heart wants nothing to do with the protective shield I'm trying to put in place around it.

Chapter 5

I step out of the car and look up at Arlington Hall as Jude takes my hand. "Is this allowed?" he asks. I give him a tired look, and he shrugs. "I've never done this, Amelia, so you've got to help me out."

He's never dated? Is that what we're even doing? I sigh, exasperated by my own questions. If I don't know, how the hell do I expect Jude Fuckboy Harrison to? I'd tell him we should just go with the flow, but I know the flow would take us straight to his bed and have us naked faster than Katherine can whip out her claws. Speaking of which, is she still gracing the rooms of Arlington Hall with her toxicity? I frown and pull my hand from Jude's. I don't know how to play this, which begs the question of why I let him bring me here. All I know is that I feel vulnerable while feeling incredibly settled, and it's fucking with my head.

"Ouch," Jude murmurs, stepping back, shaking his head mildly. "Doesn't this uncertain energy between us feel wrong to you?" he asks, appearing genuinely perplexed. "Our relationship started off with a bang, Amelia."

"But it was a lie."

"No, baby." He rakes both hands through his hair before coming close again, dipping to my level. "It wasn't a lie. It was incredible."

I wince, my gaze low.

"You're not letting yourself be fully present." Jude hunkers down some more, forcing me to look at him without touching me. "You want to hold my hand, so hold my hand."

I want to do more than hold his hand, but I'm so scared I'll lose sight of my objective. Which is what? To punish myself? Punish him? Or simply to figure out if Jude Harrison is a man I should trust with my heart before I hand it over on a plate? *It's too late.*

I look up at Arlington Hall again. I want to ask about Katherine. Where she is now, what was said between them. But I also don't want to know. I can't stand this uncertainty, swaying between happiness that he's back in my life and fear that I'm setting myself up for heartbreak.

Jude's hand appears before me, and I stare at it, desperate to take it. I was a bet. But he won the bet and still came back for me. And he's here now. Apologetic. Determined. And the frightening fact is, I will never know if I can trust him if I don't throw caution to the wind and give him the chance to prove himself.

So, on a deep breath, I take his hand and watch as he threads our fingers, squeezing.

"Thank you," he murmurs, gently encouraging me onwards.

The lobby is quiet, and so is the Library Bar when I peek inside as we pass.

Jude leads me to his apartment and escorts me inside. "I'm going to cook," he says as we enter the kitchen. I notice a basket of fresh vegetables on the oak island, along with a parcel wrapped in greaseproof paper and knotted with twine. Meat?

"Did you call ahead and have this arranged?"

"I was being optimistic." He slides a wooden chopping board out from behind a toaster. "How's your hand feeling?"

My hand is fine. It's my heart I'm worried about. "It's okay. I'm going to use the bathroom."

"Help yourself." Jude plucks a few courgettes from the basket and a knife from the stand. "I'll be here grinding away over a meal for two, instead of grinding into you."

"Ha. Ha."

He quirks a brow. "I'll do dessert too. It sounds like I've already exhausted my optimism for this evening."

I roll my eyes as I walk away, heading for the bathroom. And, naturally, as I pass through his dressing room, I falter by the sliding door where I found those gorgeous green shoes. I try so hard to carry on walking. And fail.

I slide the door open, and my heart sinks when I see they're still there. I can't ignore this. Inhaling, I pluck the shoes out, walking back through to the kitchen and putting them on the island. Jude pauses chopping. Looks at the shoes. Peeks up at me.

"I'm just wondering how you'd feel if you found something that belongs to another man in my wardrobe."

He sets the knife down and slowly wipes his hands on a towel. "Well, for a start, I wouldn't rummage through your wardrobe."

"I'm a little bit sorry."

He huffs under his breath, resting the towel on the wood and bracing his hands there. "You're wondering whose shoes they are."

"Maybe."

"Then let me enlighten you." He circles the island and collects me, leading me back out of his apartment and down to the hotel lobby. He stops and motions to the portrait of his mother, and I frown, looking too. Not that I need reminding. She's divine in her cream Chanel dress and cute blue suede kitten heels. "Wait." Jude pulls out his phone and starts working the screen fast, eventually turning it towards me. And there on the screen is his mother in the same dress.

But different shoes. Emerald-green kitten heels.

"Oh God," I whisper. "They're your mother's?"

"Yeah, they're my mother's." He tucks his phone away. "She was wearing them the day she stumbled upon Arlington Hall and lost one as she was wading through the brambles and overgrowth." His face is pained, and I positively hate myself in this moment. Jude holds his hand out, and I take it immediately, letting him walk us back to his apartment. "We tried to find it when we started the work. I had excavators, groundsmen, everyone looking for that damn missing shoe." He smiles across to me. "They were her favourites. My dad brought them back from Paris for her. When she had that portrait done during the work on Arlington Hall, she was devastated she couldn't wear the green shoes."

"They're beautiful shoes," I murmur, so disappointed in myself. "I'm sorry."

"And that's why my mother would love you."

"Because we have similar taste?"

"No, because you can hold your hands up when you've fucked up." He turns a sardonic smile my way. "You thought they were Katherine's."

I absolutely did, and I hate myself for that too, because thinking they were Katherine's would put her in the same class bracket as Evelyn Harrison, and Katherine is miles off Jude's mother's league. "I'm not liking myself much at the moment."

"Get over it. I feel like that most days."

"What do you mean?"

"Nothing."

Oh no, he does not get to brush that statement aside. I stop him when we reach the top of the stairs and force him to face me. "What did that mean? Why don't you like yourself most days?"

His shoulders drop. "Because I hurt you, Amelia. And I realise I don't deserve a second chance, but by some miraculous act of God, you, you beautiful, graceful woman, have given me one." He hooks his forearm around my waist and hauls me up his body so our eyes are level. "I won't fuck this up."

"This isn't allowed."

"Oh, sorry." Much to my horror, and surprise, he puts me down and backs off. What the hell is he doing? I dive at him and wrap every limb around his hard body, clinging to him, burying my face in his neck and getting a needed hit of his manly scent. "So it's one rule for you, another for me, is it?" he asks, holding me under my arse.

I open my mouth and suck the flesh of his neck, bobbing up and down as he walks on. "It's just a hug," I whisper in his ear.

"Tell that to my dick."

I chuckle, finding his face as he walks. "So you found the shoe."

"A dog found the shoe."

"Seriously?"

"Yeah, the farmer's collie down the road dropped it off on the steps a few years ago."

"That's insane."

"I know. Do you know what else is insane?"

"What?"

"I'll show you." I'm put on my feet when we reach the dressing room, and Jude slides another door open. "He found your shoes too."

My jaw drops when I'm faced with the heels I wore last week and lost in the brambles. "Jude, that's spooky." I reach in and pluck them out. They're spotless. It was raining, muddy. Did he have them cleaned up?

"Why were your shoes in the bushes outside Arlington Hall?" he asks.

"I lost them the night I . . ." My lips twist, not wanting to relive that hideous scene. "The night I left."

"I didn't notice you were barefoot when you got in the car."

I nearly crick my neck when I look at him. "You were there?"

"I needed to make sure you were safe. It was dark out there. Remote."

He stood there in the rain watching me? Jesus, I was crying so hard.

"It shook me, Amelia," he says quietly. "Seeing you like that, knowing I was responsible." He turns into me and takes my hands, being careful of the dressing as he gently feels them. "I wanted to tell you about the stupid fucking bet. I had every intention of telling you, I just didn't know how."

"With words."

"I'm not very good at talking."

"You underestimate yourself."

An adorable, lopsided grin adorns his face, and he nuzzles my cheek. "I underestimated you, actually."

"This isn't allowed."

"Oh, sorry." He drops me and moves back, and I grin, diving into his arms and smothering him with my mouth, kissing him deep and long, and with all the adoration I feel but can't admit to him.

"You need to furnish me with the rules of this game," he mumbles around our swirling tongues, "because I'm getting a bit confused with all these mixed messages."

"Poor thing."

"Hmm." He carries me back to the kitchen and puts me on a stool, indulging my demand for his mouth. "Are you going to let me cook for you, or am I taking you straight to bed?"

"That's not allowed."

He chuckles and tears his mouth from mine, gazing at me as he braces his hands on my thighs. I pout and move in, wanting more. But he dodges my attempt to get another kiss. So I try again, scowling when he moves his head to the side to avoid my lips.

"That's not allowed, Amelia," he whispers, pushing off my legs and stepping back, unable to hide his smug smile.

So he wants to play that game? Fuck, I'll lose. I already know Jude's got some superpower that enables him to walk away from me during highly charged sexual moments.

He pulls his phone out and wanders around the counter, and I look up at the ceiling speakers when Lana Del Rey starts singing softly to RIOPY playing the piano. I smile, turning myself on the stool. "What are you cooking?" My thighs tense and squeeze together in an attempt to stem the pulses.

"Lamb and roasted vegetables." He pushes a chopping board across and places a peeler and a knife on it. "You're in charge of the carrots."

I raise my brows and collect a carrot. "Are these from the Kitchen Garden?"

"Everything in the basket is from the Kitchen Garden. Use the big carrots. You need to peel them and slice them into discs around five millimetres thick."

"What qualifies as big?"

"About eight inches long, two inches thick."

I frown to myself and pout as I try to measure out eight inches between my hands. "I don't know how big that is."

"Think of my cock," Jude says, peeking up from slicing the courgette. "Erect."

I cough over my laugh. "That's not allowed."

"Sure," he murmurs. "Get on with it. I want to get to the *really* not-allowed stuff."

God damn me, so do I. It was foolish to slap conditions on this. Our sexual chemistry was the catalyst to us. And truly, we're not really *us* without our intimacy. I see a more vulnerable side to him when we connect like that.

I reach for a carrot and assess the length. The girth. Peek up at Jude, who's merrily chopping his way through the Kitchen Garden. Smirking to myself, I get off the stool and round the island, and Jude stops chopping, eyeing me until I'm next to him.

"Excuse me," I say, lowering to my knees.

His eyebrows shoot up as I stroke over his crotch. "What are you doing?" he asks, his voice unmistakably gruff.

"I take my job very seriously."

The knife drops from his hand, clanging against the oak. "Shit, Amelia."

I unzip his fly and reach into his boxers, taking hold of his hardening cock, and Jude grunts under his breath, clenching his eyes briefly. "Is this allowed?" he asks, as I continue to massage him.

I smile and pull out his raging hard-on, inhaling at the sight of the swollen, taut head weeping. I lean in and lick the head, humming my happiness. The smell of him, the feel, the taste. *Home.*

"Fuck," Jude barks, his eyes dropping, hooded and dark. "Suck me, baby."

"You want me to suck you?"

"Do it."

I consider his demand for a few seconds, then smile and hold the carrot next to his dick, humming. "I think it's just shy of eight inches, actually," I muse, dropping him and standing. "Your dick, not the carrot."

Jude lets out a sharp bark of laughter, grabbing the counter for support, as I make my way back round the island and slap the carrot on the chopping board, holding it gingerly with my damaged hand and bringing the knife down on the end. He jumps. The top flies off and shoots across the kitchen, and both Jude and I follow its path until it lands by the doorway.

"Now it's seven inches," I murmur, making Jude fold over the counter in complete hysteria. It makes me stop and take a moment to appreciate it. It's the most gorgeous sight, Jude Harrison in a full-blown laughing fit, having to hold himself up. I rest my arse on a stool and split my attention between peeling a carrot, holding it cautiously with my dressed hand, and watching him gather himself, odd chuckles escaping. He wipes his eyes. "Alright there?" I ask.

He grins down at the half-chopped courgettes. "Amelia," he says, turning his gaze up. His eyes are so green right now. I tilt my head in question. "I . . ." His mouth closes, and he inhales. "I'm really happy you're here."

I hardly want to admit it. *Hardly.* "Me too."

Jude nods, thoughtful, blindly lowering the knife to the wood again, and the way he's looking at me has sparks lighting up my insides. My body burns for him. I can't stop it. Don't want to. I lower the peeler, my lungs screaming with the effort to breathe easy. Just look at him. This beautiful, complicated man. My breathing becomes even more strained when the track changes and Kidnap and LYDY MAY's "Cold Water" joins us.

"Oh God," I whisper, feeling the throb between my legs get more violent.

"To hell with your boundaries." Jude comes round the island and grabs me, getting his mouth on mine and attacking me full force. I reach for his shirt to tear it off, forgetting myself, and pain shoots through my hand. I hiss, retracting, trying to maintain our kiss. "Careful," he says gently, forcing my backwards steps towards the bedroom, keeping our kiss up as he unbuttons his shirt, and I wriggle out of my sweater. The backs of my legs meet the edge of the bed, and I drop to my arse, flinging my top aside and trying and failing to unfasten my bra with one hand. "Leave it." His chest swells as he shrugs out of his shirt and drops it. My panting is out of control, Jude looming over me as he strips, his eyes hungry and full of intent. His trousers hit the floor. I inhale. His thumbs slip past the waistband on his boxers. I peek up at him and bite my lip, my mouth watering as he eases them down his thighs and kicks them aside. And he's naked. A polished mass of manly perfection. I swallow back my awe and reach for his hip, tracing a line down one side of his V to his pubic bone. His cock is at mouth level, and I won't pass up that kind of opportunity again. Licking my lips, I take hold of him gently and circle the tip with my tongue, gazing up through my lashes to see him watching me intently. "Taste good?" he asks.

I hum my approval but don't get to indulge myself more. Jude pulls away and shoves me to my back, taking the waist of my leggings and drawing them down my legs painfully slowly, followed by my knickers before he yanks down the cups of my bra.

Then he pulls my legs apart and lashes straight up my centre with his hot, wet tongue.

I nearly go through the ceiling, my back snapping into an arch, the pleasure unbearable. "Jude!" I yell, feeling him bite each nipple as he passes, crawling up my body until he's settled on top of me.

"Delicious," he mumbles, taking the wrist of my injured hand and putting it above my head, holding it in place for me, because he knows I'll fail to keep it still and out of the way. He looks at me, his dick throbbing against my lower tummy. His lip twitches at the corner. "Is this allowed?"

"Shut up." I lift my head to catch his lips.

"Do you want me inside you?" he asks, and I groan, exploring his mouth with my tongue, my temperature rising, my body throbbing with the music. "Do you want me to fuck you, Amelia?"

"Jude," I whisper, aching for him, my internal walls pulsing. "Please."

"I can't fuck you."

"Yes, you can."

"But you said we need to take this slowly."

"Jude!"

"Have you changed your mind?" Biting my bottom lip, he pulls away, and I growl my annoyance, making him smile. "Answer me."

"I can't resist you," I admit, and he nods lazily. Understanding.

"I can't resist you either, baby." He lifts his hips, lines up, and pushes into me infuriatingly slowly, the friction and heat sending me wild and dizzy, my hand twitching in his hold above my head while my other claws at his back. Air hisses through his teeth, his jaw tight, sustaining the absolute rightness as well as enduring my punishment of his back. "Are you going to argue with that?" He strains the words, reaching the deepest depths of my pussy and holding still, allowing us both a moment to get a hold of ourselves.

"Never," I cry out, my muscles out of control, clenching and releasing him, the pressure both unbearable and wonderful. "Oh God."

His head drops, hanging heavy. "Fuck, baby, we feel out of this world."

"Yeah," I whisper, finding some patience and waiting for him to start moving. And when he does, I can't describe the pleasure, his slippery flesh sliding easily through me as he withdraws and hovers briefly before advancing again, steadily and accurately. I groan and close my eyes, flexing into his hips each time he rolls into me, my falling heart pounding with something more than the strain of sustaining him making love to me.

"Open your eyes, Amelia," he orders hoarsely, nodding when I do. He scans my face, every inch of the ecstasy coating it. "This is my favourite view."

It's mine too, his hair in disarray, damp, and falling into his eyes, his green gaze alive but heavy, his rough jaw pulsing from the effort of holding himself together. I release my nails from his back and slide my hand onto his upper arm, feeling his muscles flexing with his pumping hips.

"For years I've had to think about every breath I take, Amelia," he whispers, dropping a light kiss on the corner of my mouth, not wavering in his delicate pace, keeping me in a constant state of euphoria. "You're all the air I need." He brushes his lips over mine, and I melt under his soft words and handling of me. My tongue leaves my mouth and finds his, and they dance, rolling delicately, each swirl pushing me higher. I don't know how he's maintaining his rhythm, how he's keeping his torso raised.

I love you!

"Jude," I mumble into his mouth, my toes curling as I hook my legs around his waist and cling on.

"Is it coming?"

"Yes." Urgency is coming too, my release tinkering just out of reach, needing a few more strokes to get me there.

"I've got you." He's so calm, but his hips move faster. "Wait for me."

"I can't." I shake my head, making his lips slide onto my cheek. He bites down gently, panting harshly, his hold around my wrist getting tighter.

"You can." He finally collapses onto me and buries his face in my neck, and my eyes close, my hips meeting every one of his thrusts, chasing the pleasure. Then I hear him gasp and curse, before he quickly lifts his upper body and kneels, taking me under my knees and using his hold as leverage to yank me back and forth onto him.

I throw my other arm over my head and cling to the headboard, watching as Jude controls every bit of my body and our pleasure, feeling him expand inside me. "Fuck!" he roars, pumping harder. Faster.

I can't talk to let him know I'm about to fall over the edge, my chest hurting from holding my breath, my eyes fixed on the Adonis before me on his knees, wet, hard, fucking gorgeous. My clit throbs. My thighs tense. My back arches.

And I come, releasing the air I've held on a loud yell, immediately shaking with the force, twitching, convulsing, shots of intense pleasure firing from my pussy to my toes, making them point. "Oh my God," I wheeze, everything out of control, my body at the mercy of my orgasm.

Jude goes rigid, his jaw stiff, his head thrown back, as he comes hard, jolting over and over until it unbalances him and his arse drops to his heels, my lower body in his lap, his cock still held deep inside as he comes in powerful surges. Moaning.

I'm out of my mind.

I don't think I'll ever recover from that.

Our breathing is loud and chaotic, as I watch him ride the wave with me, a wildfire blazing inside, burning through all my doubts.

I love him. And I can't fucking help that. Can't stop it.

"Shit," Jude gasps, dazed, appearing to shake his vision clear, his damp hair sticking around his eyes, the pieces flicking out from his nape starting to clump into wet locks. "Shit, shit, shit." He drags a hand down his face, his body spasming every few seconds, the aftermath of his climax lingering. I'm spent. Dazed.

Still full of him.

My lids heavy, I let them close and listen to the pounding of blood in my ears as Jude somehow keeps himself inside me as he negotiates my body so he can come down on top of me. Falling onto his side, he pulls me close so we're face-to-face, still connected, his dick softening against my walls.

"I'm not ready to leave you," he says, breathless, kissing my damp forehead.

I don't argue, moving in closer to his chest and entwining our legs. So sweaty. So hot.

So right.

Chapter 6

Whales call to me, the sound distant but clear. Light invades my eyes as I cautiously peel them open, finding Jude's neck in my sights. The feel of his hands stroking through my hair registers, along with the warm softness of his cock still inside me.

Then the whales register again, and I push myself off his chest in a panic, wincing when he slips out of me.

Jude hisses. "What's up?" he asks sleepily as I scramble to sit up.

"Fuck!" Pain slices through my hand, and I clench it to my naked boobs. "Ouch, ouch, ouch."

"Careful," he warns.

Disorientation gets me as I blink my eyes clear, snippets of last night coming back to me. I look at Jude, who's rolled onto his back, apparently not concerned that we've slept through to morning. "Shit."

"Amelia, what?" he asks, not opening his eyes.

I reach for the machine by his bed and shut up the whales. "Oh my God," I blurt when I see the time. "Jude!" I jump up and run aimlessly around his bedroom trying to find my clothes, still not fully awake. "It's eight!" I'm going to be so late! And I have a shit ton of stuff to get done. "Jude, help me."

At a loss and unable to locate my clothes, I go to the edge of the bed and nudge him. Even if I knew where my clothes were, I probably wouldn't be able to see them; my vision is still foggy. That was a deep sleep. I shouldn't be surprised. I've hardly slept for a week.

"Jude, wake up."

He opens one eye and slowly props himself up against the headboard. "What?"

What? He must have been in a deep slumber too. "It's eight o'clock."

He frowns and looks at his whale machine. "In the evening, Amelia. For fuck's sake." He scrubs his hands down his face, exasperated, before reaching for my wrist and hauling me back into bed. "I don't know why my alarm's going off—I must have set it wrong."

Evening? I fight Jude's clutch and look towards the window. It's dusk. If it were morning, it would be lighter. "Oh." I fall back to the mattress and breathe out my relief, looking down at Jude's hand on my tummy. I know I'm about to face some resistance, and, no, I don't want to go, but I have some prep I need to do this evening for my lunchtime meeting tomorrow and my diary is jam-packed with calls in the morning, so there's no chance of finding the time then, not to mention the fact that I need to pack. "I've got to go." I roll onto my side and shuffle to the edge.

And immediately get tugged back.

"Jude, I've got to go."

"Not a fan."

I roll my eyes and make to move again, getting precisely nowhere, as Jude keeps me safe and close to his chest. "Come on, you promised to let me leave."

"I made no promises. I think you'll find that what I actually said was I'd think about your proposal. I've thought about it. And I have my answer. It's a no."

"Do you want some more time to think about that?" I ask on a laugh.

"It took me a split second to think about it. I just took longer to inform you of my decision."

"And do I get a say?"

"No again." He hugs me tight, pushing his nose into the crook of my neck and breathing in deeply. "You don't want to leave me anyway."

"I have so much to catch up on," I say, really wishing I didn't. "Clark's wedding took up all of Friday and Saturday, I did nothing to prep for my week, I have investment reports to wrap up, and I've got to pack." I feel Jude sag against me. "Can we negotiate?"

He stills for a moment, obviously thinking. "Okay." Then he helps me turn around to face him, both of our heads settling on the same pillow. "Negotiate." He pouts at my exposed boobs and starts circling my nipple.

"I'd like to negotiate without any distractions." I take his hand, remove it from my boob, and pull the cups of my bra into place. His gorgeous, sleepy face contorts with disapproval. "My job is very important to me."

"I know that. Support that."

I raise a brow, and he visibly sags.

"Please state your case," he breathes tiredly. "Whilst also remembering that I'm a little bit obsessed with you and have a habit to feed."

Such a comment shouldn't make me grin in delight, and yet it does. "Duly noted."

"Good. Proceed."

"I have to go home to pack and prep for tomorrow. I've not exactly been operating at full capacity this past week."

Jude falls onto his back and theatrically pretends to stab himself in the heart.

I sigh and crawl onto his sprawled body, sitting up on his waist. "That wasn't intended to make you feel bad."

"But I do," he says, sliding his palms onto my thighs. "I really do."

Dropping my front to his, I frame his head with my bent arms and play with some locks of his hair. "I know."

"So if I can't keep you tonight, can I have you tomorrow night?" His hopeful face melts me.

How can I refuse him? "I can live with that," I whisper, sealing our lips.

"Good. Negotiations are over." He rolls us and gets himself into position, sliding into me easily on a hitch of breath from us both. "Fucking hell, there's no place better in the world."

I reach for his arse and sink my nails into his hard flesh, humming, flexing up into his drive. His face nuzzles mine, prompting me to open my eyes.

And I look into his as he rocks into me, and we both come on long exhales.

Taking it slowly was never going to work.

Chapter 7

I managed to avoid bumping into Abbie outside her apartment by the skin of my teeth when I got back to her place last night, letting myself in just moments before she got home. It was so close, I was certain she must have passed Jude as he drove off, but she didn't mention it when she found me elbows deep in clothes, packing. Instead, she got a bottle of wine and sat herself on my bed while I folded and packed, and we chatted about how wonderful Saturday had been. I gave her a half-true version of how I cut my hand. The whole time, a confession hung on the end of my tongue waiting to fall out, but I bottled it. I know she and Charley won't be impressed that I'm seeing Jude again, and I can't face their judgments. Or the fact that they might be right when they tell me I'm crazy for giving him another chance.

As soon as I get to the office, I go on the hunt for Gary to make sure he got my message about XYZ and find him hunched over his desk, looking weary. "Okay?" I ask.

He lifts his eyes but not his head. "Long weekend."

"Did you get my voicemail?"

"What voicemail?"

"The one about XYZ?"

He sits up straight. "What about XYZ?"

Oh shit, he doesn't know? "You didn't check the *Financial Times* on Saturday?"

"No, I spent the weekend up a mountain or on a lake." He scrambles for his phone and loads the app, scrolling through the endless articles that have been released since Saturday. "Oh fuck." His fist comes down on his desk hard.

"I'll leave you to it," I say quietly, slipping out before he really goes off the deep end and I'm caught in the cross fire. I shut the door, cringing as a loud string of curses comes through the wood.

"What's going on in there?" Leighton asks, craning his neck to see through the panel of glass next to Gary's door.

"He didn't see the article on XYZ over the weekend."

"Oh holy hell." Leighton's eyes bug. "How did he miss that?"

"He was away with his wife."

"Fuck me, I'll be staying out of his way today," he says, just as a ton *more* "Fucks" fly around Gary's office. I tense, my face bunching.

"Hey, what happened to your hand?" Leighton helps himself to it and inspects the dressing.

I reclaim my limb as I peel my back away from the door and get on my way to the kitchen for coffee. "I cut it on a broken glass."

"Ouch. Good weekend?" Leighton tracks me a few paces behind, and I look back to see he appears genuinely interested. "Your brother got married, right?"

"Right." How does he know that? "And it was lovely, thank you." I enter the kitchen and put a cup under the machine, spotting Sue bent over, reaching into the fridge. I clock Leighton eyeing her backside and cock my head when he sees I've caught him being a sleazebag. "Hi, Sue," I say, eyes still on Leighton.

He clears his throat and gets his wandering eye under control, as Sue unbends her body and faces us, a smoothie carton in her hand. "Hey, kids," she chirps. "Good weekend?"

"Excellent," Leighton and I chime in unison, making both of us frown and glance at each other briefly before he clears his throat again and grabs a glass from the shelf, handing it to Sue. "You?" he asks.

"Well, I hammered my husband at golf, so yes. And we took our eldest back to university, so no." She accepts the glass on a telling half-grin. "Thank you, Leighton."

"Welcome."

God, he's such a suck-up. Sue toasts her empty glass at thin air. "Must get on." She passes between us. "Don't forget to keep an eye on that merger, Amelia. The whispers are rife," she calls, looking back at me. "Gary said he mentioned it the night we were out for drinks."

I try so hard to hide my smile, feeling Leighton's equally poorly hidden scowl on my profile. "I will."

Sue winks and leaves, and as expected, Leighton is on me like a rash. "What merger?"

I hit the button for a black Americano, pondering whether I should tell him. Tilda's words come back to me. *You're not a vulture, Amelia.* I'm also not a dickhead. And speaking of Tilda Spector, has she made any decisions yet on where and who she's passing her clients to? Should I touch base with her? Check in?

I sigh—I honestly don't know—and get back to the matter at hand. Leighton Sleazeball Steers. "There are whispers on the grapevine about two of the big investment banks merging."

Leighton reaches for a spoon and hands it to me. How helpful of him. "Sugar?"

"I'm sweet enough," I quip on a sickly-sweet smile.

"You are."

God give me strength. "It's Gleneagles and Hollenbeck," I tell him before he's forced to butter me up some more as I pull my cup off the stand and take that first glorious sip. "I think one of them is secretly struggling, but who is yet to be determined. If the merger is handled well, it could skyrocket the shares."

"And if it doesn't—"

"Crash and burn," I whisper, sounding menacing.

"Fuck, I have both in some of my clients' portfolios," Leighton muses, looking off into the distance.

"Me too, hence I'm keeping my ears open." I walk off, feeling Leighton's eyes on my arse. I glance back. I wasn't wrong.

He smiles, folding his arms over his chest. "You're a fair player, Amelia. Just let me know how I can repay you."

He can repay me by keeping his slimy eyes off me. "Have a good day, Leighton." I shudder, bumping into Shelley in the doorway. "Hey."

"Morning," she chimes.

"Here's the birthday girl!" Leighton sings.

"Wait, it's your birthday?"

"Thirty-five today," Shelley says, giving Leighton pursed lips as she passes him on her way to the fridge. "I don't need a birthday kiss."

I laugh.

"You sure?" he asks, puckering.

"I'd rather burn in the deepest depths of hell."

"Be careful, sweetheart—a PA is written in my stars, and I'll choose you," he declares, getting himself a coffee.

I widen my eyes, and Shelley looks like she could throw up all over the kitchen. "I'd quit first, Steers."

He sounds sure he's going to make partner and therefore get a PA thrown in with the role. Does he know something I don't? I eye his back as he waits for his coffee but force the question down my throat—I don't want him to think I'm worried—and walk back to my office, thoughtful, entering and coming to a startled stop when I find a bouquet of flowers on my desk. I already know they're not Jude's doing. He doesn't do small when it comes to flowers. "Shit," I breathe, approaching with caution. I spot a card nestled amid the carnations and pluck it out, cringing all over the words from Nick.

You looked beautiful on Saturday. It was so good to see you. Nick. xxx

I groan and drop to my chair, tossing the card onto my desk. Did he forget I ignored him hammering on my hotel room door?

"I've never seen someone so pissed off after receiving flowers," Sue says, her head popped around the door.

"It's my ex," I explain, moving them to the side.

"Oh, I see." She slinks in and looks out to the corridor before shutting the door.

"Are you okay?" I ask. She's acting shifty.

"I'm great." She puts herself in the chair opposite me. "I didn't want to mention it in front of Steers."

"Mention what?" I ask as she slips a card towards me. I pick it up, scanning the bold silver writing. "Leo Lombardy? Who's Leo Lombardy?" I flip the card over and find a telephone number.

"He's a potential high-wealth client," Sue says, getting my attention. "He's in the yacht industry. As in, he builds them."

"Oh?"

"He's recently parted ways with his adviser, and I thought you'd do great with him."

"Parted ways with his adviser?"

"Lost him in his divorce."

"Ohhh," I breathe. "And you?" Why isn't Sue advising him?

"He's a friend. I don't mix friendships with business—it can be messy. Amelia, he's worth a lot of money. Strike up a good rapport with him, he could push you way ahead, if you know what I mean."

I scrunch my nose, flicking the card over in my hand. Steers has got those Liverpudlian twins on his radar, and that, I admit, is a concern. "I appreciate this, Sue."

"I know you do." She smiles and stands. "If anyone asks, I didn't facilitate this, okay?"

"Understood." I nod. I wouldn't throw her under the bus and give Steers the opportunity to squeal favouritism. "My lips are sealed."

She nods and leaves, and I waste no time calling Leo Lombardy before my scheduled calls start at ten. It rings and rings, and just as I'm about to ready myself for the voicemail to kick in, he answers. I sit up straight. Italian? "Hi, Mr. Lombardy, my name is Amelia Lazenby. Sue Prescott passed on your details to me."

"Ah, Amelia, yes, yes. Very good to hear from you. Let's do a dinner meeting. Say tomorrow? What do you eat?"

I blink. Wow, this is moving fast. "I'm easy." I wince. "I mean, I like everything."

He laughs. "Do you like Italian? I know a special little place in Shoreditch. Nonna's. Bellissimo!"

"I love Italian food, and I've always wanted to try Nonna's, but it's like a three-month waiting list," I say, making him laugh again.

"Leave it to me. I'll have my assistant make the reservation. Seven thirty tomorrow. Ciao, ciao." He hangs up before I can say bye in return, and my phone immediately dings. Smiling, I open the message from Clark. There's a picture of him and Rachel on a beach. I quickly reply.

Looks gorgeous. Have fun, and please please please let me be there when you tell Mum and Dad you got Rach up the duff out of wedlock

I get a rolling-eye emoji in reply, then a question.

Have you dropped the cake stand off with the cake maker? xxx

"Fucking hell," I breathe. *The cake stand!* I get up and start walking circles round my office, calling the hotel to speak to Martina. She told me she'd found it. Was she lying, just to get me into a suite with Jude? When someone finally answers, I'm told Martina isn't in until later today, so I leave a message for her to call me back before texting my brother to let him know the cake stand is safe, even though I have no idea where it is. "Shit," I grumble, putting myself back at my desk and starting to clear my emails down. I falter when a new one lands. From Jude.

To: amelialazenby@lbandbfg.co.uk
From: JH@arlingtonhall.co.uk
Re: You're staying the night

Don't argue with me.

Sincerely,
Jude Harrison
Arlington Hall Luxury Hotel & Spa

I smile, despite myself, falling into a daydream, feeling every one of his touches from last night on my skin again, every kiss still lingering on my lips. The way he looked at me as he made love to me. Slowly. I pout to myself, silently admitting that I miss him. I'm hooked. I can't wait to see him later, squeeze him, eat him alive, smell him. *Oh dear, Amelia.*

A call comes through from Abbie on FaceTime, snapping me back to the present. "Hey," I chirp, mentally ordering the heat in my cheeks to calm.

She frowns. "Why are your cheeks red?"

"It's stupidly hot in this office." I get up and walk to the window, opening it as far as I can. Which is about an inch.

"What are you up to?" she asks.

"Just worky things."

"Gym after the worky things?"

Jesus, I can't stop cringing today. "I've got to pass."

"Why?"

"I have more worky stuff to sort." I smile like an idiot, surely looking as guilty as I am.

"Amelia Gracie Lazenby," Abbie says, her voice tired. "I have known you for how many years?"

"Twenty-three." I know exactly where this is heading.

"And how many times in those years have you got away with lying to me?"

I flop back in my swivel chair, scowling. "Never. You're like a real-life human lie detector."

"Which is how I know you're lying now. So why can't you come to the gym?"

My jaw rolls from how hard I'm clenching my teeth, trying to stop myself from confessing and therefore enduring a lecture. I know it's coming—I can't keep this from them—but I can't face it now. Plus, I don't have time. "I told you. I have worky things to do."

"Amelia!"

God damn it. "You know why," I grate, throwing my arm up heavily and dropping my head back.

"You're seeing him?"

"It's complicated." My injured hand balls and, as a result, hurts like hell. "Fuck," I curse.

"It's not complicated. He fucked you over, and you're going to let him do it all over again?" There's a rustle, a few beeps, and the next minute Charley's face appears. "She is," Abbie says, looking as outraged as she sounds. "She's seeing him again."

"Amelia!" Charley cries. "What the hell are you thinking?"

I feel a lump in my throat growing, my brain not helping me out. I have plenty of words, many reasons and justifications. I just can't find them now as my best friends glare at me, waiting for an explanation to my apparent madness. Apparent? Am I mad?

"I can't do this right now, girls," I say, hanging up on them for the first time in our lives. I drop my phone and cover my face with my palm, sucking back the emotion before it makes a fool of me at work. I take a deep breath. And another. And a few more. "Shit," I whisper, looking up at the ceiling, ignoring my phone ringing on my desk. I *really* can't do this right now. I don't want my best friends to hate Jude. I can't blame them, but I don't want them to. Sighing, I swivel my chair and face my screen, scrolling through the emails that need dealing with, happy to take the distraction.

◆ ◆ ◆

At five, I look away from my screen, squinting. All of my calls are done for the day and my inbox looks a lot prettier, but my mind is still playing back Abbie's and Charley's reactions to the news that Jude's back in my life. I have no idea how I'm going to navigate that situation. Jude's got wide shoulders, but I have not. My friends' opinions matter, and I hate they have such a negative perspective. And yet, again, I can hardly blame them.

I look at the flowers on my desk and grimace. And then there's Nick. Dad told him I'm not seeing anyone now. Is there anyone in my life who will be happy for me? I sweep up the flowers and pace to Shelley's desk, popping them on the edge. She looks up over the blooms.

"Happy birthday," I say, smiling.

"For me?"

"For you," I confirm. "I hope you've had a wonderful day." I hear a commotion going on in Gary's office. "The hostile takeover at XYZ?" I ask, as various partners pass us, joining Gary.

"No, actually. It's a bad day." Shelley twiddles her pen, looking over her shoulder to Gary's door. I can only imagine the abuse Shelley's poor ears have endured today. "The Gleneagles and Hollenbeck merger was announced an hour ago, and the shares have absolutely tanked."

"What?" I stare at Shelley, hoping she corrects herself and tells me there's another reason for Gary's nonstop expletives. An hour ago? And I missed it?

"The Gleneagles and Hollenbeck mer—"

"Fuck!" I rush past her and fall into Gary's office. "What's happened?" I ask, looking around at the partners, noting they all appear a little pale. I can feel the blood draining from my own face rather fast too. God, no, I have endless recommendation letters drafted advising my clients to authorise me to reinvest their kickout plans into Hollenbeck. *Please don't tell me I've missed something critical!*

Gary throws his pen down and pulls his glasses off, rubbing his eyes. "The merger. It was announced at four. The board lost confidence, PR fucked up, and an anonymous source has taken to social media and blown the whistle on Hollenbeck's dire financial situation, *and* the fat bonuses the board has taken this past year."

"Shit," I curse.

"You saw the reports that started coming in at lunchtime, didn't you?" Gary asks.

"Yes," I squeak.

"So you've spent the afternoon reworking any proposals involving Hollenbeck, right?"

"Of course!" I smile. "It's all in hand."

"Oh, good, because those letters are going out—"

"First thing in the morning." I dash back to my office, swearing all the way, checking the time on my phone. "Oh Jesus." Keep an ear to the ground, Gary said. I haven't. *Fuck, fuck, fuck.*

Leighton is strolling down the corridor with a coffee in his hand, apparently unperturbed by the shitty news. He stops. Notes my fluster. "Oh, you didn't?"

I growl at him as I hurry past. I haven't got time for his ego right now.

"You did!" He laughs. "After everything you told me this morning, *you* missed the news?"

"Fuck off, Leighton. I didn't miss the news." I want to punch my own face in. I've been so lost in emails, calls, and other outside lingering thoughts, I've not watched my notifications.

"Sure. You should have come to me, babe," Leighton sings. "I would have shared my inside information."

I stop, facing him. "What inside information?"

He smiles, smug, and gets on his way.

"Fuck it." I grab my phone and call Jude. "Hey."

"Hey, baby, how's your day been?"

I push my way into my office and try to breathe. Can't. All I can think about are the dozens of drafted letters on my computer waiting to be sent in the morning. I'm also considering the merits of calling the fuckhead at Hollenbeck who convinced me the plan was a no-brainer and threatening physical pain. It *was* a no-brainer, God damn it. Unless, of course, the bank's on the brink of ruin. Which it was. That fucker must have known.

"I've had better." What the hell am I going to do? It's the end of the financial year, and I have precisely . . . I look at my mobile and breathe in. I have sixteen hours before the letters are sent and only another few days to get my clients' approval to reinvest their money before the year-end deadline.

"Let me fix that. I'm just pulling up outside," Jude says, and I cringe.

"I can't come." I switch my phone to my left hand so I can take my mouse, hissing and switching it straight back to my right hand.

"What?"

I look down at the dressing and see a few spots of blood seeping through. I need to change the dressing. "Can we do tomorrow night?"

"No," he says, flat-out refusing. "We negotiated, and you agreed I got tonight."

"Something's gone wrong, Jude, and I need to fix it," I explain, trying to give him some context. "I have a pile of letters in my email waiting to go out to clients tomorrow morning, and I just heard a merger has gone horribly wrong, so the shares have dropped like a rock. I have to stay late and rewrite my recommendations." I place my hand over my head and breathe in deeply. This is a fucking disaster.

"Pack your laptop," he says. "Bring your files."

"What? And work at Arlington Hall?"

"Yes," he says simply, as if it's that simple.

"Jude, I *have* to work." He'll never let me concentrate, and neither will my mind if I know he's nearby.

"I promise I will let you work. I've got to see you, Amelia. Today's dragged unbearably. You can do what you have to do, and I won't disturb you, I promise. I just want you close."

He wants me close. *Oh my heart.*

"You've not missed me?" he asks.

"I've missed you." Terribly. It hurts.

"Then pack your files and get that gorgeous arse down here."

"Okay." I can't argue. I'm going to need a cuddle after this mammoth mission. "I'll be downstairs in five." I literally sweep my arm across my desk and shove everything into my bag, before gathering the files I need and rushing out, hurrying to the elevator.

I'm fidgety the whole way down, running over where to start, who with, what I can copy and paste, what I can't. And, more importantly, what the hell am I recommending that's equivalent to the Hollenbeck plan? I can't even ask Gary, or any of the other partners, because then they'll know I've fucked up. They can't know I've fucked up.

As soon as the doors open, I worm my way past the crowds of people leaving the building and run across the lobby, and I'm thrown when I find one of the Rolls-Royces from Arlington Hall is waiting by the kerb, Humphrey at the wheel.

Jude gets out the back and comes to me, and God, he's a sight for sore eyes. Suited. Stubbly. Drop-dead gorgeous. "You're not driving?"

"I had an early dinner with my brother."

"Which one?"

"The one who recently starred in his very own sex tape."

"Oh my God, has it surfaced?"

"No." He grabs my face with both hands and kisses me hard on the lips, a moan of happiness reverberating at the back of his throat. Listless, I absorb every little bit of him against me.

"You look lovely," I say, as always trying to find air after he's kissed me like that.

Jude raises his brows and looks down his front. Then he takes in my cream dress. Smirks. "You were wearing this the first time I saw you."

"It's a favourite."

"It should be. You look gorgeous in it. I think it's one of mine too. Tell me about your day."

"It started great. One of the partners, Sue, passed on a referral to me. It sounds like a big account to land. But I dropped the ball on a merger and now I'm paying for it, hence it's ending on a low."

"It's not ending on a low. Approximately how many hours of work do you have?"

"Too many."

He groans. "Okay." Taking my bags, he claims my hand and leads me to the car. "How's your hand?"

"Fine if I stop forgetting it's sewn together," I mutter, assessing it. More blood.

"Shit, Amelia," he grumbles, throwing my bags in the back of the car and taking my hand, wincing as he checks it. "Did you change the dressing this morning?"

"Yes, sir."

"Don't be smart." He lifts it to his lips and kisses the edge. "This is being changed before you do anything. Have you got your spare bandages?"

I smirk. "Yes, sir."

"Oh, you're a bad, bad girl."

"Don't punish me, sir."

He chuckles and helps me into the car. "Only if you're lucky." Once I'm in the seat, Jude helps himself and pulls out my laptop, opening it and setting it on my lap. "Is there anything I can do to help?" His gaze falls down my cream dress as he leans across and puts his mouth to my ear. "Help you relax and clear your mind?"

I go lax, closing my eyes, succumbing instantly to the power of Jude, a hard, intense throb dropping to between my thighs. My toes curl. *Fuck.* My eyes snap open, and I push him away. "Back off, Harrison," I warn, opening my documents and gathering myself, willing the buzz inside to fuck off and give me time to fix this crisis.

Throwing me a warning look, he slowly lifts his wrist and looks at his watch. "Get to work."

◆ ◆ ◆

I blink repeatedly, trying to moisten my dry eyes, looking up as Humphrey pulls through the gates of Arlington Hall. Stretching feels glorious. I glance across to Jude, who's lost in the screen of his mobile. "Everything okay?" I ask.

He breathes out. "Rhys's publicist is being a diva."

"She's being a diva how?"

"She's hell-bent on finding the sex tape that can't be found, which makes me wonder if it even exists. It's as if she wants it to be found so she can swing into PR heaven and save my brother's reputation and career."

"It sounds like she needs telling to stand down."

He hums, frowning to himself. "Rhys and I talked about it over dinner. I think he's actually listening to me. And I didn't think pigs could fly."

Now this is another side to Jude. The caring brother. I like it. "What does Rhys do?" I ask, remembering Jude talking about going to Ireland to try to sort out his drama.

"Plays rugby."

"Ohhhh. Who for?"

"Dublin Harriers." He raises his brow. "And England."

"You're kidding?" I breathe as Jude reaches for my laptop and snaps the lid shut.

The second the car rolls to a stop, he's out, taking my bags and pulling me along behind him. "Not kidding. But if he carries on with the partying and getting himself in sticky situations, he'll be thrown out of both teams."

"Big brother to the rescue," I say, smiling fondly at Jude's suit-covered back as he leads the way.

Naturally, I peek into the Library Bar as we pass, seeing it's busy. But no Katherine. I do see Anouska, though, talking to Clinton over the bar. They both look this way, smiling. It could just be me, but they look pleased to see me.

"The Amelia is going down a storm," Jude says over his shoulder, an ironic smile on his face. I still can't believe he's named a cocktail after me. "Want one?"

"Maybe when I've finished working."

He walks us up to his apartment and leads me into his bedroom, where he sits me on the bed. "Let's sort that hand out," he says. "Where are the dressings?"

"Can it wait until I'm finished working?"

"No."

I drop my head back. "Jude, it's stopped hurting, and the second I peel off this dressing, it'll be sore again." Typing with only one fully functioning hand is tricky enough without the added bonus of pain.

He frowns and takes my hand, checking it over. There's no more blood than when we left London. It's stopped bleeding. He must conclude the same because he relents and pulls off my heels, plumps the pillow, and gets me in place, opening my laptop and resting it on my thighs before getting my files and phone, putting them next to me. Then he disappears and returns a few minutes later with a bottle of water. "There," he says, placing it on the nightstand. "Do you need anything else?"

I shake my head. "Thank you."

"Oh, wait." He's off across the bedroom again, disappearing into the dressing room, and is back moments later carrying something.

"My hoodie?" I ask, setting my laptop aside.

"It was in the bag you left behind the night you . . ." Jude's lips twist. "It was in the bag."

"And you went through it?"

"It was lying on top." He sits on the edge of the bed and puts it over my head, feeding my hands through the sleeves carefully. "There."

He smiles down at it and leans forward, pushing his mouth to mine and holding it there for a few moments. *Oh no.* My body naturally responds and screams for him. "I want a cuddle that leads to sex when you're done," he whispers.

"Okay."

Jude grins and gets up, leaving me in breathless anticipation on the bed. "I've got a few things to sort in my office," he calls. "Work fast."

He's a man of his word. I'm left to power through my rewrites with no interruptions. I find an alternative plan to recommend, thank God, and the rest wasn't half as painful as I feared. I'm wrapping up on my final letter just after eight when Jude appears in the doorway. His eyes jump from me to my open laptop as I look up at him through my lashes.

No. Focus. I'm nearly finished.

I get back to my screen to tweak the closing paragraph of my final letter, my good fingers working fast over the keys, the ones on my injured hand struggling to keep up. And it's sore now. Achy.

My fingers pause on the keys when I feel the bed dip, and I see Jude kneel on the end in my lowered vision. Peeking up, I watch as he tugs at his tie. *Fuck.* I drop my eyes again, forgetting where I was, so I reread the last sentence. Based on this, my recom . . .

My brain short-circuits, the feel of his hand wrapping around my ankle sending a rush of heat through me.

Based on this, my recommendation . . .

"Jude," I whisper, as he licks the instep of my foot, the heat radiating up my legs. He hums, watching me fight my knee-jerk reaction to toss my laptop aside and devour him.

Based on this, my recommendation would be to . . .

He nibbles my little toe.

"Jude."

Circles my ankle with his tongue.

Fuck. I'm gone, slamming the lid of my laptop and pushing it off my lap. I wriggle down the bed and stretch, sighing, and Jude chuckles, satisfied. *Don't care.* Crawling up the bed, he straddles my hips and drops to his fists, hovering above me. I smirk, grasp his tie, and haul him down onto my mouth. His weight on me feels glorious, his smell intoxicating, his tongue rolling languidly around mine utter bliss. We kiss forever, soft and slow, our hums and moans the music while our tongues dance. This is my reward. *Him.*

After pecking across my cheek, he nibbles at my ear, and I shudder. Then he moves to the other. Licks the shell and kisses below my lobe. "Are you done?" he whispers, pushing his torso up, taking my hand, and lacing our fingers.

"Crisis averted," I confirm.

"I don't know about that." He flexes his hips, forcing a lumpy swallow as his hardness pushes into me. I grab his forearm with my spare hand.

"Fuck," I hiss, retracting quickly as pain flares across my palm.

"Oh, baby." His face contorts as he takes my wrist and inspects the dressing. "There's more blood."

I pout as he lifts off me, collecting my bag from the floor and rummaging through. "Time to change your dressing."

"I can do it." I sit up and cross my legs, then start to peel at the edges of my bandage. "I need some warm salty water." I glance at him. He's still, my bag on his lap. "Jude?"

He turns his eyes my way, and I seriously don't like the deep dark-blue shining back at me.

"When did he send you flowers?" he asks, holding up a card. *Oh shit.* My mind empties as Jude glares at me, angry.

"Today," I say on a sigh. "It's nothing."

"Nothing? He sends you flowers, and you think that's nothing?" Getting up, he drops my bag to the floor and starts pacing at the end of the bed.

"Okay, it's nothing to me."

"So he wants you back?"

What can I do? Lie? "I get that impression, yes." What a cop-out. "I've made it clear to him there's no going back for me, and he just doesn't seem to be listening. Not even when he knew I was seeing someone."

He looks plain horrified. I don't suppose I can expect anything less. Jude doesn't mix well with other men he deems a threat. "You told him you were seeing me?"

"Not exactly." I feel myself wilting. "He saw the flowers you sent me before we . . . I don't know, before we broke up." Did we break up? Were we even together enough to classify it a breakup? Fuck, my head.

"How did he see the flowers I sent you?"

Oh crap. I need to shut the hell up; I'm just making this worse. "Just leave it, Jude."

"No, I won't leave it. How did he see the flowers I sent you?"

"Because he stopped by my parents' when I was there."

His head slowly tilts. "Why would he stop by your parents'?"

Oh God, I don't like the obvious tensing of his entire frame as he stands at the end of the bed, heaving a little too much. He's holding back his anger. Or trying to. Not doing a very good job.

"My parents wanted me to try and work things out with him." I withdraw, holding my breath, watching as Jude continues his battle not to lose his shit. I should shut up now.

"But you don't?"

"Of course I don't." What kind of stupid question is that?

"You said he's out of the picture."

"He is."

"But he still pops in to visit your family? Sends you flowers?"

And attends my brother's wedding. "Jude, I can't con—"

"Why the hell is he sending you flowers?" he barks, his handsome face twisting as he begins a dogged march around the bedroom.

I breathe out tiredly and follow his path, remaining quiet, since I seem to poke the bear harder each time I open my mouth. "Calm down." And I say that?

"So you think it's okay that he's still sending you flowers?" he asks, his dark eyes landing on me with a bang. The wrong kind of bang. He's fuming.

"Did you hear me say it's okay?" *Do not roll your eyes, Amelia.* "And *you* think it's okay to react like *this?*"

"How the fuck do you want me to react, Amelia? You've just told me your ex is sending you flowers, and your parents want you to rekindle whatever the fuck it was you had with him."

I stare at him, flummoxed. After Katherine's performances, trying to stake a claim on Jude, he has the nerve to behave like an ape? And yet I hold my tongue because tit for tat will get us nowhere.

"He knew you were seeing someone else, and now he's sending you flowers?"

"He doesn't think I'm seeing you anymore."

"What?"

"My father told him I wasn't seeing you anymore."

"Why?"

"Because I wasn't, Jude," I say, exasperated. "You ordered flowers at Abbie's with my mother, she brought them home, my father saw them, so I told them I was seeing someone, and then Nick walked in and overheard. Then I found out that I was a bet, and surprisingly, it kind of hurt, so I was a little bit off sorts and my family noticed. I told them things didn't work out between us, and my dad must have told Nick at the wedding."

"He was at your brother's wedding?" he practically shrieks, recoiling.

Fuck. "He was an usher." I flop back to the bed, waiting for more eruptions. "I asked my brother to uninvite him, but he didn't."

"Great. So you spent a lovely romantic day with your ex while I was tearing myself apart with guilt and regret, trying to figure out how I could show you that I lo—"

"Are you actually making yourself the victim right now?" I sit up, outraged.

His lips twist, his nostrils flaring. "Does he know you left halfway through the day to fuck me in the back of my car?"

Fuck this. I get up and gather my things. "Okay, I'm leaving. I can't deal with this bullshit." He's like two people, my perfect man and an absolute possessive nightmare.

"Bullshit?" he asks, laughing. "This is bullshit?"

"Yes! It's fucking bullshit." I ram my laptop in my bag and swing it onto my shoulder, stuffing my feet into my heels. "Like how you've behaved each and every time you've seen me talking to a man is utter bullshit."

"Or kissing them in steam rooms."

Laughing under my breath, I don't bother reminding him that it was a mistake. He's being ridiculous. Is he ever going to let that go? "Fuck off, Jude." A man has never drawn such reactions from me. I huff to myself as I storm out of the bedroom. Well, the honeymoon period was short-lived. And his performance is a stark reminder that Jude Harrison has some chinks in his armour. What the hell is wrong with him?

"Do I need to remind you about your reactions to Katherine?" His voice is getting louder. Of course he's following me. And how fucking dare he!

"She comes here to have sex with you!" I yell. *Fuck. Keep it together.* "I'm going." I feel like I could pop. Or slap him. He's so fucking wonderful, and then completely unbearable. I yank the door open.

And gasp when it's slammed shut again, my arm nearly wrenched from the socket. I stare at his palm on the wood in front of me, his arm stretching over my shoulder. His breathing is loud in my ear. "I'm sorry." The words are spat out, clearly an effort. "Fuck, I'm sorry," he repeats, this time softer. "I . . . shit, I don't know."

I remain where I am, questioning whether to just leave anyway. I don't like this side of him. He seems so volatile. And then I remember what his brother said. *Jesus, Jude, what the hell have you got yourself into? You're the eldest. You're supposed to be the most stable.*

Is Jude taking the pills? I feel like I should ask. I also don't want him to think I've been snooping.

"I don't like the thought of you with another man," he goes on. "In fact, it sends me wild."

And what can I say, really? I was feral over Katherine. I'm blaming Jude.

"Please stay," he whispers, taking the strap of my bag on my shoulder and easing it off. I turn my eyes onto him, seeing an entirely different man to a few minutes ago. A softer man. Sheepish. *Sorry.*

He lowers my bag to the floor, never taking his eyes off me, and turns me by my shoulders into him. "I'm sorry."

My body deflates from my supressed sigh. "I don't want him back," I say, for the sake of clarity. "I'm not particularly loving the fact that I'm hurting someone, and that's why I didn't want Nick to know I was seeing someone else. But then he did know. And now he doesn't again."

He frowns. "So Nick doesn't know you're back with me?"

I shake my head. "And neither do my parents. Or my brother. Only the girls. And they're not happy."

"You told them about the bet."

"I didn't have much choice, Jude." One minute I was coming to tell him I was falling for him, the next I was a soaked, barefoot wreck on Abbie's doorstep. "I was kind of a mess."

Slipping his finger under my chin, he lifts my face. "I'm sorry."

"I know Nick has to know about you eventually, but I can't deal with that right now. I have so much going on at work." I raise my brows. "And with you."

"I understand."

"You do?"

Jude quickly covers my mouth with his, swallowing me up and blanking my mind. The hum that rumbles up from his belly is carnal and content. "You're staying the night."

"As long as you stop being a bull."

"I will. I'm sorry. We both need to let off some steam."

"I'm fine," I say around his lips, hooking my arms over his shoulders, giving in to the spark that leads me back to Jude every time. "It's you who needs to let off some steam."

"You can help me." He starts guiding my backwards steps to the kitchen. "But first we fix your hand." He lifts me onto the counter and dumps my bag next to me. "I'll get some antiseptic." Going to the cupboard, he pulls down a small bag and brings it over as I start peeling the edges of the bandage again. "Sore?"

"A little," I admit, easing back the dressing, my teeth clenched. The cut is jagged, Z-shaped, and it creeps from the side of my hand onto my palm. It's ugly but, thank God, in a discreet place.

I hold it out to Jude and watch him closely as he concentrates on cleaning the fresh and dried blood away, dabbing carefully, checking my face for discomfort. "Okay?" he asks every so often. I nod each time, quiet. That changes when he sprays the antiseptic.

"Fuck!" I tense from top to toe, bringing my hand to my chest protectively. "Oh God, that stings."

"I'm sorry, baby," he says softly, wincing with me. "You've got to keep it clean."

"I know," I grate, breathing through the pain until I'm ready to let him dress it again.

"How did you shower this morning without getting it wet?"

"With great difficulty," I admit, reliving the whole awkward scene. "I tried a plastic bag over it, but I couldn't tie it up well enough to keep the water out, so I ended up holding my hand outside the cubicle while I did everything with one hand."

Jude chuckles, finishing up with a little extra tape. "So you know the solution to that, don't you?"

I grin as he lifts me down. "I have to shower with you, so I have three hands."

He peeks at the motif on my hoodie with a cocked brow. "Give me a hug that'll lead to sex."

I walk straight into his open arms and let him cuddle me half to death, feeling his remorse. I relax into it for a while, eventually breaking away and looking up at him. "My friends hate you," I whisper. He definitely flinches. "I don't want them to hate you."

"So I need to prove myself." He seals our mouths and walks me back to the bedroom, kissing me all the way there, releasing me only to lift the hoodie over my head. Then he kisses me down to the mattress. "And I will." He starts at my neck and works his way over my dress to my thighs, and I melt into the sheets on an exhale as he hitches the material up and brushes his finger across the lace of my knickers, biting at the insides of my thighs. "Do you trust me?"

"Yes."

He comes back up and pulls his trousers open, freeing himself. "Get your knickers off," he orders, prompting me to wriggle out of them as he holds himself up, getting his trousers and boxers down just enough. One swivel and he's inside, and we both groan at the inexplicable rightness of our bodies coming together. His head hangs as we adjust, before he looks at me, resting on his elbows and framing my face with his hands. He's still and silent for a few moments before he eventually speaks quietly. "I feel like you've got an arrow aimed at my heart, Amelia."

I breathe in my surprise. Then we're on the same page. Except Jude has fired and hit his target already. Should I confirm that?

He retreats and advances on an exhale, our breathing heavy. My hands stroke through his hair as he gazes down at me, his eyes green and soft. I feel like I've waited a lifetime for this feeling. For him. And yet it's happened so fast and been so tumultuous, I'm struggling to grab hold of my thoughts and make any sense of them. How fast can love happen?

What dictates it? Chemistry, lust, banter? My heart beats harder with him. It hurts when we fight.

"What are you thinking?" he asks softly.

The words hang on the end of my tongue, but I quickly remind myself that this is still very early days, and I don't mean since we got back together. I can't show my hand, expose myself. "Nothing."

Jesus Christ, this wasn't supposed to happen. Jude is comfort but unpredictable. Patience but frustration. I want to keep him at arm's length and be sensible, but my plan goes to shit each time, because when I look at him, something inside kicks, and I love the feeling, but fear it.

He starts grinding slowly, the intensity of his lazy eyes on me unmoving. I shake my head, unable to articulate how I'm feeling while also trying to deal with the sensations being inflicted on my body.

"What are *you* thinking?" I ask, throwing it back at him.

He stills for a moment, throbbing inside me, his eyes darting across my face. "Nothing," he whispers back. And he kisses me, rolling his hips and sending me out of my mind on Jude Harrison. He groans and starts moving faster, firmer, kissing me to match our new pace. "We're fucking idiots," he mumbles, biting my lip and pulling out, wrestling me out of my dress, then stripping himself. He turns me onto my side, curling his body around mine, guiding himself to me. Slipping in smoothly from behind, he slides his hand over my thigh, using it to pull me back onto him, yelling, sounding angry, and I cry out, closing my eyes, knowing soft and slow has left the building.

And more frustration has joined us.

Jude subjects me to a brutal pounding, his shouts loud, his force merciless, and I take it all, wishing I were brave enough to speak my truth.

I love him.

And to Jude's point, am I an idiot?

Chapter 8

The flesh around his nipple puckers as I circle it with my fingertip, my head in utter chaos despite my body feeling sated and calm. Jude hasn't murmured another word since he bellowed a few curses on his release, digging his fingers into my arse after he got me on my hands and knees and hammered into me to finish us both off.

I look up at him from where I'm sprawled across his chest, seeing his eyes closed. My mind races some more. It feels like there's something hanging between us, something awkward.

I'm worried we're not aligned to what that something is.

I love him and I don't know if I should. And, worse, I'm worried Jude hasn't entertained that possibility. The possibility to love. Loving being inside someone isn't the same as loving someone. Missing them isn't the same as loving them. My head starts to ache with the weight of my thoughts as I gently peel my body off his and get out of bed, padding on bare feet to the bathroom. I use the toilet, my eyes fixed on the cupboard as I pee. I hate myself for it, but as soon as I'm done, I find the box and check.

I don't know what to think when I see no more pills are missing. I put them back and rest my arse on the edge of the tub, my mind spinning. The answer for his erratic moods could be in that box. Allowing myself to conclude his irrationality and possessiveness are simply Jude being Jude isn't something I want to do. Or could the answer to his quirks be something else? I bite my lip, remembering his face when I told him I was falling for him. He looked shocked. No, he looked worried.

We're both idiots.

Am I wrong? Has he entertained the possibility? I bury my face in my palms, my overthinking head hurting some more. *God damn it.* I have to talk to him. I feel like I'm going insane, wondering if I'm wasting my time and love on a man who is incapable of feeling the same. Wondering if he's a man who thrives on the chemistry, but that's all it is. Good sex.

Possessive.

"Fuck," I whisper. He's *so* possessive. Is that what I want? A man who flies off the handle if another man so much as enters a five-mile radius of me? A man who sees me as a possession? A domineering, arguably volatile man who could have me walking on eggshells around him? Supressing myself? Being wary of every move I make? Jude's words to his brother come back to me, and I once again wonder what he was talking about.

Well, I feel fucked, to be honest.

The bet? It would make sense, but I just feel like there's more to it. He feels fucked.

"You and me both," I whisper. Ask him about the pills? Don't? Stick around to be hurt? Don't? Go back to my original plan of focusing on work and wine for a while? Don't? But the universe is telling me this is the one. Flaws and clashes aside, he's the one.

The pressure of my nonstop racing thoughts makes my head feel like it could explode. I squeeze my eyes closed, and on a sigh weighed down with hopelessness, I pull my hair into a ponytail. I need to talk to him. Have it out. Tell him how I really feel about him and see where that takes us. If he withdraws, my questions are answered. I'm wasting my time. *So much for taking it slowly.*

I head back into the bedroom.

And jar to a shocked halt on the threshold. "What the hell?" I blurt.

Jude catapults up in bed, startled, his sleepy eyes blinking rapidly as he tries to figure out what's wrong with me. "Katherine?" He grabs a pillow and pulls it over his groin. His move reminds me that I'm standing here completely naked.

"Is this a joke?" I spot one of Jude's T-shirts hanging over the back of a chair and quickly get into it.

"What the fuck?" Jude gets off the bed, pillow in place.

"Oh, she's here," Katherine says, casual.

My mouth falls open and Jude winces. "Get out, Katherine."

"I'll come back when she's gone." She turns and struts out, and my mouth falls open a little bit more. I can't believe this. She's still here, still sniffing around and spitting her venom.

"Isn't it about time you told her we were a thing?" she calls over her shoulder.

"What?" I gasp, looking at Jude to tell me she's talking out of her arse. A thing? What's a *thing*?

"It's complicated," Jude says, cursing and throwing the pillow down on the bed.

"Complicated how?"

He supresses a sigh. Oh, *he's* exasperated? "We have a history." His reluctance is clear. It's also worrying me, and my withdrawal spells that out.

"A history?"

"We were together."

I blink.

"Many years ago." It's him withdrawing now, backing away, putting space between us.

"She's your ex?" I ask, my voice high. Jude deflates, his eyes dropping. "Oh my God."

"I wanted to tell you myself, but, well"—he laughs under his breath—"Katherine fixed that."

"Oh, like you were going to tell me about the bet?"

His face is a landscape of impassiveness. "Yes."

"You said there was nothing significant to share when I asked you about your previous relationships." After I told him about Nick on our first *date*. Nick, who I *wasn't* still fucking. I can't believe this.

Tearing his T-shirt off, I go to my dress on the floor by the bed and snatch it up, starting to fight my way into it. Jude tenses as a result, looking like he's getting ready to stop me from walking out. "You have the audacity to make a fuss over some poxy flowers, and you're fucking your ex? Who, by the way, is fucking married!"

"It's fucked up, I know. And I *was* fucking her, Amelia. *Was.*"

I wrestle with the zip on the back of my dress, struggling with my stupid, lame hand. "Fuck!" Getting involved with a man quick off the heels of a breakup has already made a mockery of my plan. But getting myself caught up in a love triangle would be monumentally foolish. This was old news. Katherine was old news. But she's just made it very much new news, and somehow now it all feels so much more serious. She's his ex? Which means he *has* loved.

Incensed, and feeling so fucking stupid, especially after my tidal wave of thoughts in the bathroom, I leave my dress hanging open. "You're just one big bag of surprises, aren't you?"

Jude huffs a breath of unamused laughter. "You're the biggest surprise in this situation, Amelia, believe me." He grabs some boxers and yanks them on. "I've told you before, I'm fucked up. Leave. Save yourself."

Save myself? Too fucking late! "You should have told me. I should have known who she was so I could manage how I deal with the situation."

He keeps his eyes on me as he pulls his trousers up and his shirt on. "You managed just fine when you were trying to claw her eyes out a few weeks ago."

Is he going to continue with the proverbial slaps? "I think we're done."

"We are so far from done." He looks at the ceiling, exasperated, and I freeze, not liking his persona. "We were engaged."

My jaw goes lax, my eyes like saucers. *Engaged?*

"Briefly," he adds, as if that takes the sting out of this new bombshell. "Before I ended things." He blows his cheeks out, starting to pace up and down, fidgety. "I called it off, she met Rob, and that was that."

"That was that?" I ask in disbelief. "You still fuck her!"

"Not since I met you!"

"Oh, how admirable of you." Emotion is sneaking up on me, my voice becoming wobbly, my throat tight. What the hell have I got myself into? And how many times will I ask myself that stupid fucking question before I, in Jude's words, save myself?

I pull the hoodie on to cover the gaping back of my dress and collect my things.

"You're leaving," he says on a sigh. "Of course you are."

I turn and face him, resolute. "I'm taking your advice and saving myself." I walk out, knowing he's following me but keeping his distance. He was engaged to be married? Somehow, stupidly, that hurts way more than knowing he fucked her.

He *must* have loved her. The sting is real. I've never loved anyone like I love Jude, and I currently hate that. *Hate it.*

I sniff and roughly wipe at my face, and when I reach the lobby, Katherine is in the doorway to the bar, a gin glass in her hand. A smug smile on her face. And here I am, a mess.

I don't have the energy for her, and what would be the point anyway? She keeps firing her bullets, and they keep fucking hitting.

"Amelia," Jude calls after me, surprisingly calmly.

I step outside and feel untold relief when I see Humphrey beside one of the cars. "Can you take me back to London, Humphrey?" I ask, seeing him look past me. I peek over my shoulder and find Jude outside the doors. He stuffs his hands into his pockets, studying me, his jaw twitching with how tense it is.

He eventually tears his eyes away from me. "Take her," he says.

And then he turns and walks back into Arlington Hall.

And I feel like all my limbs have been cut off.

Chapter 9

I felt like I'd done a whole day before I even got to the office this morning. I went to the gym, picked up the cake stand, shot across town on the Tube to drop it off, shot back to sign the papers on my new rental, ready to collect the keys on Friday, and miraculously got into the office five minutes early. The weight that left my shoulders when I hit send on the various reinvestment recommendations was indescribable.

So is the infinite sense of stupidity. And hurt. His fucking fiancée? They were going to get married. That sounds pretty fucking serious. And the fact they were still fucking? What the hell does that even mean? They're not over each other? Jude can't let go? He regrets ending it? He's jealous she's married to someone else?

I growl under my breath and scratch my palm, the damn thing itching and driving me nuts. When my phone dings, I cautiously peek at the screen.

You're avoiding me

I shrink over my desk. Yes, I'm avoiding her. Because now I have to tell them that I'm not, in fact, back with Jude. So, cowardly, I ignore Abbie's message and call my mum instead.

"I'm still on a high!" she sings. "Oh, what a wonderful day it was. I want to do it all over again."

I smile with effort as I flick through my emails, earmarking them in order of priority. "It was."

"We haven't seen you for a few days."

"I've been a bit busy. I'll call round after work, okay? I have a dinner meeting at seven thirty, so don't cook for me."

"Okay, darling. Have you signed the paperwork for your new apartment yet?"

"This morning. I get the keys Friday."

"Lovely, I can't wait to pop round and see it."

"You'll be sitting on the floor." Jesus, that's something else I need to do. Furniture. "I'll see you after work." I hang up and head for Sue's office.

"Amelia." She sets her pen down.

"Has Gary calmed down yet?" I ask, shutting the door.

She laughs. "He's stable. What can I do for you?" She motions to the chair, and I lower to it.

"I wondered if there's anything I need to know about Leo Lombardy. We have a dinner meeting this evening."

"Oh, well, first of all, he's super casual."

"In attire or personality?"

"Both. You wouldn't look at him and think he's a multimillionaire, anyway. He's also casual with his money. To be honest, he's got so much it's neither here nor there to him if he loses some, so he'll be happy with high risk. Will probably push for it, actually, but keep your head on straight. That's why I put him your way, Amelia, and not Leighton's. Steers would undoubtedly take that as a green light to get silly. You are not a maverick, and Lombardy does not need one."

I nod, understanding. "Thank you for the insight." I stand. "I'll let you know how it goes."

"You'll get on like a house on fire, I'm sure. He's chilled, and you're just the right amount of cautious that he needs."

"Thanks, Sue."

"And Amelia?"

I look back as I pull the door open.

"You're doing everything right, okay?"

My heavy body lifts, and I nod, thankful for the pep talk when I'm uncertain about so much of my life. "Thanks, Sue." I leave and take a few breaths, but still when I hear Leighton in the distance. I can't promise I won't launch him into outer space with my good hand if he spews any of his smarminess all over me, so I hotfoot it back to my office and grab my things, before exiting the office swiftly.

◆ ◆ ◆

I walk through the front door and drop my bags, calling out a hello.

"Grand Girl!"

Poking my head around the lounge door, I find Grandma and Grandpa in their obligatory spots on either side of the fireplace. "Hey, you two."

Grandma beckons me, so I perch on the arm of her armchair as she sets her knitting needles down. Her grey eyebrows lift. "How are you?"

Since I last saw her? Well, I got back together with the man who gave me fanny flutters, and we've split up again. Things are peachy. "I get the keys to my new place Friday."

Grandma rolls her eyes. "Boring."

"I'm fine, Grandma," I assure her. *You silly, silly girl.* She wasn't wrong. *The best kind of love hurts the most.* I don't want to love him! "Have you spoken to Clark and Rachel?"

"Yes," Grandpa chirps up, snapping his *Financial Times* shut. "Video call, Amelia. It was like I was in Greece with them!"

I laugh, looking back to the kitchen. It's quiet. "Where's Mum and Dad?"

"Having a discussion in the garden," Grandma says, craning her head to look back too. "Your mother wants to do more shifts at the florist and your father would rather she didn't."

"Oh God," I breathe, getting up and heading out the back, ready to split them up. I see them out the window on the patio, Mum with a gardening fork in her hand, Dad with a watering can and a scowl on his face. It looks like it's getting heated, so I hurry to the back door.

"You're not even retired!" Mum hisses. "You've been in the office every day this week!"

"Every day?" Dad laughs. "It's Tuesday, for Christ's sake."

"And will you go in tomorrow?"

"I have to, Clark's on his honeymoon."

"You have three managers!"

"Hello," I say, resting my shoulder on the doorframe. Mum slaps on a smile and whips off her gardening gloves, and Dad drops the watering can. "What's all the noise about?"

"Nothing, darling."

"What happened to your hand?" Dad asks, coming to me.

"It's fine. I cut it and needed a few stitches."

"How did you cut it?" He lifts it and checks the bandages. "You're leaking. This needs changing. Jenn, Amelia's dressing needs changing." He looks at Mum, who glances between us. She's a little red in the face. Exasperated.

"You do it," she snaps. "I have dinner to cook." Stomping past us, she throws him a filthy glare, and Dad recoils like she could have just slapped him.

"Jenn?" he murmurs.

"You're in the doghouse," I say, pointing out the obvious. The poor man looks so wounded. Yes, he's old-fashioned to a fault, but he's a good man. "Come on, help me change this thing. I have a dinner meeting. I can't be bleeding all over the table."

Dad sighs. "What do I need?"

"Some salty warm water." I link arms with him and walk us through the patio doors to the dining room, avoiding Mum in the kitchen. "Actually, I'll get the water. You wait."

I grab my bag from the hall and go back to the kitchen, where I find Mum stirring the pot on the stove aggressively. I leave her be and get some water from the kettle and salt from the cupboard, then join Dad again, lowering and giving him my hand. "Get on with it."

He peeks up through his lashes with only mild warning, and I smile, making him shake his head. "Your mother was always the first-aider when you were kids." He peels away the dressing carefully with his big fingers as I sprinkle some salt into the water.

"I'm not a kid anymore."

"No, you're not, Amelia Gracie," he muses. "You're certainly not a kid." He winces when he reveals the cut. "Jesus Lord above," he gasps, horrified. "How the hell did you manage this?"

I grimace at my wound. It really does look angry. "I leant on a piece of glass." I take some cotton wool from my makeup bag and dunk it. "It looks worse than it is. Here."

Dad accepts and starts gingerly dabbing. "I don't want to hurt you."

I smile fondly. What Dad doesn't realise is the only time he hurts me is when he's an unwitting misogynist. "You're not hurting me."

He grunts, brushing at the cut delicately. "I had my first golf lesson today."

"But Mum said you were in the office today."

"I finished early."

I roll my eyes. That wasn't the plan, but small steps, I suppose. "How was it?"

"Harder than I thought, but my instructor said I've got a solid swing."

"Did you enjoy it?" Will he keep it up? Maybe stop going to the office every single day and actually embrace retirement?

He smiles up at me. "I did."

"That's great."

"Tell me about your day."

I nearly fall off my chair. "My day?" I murmur, my shock obvious.

"Yes, your day."

He says it like it's not really weird that after years of never asking, he's suddenly hitting me with that question. "I'm assuming you mean work."

He looks up tiredly. "Unless you want to talk about your most recent breakup, and I don't mean with Nick."

I wilt where I'm sitting. Dad doesn't know just how recent my breakup is. And that it's a whole shiny-new breakup. "I was seeing him. And now I'm not. The end."

"Him. Who is *him*?"

"It doesn't matter. It's over. And to be clear, Dad, that's not a green light for you to start inviting Nick round for dinner again."

He huffs. "I know, I've been warned."

"By whom?"

"Your mother. Your grandmother." He smirks up at me. "Don't tell your mum, but I fancy her even more when she's mad at me."

I laugh out loud, and Dad winks. It's so relaxed. So unlike Dad. And as if he's suddenly realised, he snaps back into line. "Keep still," he mutters.

"I didn't move."

"So your day?"

I don't know what's happened to change his lack of interest in my career, but I appreciate it. "I think I'm in the running to make partner, Dad."

His head lifts so fast, I'm sure he's probably going to suffer whiplash. "Partner? At LB&B?"

I nod. "I was invited out for casual drinks with the partners a couple of weeks ago."

"Well." He lets out a long, disbelieving breath. "That's very impressive, darling. Well done."

I might die of shock. What the hell is going on around here? "Thanks, Dad," I say, not wanting to make a big deal of this. But it is. It's huge. "You need to make peace with Mum."

"I just don't understand why she wants to go out to work, Amelia. Especially now."

"She's a social butterfly, Dad. Being in the shop, she'll meet people, chat with them. And to Mum's point, you're hardly retired if you go to the office every day."

"I'm just checking things are running smoothly."

"Control freak," I mutter quietly, making him gasp his disgust. I smirk. Dad scowls.

"So you're dating, are you?"

My smile soon drops. "What?"

"Dating. Like on those app things people talk about."

"I'm not on any dating apps."

"But you're dating?" he says, peeking up at me.

This is weird. "I'm not dating, Dad." I pull my hand away when he's stuck some tape over the new dressing.

"Then how did you meet the man who you're no longer seeing?"

I am *not* telling him that. "I have to make a move, or I'll be late for my meeting." I stand and kiss Dad's startled face. "Thanks for cleaning me up." Tugging my bag off the table, I throw it onto my shoulder.

"Are you sure you don't love him?"

I jolt where I'm standing, my mouth suddenly dry. "What?"

"Nick. Are you sure there's nothing you can build on?"

"Oh my God." I drop my head back. "Dad!"

"I'm just double-checking."

"And I'm leaving," I snap, marching away.

"He's a safe bet, Amelia!"

"Stop worrying about my love life and fix your own." I slam the door behind me and yell at the heavens.

Chapter 10

Nonna's is everything the endless five-star reviews promised it would be. Not that I underestimated it. What I did underestimate was Leo Lombardy. Sue was right, he's extremely casual, on all fronts. I've never been so relaxed when meeting a potential client for the first time.

"It's good, huh?" Leo says as he twiddles his fork in a pile of pasta.

"Unreal."

"Here, have some wine." He pours for me as he carries on eating, because it's really that delicious, you can't put your fork down. "So, Sue was telling me she's very excited about you."

I pause chewing, surprised, but try to play it down. "That's a massive compliment coming from Sue. She's a great adviser. Just great all round, really."

"Agree."

I pause for thought, definitely seeing a little twinkle in his eye. "How do you know each other?" I ask, appearing casual but raging with curiosity. Am I overthinking? But then Leo smiles down into his pasta and my suspicions feel quite possible. Jesus, are they . . . ?

"On the golf course," he muses quietly and easily. Too easily. *I don't mix friendships with business. It can be messy.* And mixing business with someone she's sleeping with? Well, that's against company policy. So she's passed Leo on to me? Oh fuck. Sue's married. And she told me Leo is recently divorced. Is Sue the reason why?

"On the golf course," I repeat, with a lack of anything else coming to me. *She's sleeping with him!*

Leo looks up at me, and I know, I just know, that he's sensed I've put two and two together. Fuck, I need to drop this, act dumb. I smile. "So tell me about your future plans."

Leo laughs. "I'm sixty-two, Amelia," he says, his light Italian accent smooth but grainy too. "Still young, yes? Plenty of time to think past today."

"What you just said, Leo, is literally every adviser's worst nightmare."

Leo grins cheekily, taking more pasta. "I feel like I'm about to get a lecture."

"You are. People think about the future too late. They don't make provisions for their retirement soon enough. I'm very aware that you don't count, since you're richer than God, but still. It's easier to lose money than it is to make it."

He chuckles. "Less rich now my ex-wife has . . . how you say? Fleeced me?"

"Yes." I laugh. "That." I swirl my fork in my last bit of pasta and pop it in my mouth, gazing at the remaining sauce longingly. If I were at Mum and Dad's, I would grab some bread and mop up.

"But still richer than God," Leo quips. "So what's in your future?" He finishes and wipes his mouth too, and I'm absolutely beside myself with joy when he dips into the breadbasket and plucks out a piece of granary bread, pushing it around his bowl. I follow suit.

"As of this moment, my future is work."

"No man?"

I blink, taken aback. "No man." And he's not attempted to call me or text me. I have no right to be hurt by that. And yet here I am. Hurt. "I'm career focused right now," I say, finishing my bread and washing it down with some wine.

"Well, I suppose we should exchange emails." Leo pulls an iPhone out of the inside pocket of his linen jacket. "What's yours?"

I reel it off and save Leo's when it lands, and I smile. "Sue mentioned you like high risk." I snap my mouth shut when Leo's eyebrows lift sharply. Shit. I cannot believe I said that. "I mean when it comes to investments."

Leo polishes off half his glass of wine. "Indeed, I do, but Sue told *me* that you're the perfect blend of risky and safe."

"I like to ensure I'm making conscious m—" My words fade, and my smile drops like a rock when I see Jude across the restaurant being shown to a table.

With a woman.

"What the fuck?" I breathe.

"What?" Leo says, craning to look over his shoulder.

"Nothing."

Jude's eyes land on me. And then Leo. And the instant rage on him is rampant. Oh shit. But . . . he's got a fucking nerve. Who the hell is that woman? Busty. Curvy. Platinum-blond hair. A blouse that's got one too many buttons undone. Jude says something to her, looking this way, and then starts walking through the tables towards us. *Oh fuck, fuck, fuck.*

"Excuse me." Hopping up, I grab my bag, hoping Jude follows me and doesn't confront Leo. "I need the ladies'." I head through the little nook and down a corridor, looking back over my shoulder.

I'm only a bit relieved when I find Jude in pursuit. Rounding a corner, I wait, and the second he appears, I want to weep at how fucking stunning he is in a casual beige suit and open-collar white shirt.

For another woman.

"Who the hell is that woman?"

"What the hell do you care?" he hisses back, leaning down, making a few locks of his hair fall onto his forehead.

"I don't."

"Who the hell is that man?"

"What the fucking hell do *you* care?" I pivot and push my way into the ladies', slamming the cubicle door behind me. "Fucking man," I mutter.

"Fucking woman," I hear Jude grunt.

I swing the door open. "Get out."

His eyes narrow to angry slits. "I dare you to push me over the fucking edge, Amelia," he says darkly. "I fucking dare you."

"You lied to me. You don't deserve anything from me but a slap."

"Then slap me."

"I don't want to slap you!"

He pounces, getting me up against the tiled wall and attacking my lips like a desperate madman, pushing his tongue into my mouth, the aggression of his kiss forcing my head back against the wall.

My body instantly burns for him, my mind scrambles, my thighs clench. Fuck, no! How does this keep happening? Explosions, sparks, ravenous for each other. It's unstoppable.

But I must stop it.

"No." I turn my head, breaking my lips from his, and push him back, passing him. "I'm not doing this again."

"Are you saying it's over?"

I stop at the door. Squeeze my eyes closed. I need more than chemistry and explosions. I need trust. Respect. *Love.* He's here with another fucking woman the day after we broke up. *Again.*

"It's over." I swing the door open and leave, holding back my tears as I make my way to the table. *Keep it together!* I need to nail this meeting.

Leo cocks his head as I lower to my chair, my shoulders aching from how tense they are. I can feel Jude's eyes on me. "Are you okay?"

I force a smile. "Great. My hand's a little sore."

"I didn't want to pry."

"It was an idiotic accident. It was my brother's wedding this past weekend. I had a few too many and leant on some broken glass."

"Stitches?"

"Ten."

He puts his hand on the table, palm up, and I see a scar running from the base of his little finger to the centre of his palm. "A broken bottle on the beach in Sorrento. Twenty stitches."

"You win," I quip, and he chuckles as I help myself to more wine, needing it. I freeze in my chair when Jude appears at the side of the table. *Oh God.* He looks between Leo and me, his hands in his pockets, casual, but I see the burn in his dark-blue eyes. Leo tilts his head to look up at Jude. I die on the spot.

"What do you recommend?" Jude asks, motioning to the empty bowls.

I peek at Leo, my words caught in my throat. He's smiling. "The seafood linguine is famous. A must."

I want the ground to swallow me whole. "A must," I murmur, sipping more wine. Is there another bottle coming?

"Then I'll try that," Jude says, leaving, relieving me of his passive-aggressive presence.

"Well." Leo laughs. "He was an intense creature."

I awkwardly smile at the irony, needing to get out of here, but I don't want Leo to feel like I'm trying to escape.

"The bill?" he suggests, and I sag.

"Yes, please, let me."

"Oh, absolutely not." Leo calls to a waiter, and my eyes root past him, watching Jude weaving through the tables until he disappears around a corner. They were seated in the next room. Thank God. But then he suddenly appears again, the woman in tow, a waiter motioning to a table nearby. The fuckhead. He's asked to be moved so I can see how his dinner date pans out?

I clench my fists and immediately regret it, a sharp, shooting pain engulfing my entire hand. Jude pulls a chair out for the woman, and she lowers, smiling, her back ramrod straight, her chest the showstopper of the night. He takes a chair opposite her, his back to me. But then he stands up, shifts his chair around the table and lowers next to her, looking at me briefly before picking up the menu from the centre of the table and passing it to the woman, leaning in to see it too. Close. That's what he did at our first dinner. Moved his chair to be closer to me. Then he finger-fucked me under the table until I came, clutching at the tablecloth.

My stupid, betraying heart cracks, my eyes naturally watching the tablecloth for movement.

"Amelia?"

I blink and look at Leo. He's standing. Has paid. "Sorry," I murmur, rising. "Thank you so much for dinner." I'm struggling to keep my eyes under control, which is ridiculous. I don't want to see what's going on at Jude's table.

I throw my bag onto my shoulder and follow Leo, and, fuck my life, he's walking straight towards Jude's table. "I hope you like the linguine," Leo says as he passes, and both Jude and his date look our way. She smiles, all toothy and wide, her red lips stretching. And Jude maintains his infinite, intense expression.

"Enjoy the rest of your evening," he says, eyes on me. And my heart cracks a little bit more. I overtake Leo and hurry outside, breathing in the cool nighttime air urgently.

"I assume you can get home safely," he says when he makes it to me on the pavement. There's a Bentley idling at the kerbside. Undoubtedly his.

"Yes, thank you."

"It was a pleasure to meet you, Amelia."

I feel absolutely clueless past my stress right now. We haven't talked business for long; he never really confirmed if he's interested in me taking over his financial affairs.

"I'll be in touch," Leo says, getting in the car.

He'll be in touch. Is that like date code for *I'll call you*? I look back over my shoulder to the restaurant doors, wanting to go in there and upend Jude's table. I can feel that crazy part of me I never knew existed until I met Jude Harrison rising, my blood boiling. I ended it. I have no power here.

Power?

What the hell am I thinking?

I quickly pick up my feet and head for the Tube station before I let them take me back into the restaurant and rain holy hell on Jude. But I only make it precisely five steps before I stop and turn, yelling at myself not to go back but unable to stop my legs from taking me there. *No, Amelia!* I keep walking, feeling out of control in every way. *Stop, Amelia. Go to the Tube!*

I swing the door to the restaurant open and run straight into a chest, bouncing back.

The moment I take a breath, I know it's Jude. I can smell him. I find his eyes and see the beast inside. "You are *not* going home with that man," he seethes, looking past me for said man.

"And you are not going home with that woman!"

"I don't want to!"

"Then what the hell are you doing on a date?"

"What the hell are *you* doing on a date?"

"He's a client! And he's twice my fucking age, Jude!"

He recoils. "A client?"

"I don't play stupid fucking games like you do." I shove him in his chest. "Who the hell is she?"

"It's Rhys's publicist."

"What?"

"It's Rhys's fucking publicist, Amelia. I'm firing her."

"Well, I suggest you communicate a bit better because she appears to think you want to fuck her."

"Fuck!" he yells, raking a hand through his hair and swinging around. Then he grabs my arm and walks me out onto the street and up the road a little to a quieter spot. Easing me up against a wall, he comes close. "It's all about you, Amelia," he says quietly. "I can't control Katherine or her gob, but I can make sure you know that she means *nothing* to me."

"But she did once," I whisper, hearing the need in me and hating it.

Moving in even closer, he crowds me. "It pales compared to how I feel about you."

I look away, and he curses, grabbing my face and making me look at him. His eyes scan mine. His are questioning. Mine are tearful. I'm so fucking confused. So tired of arguing and making up again.

"I wasn't expecting you," I whisper, my voice broken. "And now I'm caught up in this whirlwind of euphoria and drama and I'm questioning everything."

"Questioning what?"

"Everything. You, us, what's happening, whether I should let it happen."

Jude flinches, my words wounding him, and then he steps away, putting space I didn't ask for between us. It doesn't help my unease. But when he clenches his temples with his hands and his expression turns pained, I'm no longer uneasy. I'm scared. What the hell is he going to tell me now?

Instinct has me turning and walking away from him, unable to sustain another blow. Another one of Jude's truths.

"I'm in love with you," he says gently, almost with regret.

I stop dead in my tracks, the words hitting me like a wrecking ball to my chest. *So* hard. Could they destroy me? I bite down on my lip, shaken, staring forward, a bit dazed. My head is a riot of confliction. I don't want to turn around. Am scared to look at him.

"I love you, Amelia."

I breathe out a rush of air I hadn't realised I was holding.

"I've been trying to tell you."

I slowly turn on the spot, struggling to hold back more tears. He sighs, heavy and tired, and moves to a nearby bench, resting his arse down, his upper body curling over his thighs, his elbows on his knees. He puts his face in his hands. Hiding. He's said that, and now he's hiding? I need him to hold me. Tell me everything will be okay. That my heart is safe.

"I know it's happened fast," he continues. "I know it's intense and crazy and a lot to take in, but it's also really fucking brilliant, Amelia." Glancing up at my stunned form, he smiles a little, but it falls when he sees the tears streaming down my cheeks. "You don't believe me," he says, his voice as broken as I feel in this moment. And isn't that a worry in itself? That I feel broken? Isn't love supposed to heal? "Fuck, you don't believe me." He stands abruptly and drags a hand through his hair. Then a sense of urgency seems to come over him and he rushes to me, taking my wet cheeks in his palms. "I love you," he says, kissing my forehead. "I love you." Then my nose. "I love you." And my lips. "I love you, I love you, I love you." Pulling away, he gives me his eyes, and I can't mistake the sincerity in them. I can't believe a man would be as cruel as to say that, look like this, and not mean it. "Are you hearing what I'm saying to you?"

Yes, I'm hearing, and it's terrifying. "This isn't very slowly," I murmur like an idiot, and he smiles.

"I will do life slowly with you, baby. Make love to you slowly and softly. Stroke your back slowly and softly while you drift off to sleep, lick champagne off your body slowly. But my love is fast and hard, and it's fucking unstoppable, and I'm praying you accept it, because without you I am just a lonely man with a lot of money and no substance."

My heart doesn't crack. It melts. "You don't always have to make love softly and slowly."

Jude's eyes shine so brightly, and he hauls me into his chest, his arm hooked around my neck holding me tightly to him. I close my eyes and hear his heart beating. "I love you too," I whisper, diving in deep. The deepest. I lift my arms to his wide back and cling to him, feeling his torso deflate.

"Say it louder," he demands, removing me from his chest and pushing my hair back so he can see the whole of my surely red and blotchy face. "And to my face."

I don't hesitate. "I love you."

His smile is small but stunning. "Thank you." He slowly lowers to his knees on the hard concrete. "I'm in love with you, Amelia Gracie Lazenby. I'm tired of all this ambiguity between us."

"Me too."

"So it's official."

"Our love?"

"And that I now have myself a girlfriend."

I laugh over a strained sob, and he flashes an adorable, lopsided grin. "Jude—"

"Don't you dare put an obstacle in my way."

"I'm not. It's just, you've not even met my parents."

"Well, that's not true." He stands again. "I've met your mother."

It's not my mother I'm worried about. "You hardly know the girls, and they're not exactly your biggest fans."

"I'll fix that. We'll do dinner with your friends. And meet your parents."

Christ. That fills me with all kinds of dread. "Let's start with my friends." I feel a lot less anxious about that.

"Anything else?" he asks.

I shake my head, because there is nothing else. I'm going with this. We can work through the rest. I trust him. The fighting and making up are part of who we are, because our feelings are so strong.

"Good." He swoops in and kisses me slowly and softly. The impact, though? It hits me as fast and hard as it always does, and I breathe easy for the first time since I walked away from him last night.

"I'm staying the night," I mumble around his lips.

And he smiles.

Chapter 11

Ambient light from the blue glass shades over the bar makes the Library Bar glow beautifully, as if it could be bathed in moonlight. Jude has a quiet word in Clinton's ear, and he nods, tossing his cocktail shaker in the air and catching it expertly.

"Give me a moment," Jude says, putting me on a stool.

There's an older couple in the two chairs by the fireplace, and Jude approaches, crouching, talking quietly for a few moments. The couple get up, smiling, taking their drinks and leaving. Then he wanders over to a younger couple at the end of the bar, and after a few moments, they get up and leave too. My eyes follow as they pass me, and I smile mildly, uncertain, when they smile at me.

Next, Jude goes to a couple of women sitting by the bookcases. They listen, smile too, collect their drinks, and leave. Only the man on his own in the corner remains, but after a few seconds of Jude talking to him, he nods, snaps his laptop shut, and exits the Library Bar too.

And we're alone.

"What are you doing?" I ask when Jude comes back to me.

"Buying us some privacy."

"We could get that in your apartment." And, frankly, we'd get a bed too. I was certain that was where he'd take me.

"Here." He pushes a highball towards me. "Your drink."

"Hey Jude," I muse, admiring the masterpiece created in a glass by Clinton.

As Jude scissors the stem of another glass and pulls it towards him, he perches on the stool next to me. "I get the Amelia." He lifts the glass and holds it up, prompting me to clink it with mine.

"Are you going to tell me why you've kicked everyone out of your bar?" Just then, music joins us, and I nearly lose my breath when I register the track. I find Jude's eyes. His parents' favourite song. The song he's named after. "Jude," I breathe, watching as he reaches for my glass and helps it to my lips.

"Drink," he tells me, settling back with his own cocktail and listening. "Mum used to play this to me when I was a kid. When I was sad about anything." He laughs a little. "She told me it was about love fixing everything. About being positive in shitty situations. I honestly believed Paul McCartney wrote it for me and that Mum was talking about her love for me, because it really did fix everything."

Oh my heart, I can't take it.

"McCartney actually wrote it for John Lennon's son," he goes on. "He did?"

"But his name was Julian. I don't know how Julian turned into Jude. Three syllables versus one, I guess."

I chuckle. "*Hey Julian* doesn't have the same ring to it, huh?"

He smirks, reaching for my hand and stroking gently over the dressing. "I've not listened to it since her funeral."

My lip wobbles, my throat tightening.

"I've really never felt strong enough." He looks up at me, and my head runs amok with thoughts and visions of pills. He's never felt strong enough. God, I can't even begin to comprehend his grief. "I feel strong enough now," he adds quietly.

I'm going to cry. "I'm glad."

"Me too." He stands and takes my glass, setting it on the bar, and helps me off the stool. Going to the doors, he closes them as Clinton slips through the staff door behind the bar, leaving us.

"What's happening?"

He takes my good hand and pulls me gently into his chest by the fireplace. We're dancing? He drapes my arms over his neck and holds my waist, starting to sway us. "We're happening," he says quietly, kissing me gently. And he doesn't stop. And I can't help but think it's a ploy on his part to keep himself busy, to not let his emotions get the better of him.

And yet however he chooses to deal with it, it's still a perfectly beautiful moment. "I love you," he says, eventually breaking our kiss and sinking his face into my neck. "I really fucking love you, Amelia."

Peace envelops me. And a deep sense that this is completely right.

I cling on to him and let him circle us slowly, our bodies pressed together, every curve of mine melding with his, feeling as perfect as this moment. My fingers weave through the strands of hair on his nape, my eyes closed, just needing to hear and feel.

And we remain that way, both of us quiet, for the entire track until we're turning in silence. I don't instigate the separation of our bodies, happy to remain in this beautiful bubble of peace together.

I open my eyes when I feel his lips on my neck, staring out the window onto the drive of Arlington Hall. Whatever he needs to take from me, he can take. "Thank you," he eventually whispers.

I shake my head mildly and pull away, my eyes scanning his for a few quiet seconds, before I apply pressure to the back of his head and push our lips together, speaking with my kiss rather than with words. He hums, lifting me from my feet, deepening our kiss as he walks us to the door. When he sets me down, I'm more than dazed. My body alive. My heart alive.

"Come," he says, his voice gruff with desire as he takes my hand and opens the door. Purpose and intent radiate from his entire being as he leads me up to his apartment, anticipation hammering between my legs, every piece of me pulsing for him. As soon as the door closes behind us, he's on me, kissing me hard, his tongue inexorable. I shove his jacket off his shoulders, and he wrestles out of it, freeing his arms before finding the zip on the back of my dress and pulling it down fast. I wriggle my arms out, keeping my lips attached to his, and Jude lifts me, letting me kick my way out of my dress and heels. By the time we make it to the bed in a tangle of limbs and flying clothes, we're naked, and we fall down together, arms and legs everywhere, our mouths wild, our impatience thick. He rolls me onto my back, covers my body with his, and slides into me on a suppressed groan, his eyes clenched shut.

My world explodes into a million shards of ecstasy. I toss my head back on a cry, feeling his mouth sucking at my neck, his hips swinging into action, desperation getting the better of him.

Bliss.

Every pump takes me higher, makes me louder, my body accepting every hard, long inch of him, drawing him back in each time he retreats. There's nothing like this feeling. When we're connected so deeply, when our bodies answer each other. Know each other. He hooks an arm under my knee and lifts it, opening me up to him some more, rocking, his mouth drifting onto my chest, my breasts, and back to my mouth. A few swirls of his tongue, a few pants each time he drives in, and then he pulls back, watching me as he thrusts on. Watching me climb to my high. "I love you," he says, moving so fluidly.

I hold the side of his face, unable to talk through my pleasure, nodding my acceptance instead.

"You're pulling me in deep, baby." He turns his mouth onto my hand and kisses my dressing, clenching his eyes closed. I can feel every throb of his cock, the blood pumping, his chest matching it. Sweat beads are forming on his brow. Tingles creep up my body from my toes.

"Jude," I whisper in warning.

He drops my leg and falls to his forearms, his head hanging, driving on faster.

I cry out, coiling my legs around his waist, tensing, preparing. My vision fogs, stars jump into my sight, and our bodies start to slip as our sweat mixes on our skin. I'm holding on for dear life, knowing my climax is going to hit hard.

And when I see the veins in his neck bulge and he gasps, lifting his head to look up at me, the intensity of his eyes has me shattering underneath him on a throaty cry.

"Oh, Jesus, Amelia," he whispers, watching me come undone. My head thrashes as I deal with the intensity and the pure, exquisite fullness of him inside, banging my pleasure out of me. "Fuck," he yells. "Fuck, you look incredible coming so *fucking* hard." He thrusts one last time, holding himself deeply so I can feel the second he climaxes, before crumpling on top of me, breathless, to join me in the aftermath.

Aftershocks have me jolting constantly, the sensitivity almost too much to bear. I can't hold on to him any longer, my limbs listless. My heart feels like it could burst, both with exhaustion and love.

"Okay?" he pants, splattered all over me, hot and wet, still pulsing and twitching. That was intense. It's always intense, but that just felt different.

"I don't know yet," I admit as I stare up at the ceiling, arms and legs splayed, my mouth open, needing as much air as I can get, my lungs burning.

"Me either," he replies, a red-hot weight on top of me, but I don't have the energy to ask him to move *or* push him off. Biting at my neck with little force, Jude exhales heavily and loudly, and I close my eyes, immediately falling into a deep slumber trapped beneath him.

Burning.

Still full to the brim with Jude.

Exhausted.

Madly, deeply in love.

Chapter 12

Feathery touches down my arm wake me, and I wince as Jude lifts his hips and slides out of me, rolling onto his back with a huff and pulling me into his side. I don't know how long I've been out, but I can still hear his heart beating hard when my head comes to rest on his chest. I sigh, settled, both in body and mind, feeling like we've finally reached a common place.

"You're staying the night," he says sleepily, breathing into my hair as he plays with a strand.

I smile. "Really taking this slowly, aren't we?"

"I never agreed. You didn't want to. So here we are. Where we should be."

I scrunch my nose and turn my lips onto his chest, kissing it.

"Are you hungry?"

"No, that pasta will keep me full until lunchtime tomorrow."

"Well, I didn't get to try it, so I'm going to get room service." Easing me off his chest, he gets up and fishes his mobile out of his trouser pocket. I roll to my back on an appreciative exhale and admire his naked form as he wanders over to the window. "Hey, Audrey, can you get a chicken club sandwich sent up to my apartment?" he says. "With fries. And mayo. And extra pickles." He looks back at me, laughing under his breath. "Yeah, gotta keep up my energy."

My eyebrows lift, and I stretch out on the bed, my back arching, and it feels glorious. "I feel like something sweet." My smile is demure and really bloody teasing, and Jude's eyes instantly mist, his chest swelling from a deep inhale.

"Add the Eton Mess for Amelia," he says quietly. "And a bottle of champagne. And can you have her bags brought up from the Library Bar?" He bites his lip. "Thanks."

I brace myself when he stalks back to the bed, tossing his phone aside and crawling up to me, pinning me down by my wrists. My delighted eyes take him in as he gazes down at me. "Flirt," he whispers, swooping in and eating me alive. With ownership. It's the longest kiss. The deepest. Full of meaning, conviction and passion. He rolls us carefully, not breaking our mouths, humming, moaning, and rolling us again, back to the middle of the bed.

"Oh?" I whisper, feeling him hardening up against me. My legs open, inviting him.

"You want me again?"

"Please," I murmur, flexing my hips up, helping him fall into place.

He pulls back, observing me for a few moments, running his tongue across his bottom lip.

"Flirt." I reach for his hair and fist it, moving my mouth up his cheek to his ear as he swivels and enters me. "God, yes," I breathe, feeling him so deeply.

Jude groans, stilling, panting rapidly. "How the hell do you do this to me?"

I shut him up, claiming his mouth again, as he starts to thrust smoothly, in and out. I'm sure I could kiss him all night long, but he breaks away and pulls out, starting to kiss his way down my body. My spine bends, my eyes close, my skin soaking up the pressure of his mouth, my muscles tightening the farther down my body he gets. Cool air brushes across my opening, before his teeth nibble at the insides of my thighs.

"Yes, yes, yes," I whisper, every bit of me undulating in anticipation of his hot mouth on me.

"Hmm." His tongue flicks the tip of my clit, and I cry out, reaching for his hair and pulling. "Violence will get you nowhere," he rasps, flicking again.

My legs spread wider, my hand on his head applying pressure. I look up at the ceiling, groaning as he licks gently up my core, circling slowly, before plunging his tongue deep. My hips lift off the bed, but Jude soon forces me back down, holding me in place with one forearm across my stomach.

"Jesus," I whisper, feeling the pleasure rushing forward as he sucks, laps, kisses, moaning his way through, making a feast of me.

My mouth open, I look down my front, seeing his head bob and turn, his hair in disarray. He peeks up, his eyes misty, his mouth never faltering in driving me wild. I don't need to tell him I'm about to detonate. He must see it in my eyes, feel it in the stiffening of my body, because he tightens his hold of me, licks faster, kisses harder, sucks deeper.

"Oh God!" I force myself to keep his eyes, the sight taking me to the brink faster. It hits me between my legs like a freight train, lifts me off the bed, racks my body, shakes me violently. "Fucking hell." The sensitivity is too much. "Softer," I order, making him ease off, every piece of me sinking into the bed, twitching, as Jude laps gently, letting me ride the waves of my release. I'm sweating. Breathless. Burning up. "Oh my God," I gasp, feeling him crawl up the bed, the tip of his erection dragging across my thigh. "I need a moment."

"Tough." He rolls me onto my front and pushes a leg out, giving him room, and eases inside on a sigh, breathing in. "Jesus, you're still throbbing."

I close my eyes and absorb his pounds, clenching at the pillow, wincing at how hard and deep he's going. But I sustain it. Take it. Relish it. It doesn't take him long, and I'm grateful, not because of the power, but because I'm completely shattered. Literally, fucked to death. He collapses on my back, his hips thrusting slowly as he bites at my ear, making me shudder.

"Hmm, this is nice," he whispers, his arms coming up and framing my head. He licks the shell of my ear, nibbling the lobe.

"Stop or I'll want to go again."

"Not a problem with me."

"I need to recover."

"Then hurry up and recover."

I smile into the darkness, the weight of him covering me lush, and let myself drift off, warm, cosy, safe, and more in love with every minute that passes.

My eyes spring open when I feel Jude peel off my back. "Food's here," he whispers, sliding out of me. "To be continued." He gets up and goes to a chair, tugging on some boxers.

"Come back," I grumble, rolling onto my side, arms stretched out. "I'm cold."

"Here." Jude throws me a T-shirt and heads out, and I pull it on, mumbling my displeasure as I tie up my hair.

"Two desserts? Lucky me." I smile when I hear him laughing, retrieving my knickers from the floor and getting them on.

Jude's already got his mouth wrapped around one half of his club sandwich when I make it to the kitchen, humming his pleasure. A blob of mayonnaise sits on the corner of his lip.

"That good?" I ask, rounding the island to him. Jesus, he must have been starving; he's not even sat himself down to eat.

"The best club sandwich you'll ever try," he garbles, stilling when I lift on my tippy-toes and move in on his mouth.

"You have something here," I whisper, licking the mayonnaise away.

"Thanks." He swallows. "If I wasn't ravenous, you'd be on that counter now taking another pounding." He sinks his teeth back into his sandwich around a cheeky smile as I laugh my way round the island and hop on a stool, reaching for the metal dome on the tray and lifting it off.

"Oh, yum." My mouth waters as I sink a spoon into the meringue and scoop up some strawberries and cream. "I've had a better offer." I pop it in my mouth on a hum. My God, the cream is rich, the strawberries succulent and sweet, the meringue crisp on the outside, chewy on the inside.

"Is it gooey inside?" he asks, craning his head to see.

"Perfectly."

"Steady on," he mumbles around his mouthful as I go in for another spoonful.

"You want me to save you some?"

"Looks like I'm hoping." He picks up his plate and joins me, dunking a french fry in the pot of mayo and popping it in his mouth. The lack of creases on his tummy when he's sitting is sickening. "I've been thinking," he says, a definite edge of caution lacing his words. "About your friends."

"What about them?"

"About me meeting them."

I inhale and push some strawberries around the dish, watching them. I'm not looking forward to that. "Let me talk to them."

"Do they hate me that much?"

"No," I rush to assure him. "They're just being protective." I drop the spoon, losing my appetite for the delicious Eton Mess. I wish I had somehow avoided the girls the night I left Arlington Hall an emotional wreck. "They'll be fine." I have to hand it to Jude. At least he's committed and not avoiding them.

I hear my phone ringing in the distance and get down from the stool. "Do you mind?"

"Not at all." He takes another huge bite of his sandwich as I leave him, following the sound to the front door, where I find my bag.

I dip in and get my mobile, laughing at the irony when I see who's calling. I hold up my screen to Jude as I walk back into the kitchen so he can see.

"No time like the present," he says, taking another huge bite, filling his mouth.

I don't want Jude to hear this conversation. "I'll take it in the lounge."

He nods, unable to speak, and I leave him happily devouring his club sandwich, answering to Abbie as I go. The moment she sees my face, she checks the background, and I wait, flapping my T-shirt as I lower to one of the snuggle chairs. I'm feeling a little hot. Stifled. "Do you want to have dinner?" I ask, hitting things off.

She blinks. "Dinner?"

"You, me, Charley, Lloyd." I pause a beat. "Jude."

Her eyes narrow, suspicious. "So he can make us like him again?"

"Do you hate him?"

"*Hate* is a strong word. I wouldn't say *hate*."

"Good, because I love him." This is old news, and Abbie knows it. "And he loves me too, so here we are, Jude and I, in love, and it would be kinda nice if my best friends, whom I also love, got on with the man I love."

"He's told you that he loves you?" she asks. I nod, and Abbie blows out her cheeks. "Well, he got more than he bargained for in that bet, didn't he?"

My shoulders drop. "Can we forget about the bet? Besides, you got a luxury spa day for next to nothing as a result of that bet." God, I really don't want to tell them that Katherine is actually Jude's ex-fiancée.

"Maybe a few more of those spa days might help me on my way to acceptance."

"You're a disgrace." *Let's get this done with.* "Jude and Katherine were engaged to be married."

"Pardon me?"

"You heard."

Her mouth drops open. "God damn it, I need Charley on this call, but she's at the in-laws'."

"It was years ago."

"But he's still fucking her?"

"Was, Abbie." I stand, obviously too fast because I get a complete head rush. So I quickly lower again, shaking the daze away. I sense Abbie thinks I'm being dumb, and I hate that. I also hate the fleeting wonder. Am I? I look back over my shoulder into the kitchen. No. For God's sake, no, I'm not dumb. "Will you come to dinner with us or not?"

"I'll call Charley and see when they're free."

"Thank you."

"I can't wait to be the fifth wheel." She snorts. "Fuck my life. I take it you're not coming home tonight."

"No, I'm staying here." I blow air up onto my face, trying to cool it. "I signed the papers for my apartment this morning. Fancy a jaunt round IKEA at the weekend?"

"Oh, yes, I need some bigger pots for my plants. Sunday?"

"Perfect."

"You okay? You sound out of breath."

I stand slowly this time, pulling my T-shirt away from my body, clammy. "Fine." *Just too many orgasms.* "Let me know about Charley and Lloyd." I hang up and reach for my brow, wiping it. Damp.

I'm hot. Breathless. *What the hell?* Raising my hand to my throat, I try to swallow. And struggle. "Oh shit," I gasp, walking as fast as my suddenly shaky legs will carry me back to the kitchen. "The Eton Mess," I say, laboured, pulling Jude's eyes my way. One look at me has him dropping the last bit of his sandwich and jumping off his stool so fast, it flies back, hitting the wall. "Are there nuts in the Eton Mess?"

The panic on his face is wild as he rushes to me. "Jesus Christ," he breathes. "Fuck, I don't know. Tell me what to do, Amelia."

"My bag," I wheeze, holding on to his forearm, feeling weak and lightheaded. *I can't breathe.*

"Fuck, fuck, fuck!" He goes to leave, but comes back, his head not helping him on what's best to do.

"Go," I order him, staggering to a stool and sitting, concentrating on breathing, trying not to panic as Jude sprints to the door.

He's back in a second, throwing my bag on the counter, rummaging through with frantic hands. "What the fuck am I looking for?" he yells, his panic getting the better of him. I take over, yanking my bag towards me and slipping my hand into the side pocket, pulling out my EpiPens. I shove one at Jude, who proceeds to fumble with the protective casing, his big fingers struggling. He curses repeatedly, and I reach for his arm, squeezing. I can't tell him I need him to be cool, but he must see my message.

He inhales, trying to calm himself down, and gets the EpiPen out of the casing. I take it in my fist, ignoring the pain in my hand to remove the cap at one end, and push it into my thigh until I hear the click, holding it, waiting, counting to three in my head slowly. I feel my heartbeat immediately slow, my throat opening up and blood coming back to my head.

"Fuck," Jude whispers, watching me, keeping himself close. I exhale and breathe in, the air hitting my lungs feeling so good. "Did it work? How do you feel? Do I need to take you to the hospital?"

"I'm fine," I wheeze, removing the needle and checking my leg. I fold over the counter, heavy. "I don't need to go to the hospital. Just give me a second."

"What?"

"I've been here before, Jude."

"My God." He comes in behind me, rubbing my back. "What can I do? Tell me what to do."

"Shut up," I say, breathless.

"Charming."

I smile at the sound of his indignance and push myself up, taking in air deeply. "I'm good."

He snorts his thoughts on that and sits back down next to me, turning my sweaty face to him and wiping my brow. "So, what now?"

"I'll order another EpiPen with my doctor."

"That's it? Surely you need checking?"

"This isn't my first rodeo." I smirk, trying to lighten him up. It doesn't work. "If my symptoms return, then I'll have to go to the hospital. Trust me, okay? In all the years I've managed this, the EpiPen has done its job. I've been fine. And, bonus, you get to finish the Eton Mess."

"Funny, I've lost my appetite." He looks a bit pasty as he pushes the plates away. "And I'm never touching nuts again."

"Why?"

"Because I'd be scared to kiss you," he says, and I laugh. "You're so cool about it."

"I've never had an Eton Mess that contains nuts."

Jude's face falls. "I should have checked that. Fuck, I should have checked that."

I reach for his hand, squeezing. "Don't stress."

He laughs, not in humour, and scrubs a hand down his face. I need to distract him from his misplaced guilt, and the text that lands from Abbie is the perfect way.

"We're having dinner with my friends tomorrow night," I tell him, allowing a small part of my brain to consider the fact that my friends are obviously keen, but for what reason? To grill him? To accept him? I fear it's the former, but that might lead to the latter. *Might.* Can he take the heat?

Jude nods, taking my hand and checking the dressing. "This needs changing."

"Then change it," I say, giving him something to do. He looks shook. Dazed. "Jude?"

He gives me sorry eyes. "Please don't die on me."

What on earth? My settling heart turns in my chest, and despite not being ready, I get off the stool and put myself between his thighs, wrapping him in my arms. His raw vulnerability kills me.

And once again I think about Evelyn Harrison. And how Jude hardly ever mentions his father. "I'm not going to die." The way he clings to me breaks my heart. Now feels like the right moment to ask about the pills, but when he pulls away and looks up at me, his face a map of pain, I just can't bring myself to make him explain. He's given me so much today. So I say something else instead, hoping to lift him. "I love you."

"You came to tell me, didn't you? The night you found Katherine here."

I nod, feeling his rough cheeks, scanning every inch of his face.

"I've loved you for a while," he says softly. "I tried to tell you so many times but couldn't find the words."

"We got there in the end."

"It's not the end." Picking me up, he carries me back to the bedroom, laying me down and hugging me. "This hug won't lead to sex," he mumbles against my neck.

I sigh and sink into the mattress, Jude crowding me. Everything feels so right.

"Amelia?" he whispers.

"Yeah?"

"I've got you."

"I've got you too," I reply quietly. "Always."

Chapter 13

I've been a nervous wreck all day at work, worrying about dinner tonight with Jude and my friends, my concentration shot to bits. I couldn't even devote any attention to the fact that Sue mentioned in passing that she and Leo met at a friend's anniversary party. He said they met on the golf course, while he was smiling down at his pasta, rather coy. It's none of my business, but it would explain why Sue passed on a valuable client. Wise. And I should be wise too, so I've decided I know nothing about Sue and Leo.

As I'm leaving work, Leighton exits his office, and I groan to myself, bracing for a strong dose of him. It would have been too good to be true, avoiding him two days on the bounce. He joins me on my walk to the elevators. I can smell the mockery brewing on him.

"Good day?" he asks.

"Great."

"So you managed to fix your fuckup with the merger."

I stop and take a deep, calming breath, before I get myself fired for assault on a colleague. "I didn't fuck up."

"Oh, okay. It looked like you fucked up, but fair do's if you didn't and even fairer do's if you did and somehow managed to save the situation and convince the partners you were in control the whole time."

My teeth grind together. "Are you done being a complete bellend?"

His hand slaps on his chest. "I thought we were friends."

"Did you?"

"Would love to chat, but I'm off to meet Kimpton Kellers."

My hand pauses on its way to the call button. "Kimpton Kellers?"

"Oh, you know him?"

"Who doesn't?"

Leighton chuckles. How the fuck did he get a meeting with Kimpton Kellers? He's a multimillionaire. Could even be a billionaire. "He's got friends. Make it worth my while and I might connect you." His eyebrows lift.

"Fuck off, Leighton." I hit the button, my skin crawling, and step in the cart, groaning under my breath when I find there's no one in it. It's just us—me and him. I put myself in the far corner, giving him narrowed eyes when he stands right next to me. "There's a whole thirty-six square feet for you to choose from, Leighton."

He ignores my observation, keeping his place. "We should definitely get together sometime. Talk about some of the ideas I have once I make partner."

"We'll do that *if* you make partner."

He chuckles. "It's a given, Amelia."

He doesn't know about Leo Lombardy. Actually, come to think of it, neither do I. We had dinner, I established that it's possible Leo is fucking Sue, and I *didn't* secure his business. Should I call him? I roll my eyes to myself. *You're not a vulture, Amelia.* Good old Tilda Spector. I can't call *her* either. And for the first time in my career, I question whether I'm cut out for this. It's feeling more cutthroat that ever before. I still, stopping myself in my tracks. What the hell am I saying? Of course I'm cut out for this.

As soon as the doors open, I get my feet moving, feeling Leighton's leery eyes on my arse.

"Have a lovely evening, Amelia," he calls.

I shudder. I can't be the only person around here who sees him for what he is.

A leech.

Jude is waiting outside the restaurant when I get there, looking delightfully delicious in a grey three-piece. He spots me through the crowds of people as I approach, taking me in from top to toe, undressing me with his eyes. "Look at the state of you." He grabs me as soon as I'm close enough and hauls me into his body, sinking his face into my neck and sucking at my flesh. Now is not the time for me to come over all hot and bothered.

My eyes widen when I feel his condition past his fly. "Pleased to see me?"

"You're not allowed to look this fuckable all day when I'm not with you."

Just try to rain on my parade right now. I lean back, my hands on the lapels of his jacket. "We still have the big debate to settle."

"What debate is that, baby?"

"Seven or eight."

He laughs loudly, his head thrown back and all, the fine lines at the corners of his eyes stretching. It's such a sight to behold. My man. Laughing.

"Trying to impress?" I ask, straightening his tie even though it doesn't need straightening. It's perfect.

"They're already in there." He looks back at the restaurant door. "I thought it was safer to wait for you."

"Chicken."

Jude rolls his eyes and gives me a thorough checking over. "Do you feel okay?"

"Yes, I've told you each of the ten times you've texted and asked me that today." I break away and pull the door open, ignoring his disapproving scowl. "Ready?"

"Did you get another one of those pen things from your doctor?" he asks, taking my hand and checking the bandage.

"I picked it up from the pharmacy at lunchtime." I scan the restaurant and stop in my tracks when I see the guys. Abbie, Charley, and Lloyd.

And the babies.

My glower is instant. This means Charley and Lloyd couldn't get a sitter, and Charley went against her strict seven o'clock bedtime rule because she couldn't wait to get Jude under her microscope.

"What's up?" Jude asks, pushed up behind me.

"Charley and Lloyd brought their brood."

"Disgusting," he breathes, making me look up at him. He smirks and takes my shoulders, leading me on. "It might lighten things up."

"No, Charley will just put ear defenders on them when she wants to swear at you."

"I have wide shoulders. I can take it."

"You shouldn't have to."

"It'll be fine. Stop stressing."

We arrive at the table, and all three adults look up at us, only Lloyd standing. "Nice to finally meet you officially," he says. "Lloyd."

"Jude Harrison." Jude accepts Lloyd's hand before turning his eyes onto the girls. "Good to see you again. Sober." Both the girls smile, but Charley's is tightest. I fear the worst. They won't appreciate Jude's not-so-subtle hint that he rescued them and delivered their drunken arses home, and therefore deserves a break. "And who are these two cuties?"

I laugh under my breath, and Jude looks back at me in interest. "Sorry," I murmur.

"This is Elijah and Ena," Lloyd says when Charley doesn't speak up.

"Aunty Melia!" Elijah bounces in his booster chair, while Ena smacks the table of her high chair with a cup.

"Hey, you." I lower to the seat Jude pulls out for me and help myself to the bottle of wine in the middle.

"What the hell happened to your hand?" Charley takes it, checking the dressing, reminding me that I've not seen her since the wedding.

"She had an argument with a glass," Abbie pipes up as I reclaim my hand, catching Jude's fleeting guilty look.

"Wine?" I ask him, as he pulls the knees of his trousers up and sits. Taking the bottle from me, he proceeds to pour for everyone, me first, him last. "Thank you." I look at the girls expectantly, and both tilt their glasses a little in a half-hearted thanks too.

"Thanks, mate," Lloyd says. I don't miss the look his wife throws him. Disapproval. This is going to be tougher than I thought.

"So, what's everyone having?" I pluck a menu out of the stand on the table and start scanning the options.

"No *light* conversation before we order?" Charley says, straight in, no foreplay. She smiles, it's fake, and plucks a menu out too.

"As long as it *is* light." I smile sweetly at her before turning it onto the server when she lands by the side of the table. "Hi."

"Good evening." She smiles at everyone in turn. "Can I check if anyone has any allergies?"

"Nuts." Jude points to me. "Amelia's allergic to nuts. Severely allergic."

"Thank you." I cast him a sideways smile. "I'll take the lamb kebabs with yoghurt and mint dressing."

"Are there any nuts in that?" Jude asks.

"No, sir, no nuts."

"And there's no chance of contamination, is there?"

"Not at all, sir."

"Good." He returns to browsing the options, satisfied.

"I assume the yoghurt and mint dressing is cool," I say, popping the menu back.

"Yes, very cool."

"Great. It'll match my friend's mood."

Jude coughs, Abbie chuckles, and Charley glares at me. I lose myself in more wine and turn my attention onto Ena while everyone else orders, hoping the atmosphere improves.

"So tell me about Arlington Hall," Lloyd says.

"It's dead posh," Abbie pipes in. "You wouldn't fit in."

"Fuck off," he retorts, prompting Charley to slap her hands over Elijah's ears.

"You're welcome anytime," Jude says around his smile.

"And me?" Abbie asks. "Got any special offers on spa days coming up?"

I turn a tired look her way, and Jude shifts on his chair, uncomfortable.

"Abbie," I warn. She's not being as cold as Charley, more sarcastic, but still. Is it really necessary?

"It's fine." Jude's hand lands on my knee under the table and squeezes. "The spa's free for you to use anytime, Abbie." He looks at Charley. "And you too, of course."

"Anyone would think you're trying to buy our approval."

"No, just being friendly." Jude turns to Elijah. I don't blame him. The kids are blissfully oblivious to the lingering tension *and* far more receptible to Jude's graciousness. Jude picks up the dinosaur off the table, checking it out. "T. rex, huh?"

"Rahhhhhhh," Elijah roars.

"Ooohhh, I'm scared," Jude breathes, dropping the dinosaur on the table and backing off.

"You should be." I give Lloyd eyes to suggest I need him to carry this conversation.

The panic on his face is endearing. "So do your parents live in Oxfordshire too?" he blurts.

My jaw becomes lax, and both Abbie and Charley shrink. They know Jude's lost his parents. Lloyd doesn't, because why would Charley think to mention that? Oh God. My poor man is getting all the heat from all directions.

"I lost my mum a few years ago," Jude says. I see the struggle on him. And, again, no mention of his father.

"Oh, I'm sorry to hear that." Lloyd loses himself in his wine.

For God's sake, someone change the subject. "Lloyd's in cybersecurity!" I exclaim. Then I frown. "I think."

He blinks in surprise. "I always thought you were being polite whenever you asked how my day went."

I shrug. "I was. Wouldn't want you to feel left out when the girls are together."

"I'm happy to be left out, for the record."

Jude chuckles. "Do you play any sport?" he asks, going in safe.

"Well." Lloyd comes closer, leaning across the table. "I should have gone pro at rugby, but my ACL let me down."

"Oh, Jude's brother plays rugby," I declare, sounding almost proud. I'm not, I'm excited. Jude and Lloyd may share some common ground, and I would love that. Lloyd never jelled with Nick—they just tolerated each other for the sake of me and Charley.

"He does?"

"He does," Jude says, seeming to shy away. "For an Irish team."

"And England," I add, knocking Jude's knee. "Why are you being modest?"

"No shit." Lloyd's suddenly more interested. "Wait. Harrison? Don't fucking tell me your brother is Rhys Harrison."

"Lloyd, for Christ's sake," Charley hisses, covering Elijah's ears again.

"My brother is Rhys Harrison," Jude confirms. "You like watching?"

"When I'm allowed."

Charley scowls, outraged, and I smile.

"I'll get you tickets for the next international." Jude accepts my hand under the table when I put it in his lap.

"I'd love that." Lloyd nods, reaching over and hitting the side of his glass with Jude's.

I don't appreciate Charley's eye roll. Why the hell did she even come if she's not going to give Jude a chance?

The conversation flows easily for a while, the girls not saying much, the kids being loud, the boys talking rugby, and when our order arrives,

I busy myself eating, so thankful Lloyd and the kids are here; otherwise there would be silence at the table.

As I lower my fork, I check Jude's plate, seeing he's not eaten much. "You okay?" I ask.

"Sure." He offers a small smile. "I had a big lunch with Casey and Rhys."

"Both of them?"

"Yeah, it was nice. Unusual, but nice. We're rarely in the same place at the same time."

"So, you have two brothers?" Abbie pipes in.

"Yes," Jude says. "Both younger."

"So you're the older, reliable one, are you?" Charley asks, still feeding Ena while Elijah smears mashed potato around his plate.

I eye Charley as Jude huffs on a little burst of amusement. "Apparently."

"Or apparently not." Charley stares at Jude across the table, not backing down, and Jude flicks his eyes to everyone else, like, *Is anyone else sensing the over-the-top animosity?*

I mentally yell at Lloyd to wind her in. She's going too far.

"Charley," he warns, catching my look.

"What? I'm trying to get to know him."

"What do you want to know, Charley?" Jude breathes, as exasperated as I am. "Ask me, and I'll happily tell you."

"And now he gets cocky?"

"He's not being cocky, Charley," I snap, forcing her hands to lay over Ena's ears. Jude places his hands on Elijah's, who wipes some of his mashed potato on Jude's suit jacket for his trouble.

"I've never had to do this before." Jude ignores the mess Elijah's made of his sleeve, setting his fork down.

"What, explain yourself?" Charley laughs. It's so over the top, I could quite easily reach across the table and slap her. "I find that hard to believe."

"What's that supposed to mean?" I ask through a tight jaw, feeling Jude's hand on my leg again, silently telling me not to get worked up. Too late.

"It means I find it hard to believe it's the first time Jude Fuckboy Harrison has hurt a woman," she says, matter of fact. Abbie slides farther down her chair, as does Lloyd. "Oh, let's not forget the ex-fiancée," Charley goes on, not done. I close my eyes and take a few deep, calming breaths. "I'm assuming she was hurt when you dumped her. But then I suppose you kept her happy by fucking her when you felt like it after you decided not to marry her. Until you met Amelia, of course. Or maybe you're still fucking her."

"Okay, that's enough, Charley," Lloyd snaps, showing rare anger. "Who the hell do you think you are?"

I look at Jude, seriously not liking the shade of his eyes right now. I think it's time for us to leave, but just as I'm about to declare our departure and get Jude away from the verbal abuse coming at him, he stands abruptly. "Excuse me." He strides towards the back of the restaurant and disappears through the doors that lead to the men's, and I exhale, going heavy in my chair.

"You've gone too far." I look at Charley and see an expression I know well. Regret. Although it's a bit late now. Her lip is quivering a little, her eyes blinking more than normal to keep the tears building at bay. I've no idea why *she's* getting upset. It's me who should be.

"Yes, Charley, I've got to say, that was way too harsh." Abbie gives me sorry eyes, and I shake my head, wondering whether I should go after Jude. He was livid.

"Bad Mummy," Elijah sings, smacking his T. rex on the table.

"I'm sorry," Charley cries. "I don't know what's got into me today."

"She's been stabby all day," Lloyd mumbles, as if backing up his wife. "Jude's not the only one who's copped it."

"I'm sorry for throwing the washing basket at you," she whimpers, bursting into tears as she turns to Lloyd. "I'm really sorry."

"I'm over it," he says, pulling her into his side. "But you've got some making up to do with Jude."

I stand. "I'm going to check up on him." But I sit straight back down when I spot someone. "Oh fuck."

"What?" everyone says in unison.

"Nick's over there."

"Oh fuck," Abbie parrots, searching around for him. "Oh, fuck, fuck fuck."

"Just say hi, smile, and let him be on his way," Lloyd says.

"He doesn't know about Jude," Charley hisses.

"Oh shit." Lloyd once again shrinks in his chair, but now for an entirely different reason.

"He knew I was seeing someone. Then my dad kindly told him I wasn't."

"And he's not been updated on your relationship status?" Lloyd looks past me, worried.

"No. And I seriously don't want to deliver that blow right now in front of everyone." I know I've got to tell him eventually, but not now. It would be cruel.

"And Jude's mega passive-aggressive possessive," Abbie says, adding to my stress. It will not go well if Jude and Nick meet.

"Anyone would think he's got a bloody tracker on me," I mutter, ducking.

"Oh fuck," Lloyd breathes, the words stretched out and guilty, prompting Charley to look his way.

"What did you do?" she asks.

"I didn't know he didn't know!" Lloyd exclaims.

I recoil. "Wait, you told him about Jude?"

"No, I told him Charley and I were meeting you here for dinner tonight."

"What?" I blurt, my eyes split between Nick and Lloyd, who's getting smaller and smaller on his chair. "Why the hell would you do that?"

"Yeah, why the hell would you do that, Lloyd?"

"I was on the spot." He's suddenly scowling. "I ran into him outside the Tube station, and it was strained. I've got nothing to say to the guy, but he just hung around like a bad fucking smell, asked how you were, and because I had fuck all to say to him, I told him we were seeing you tonight."

"You prat." Charley smacks his bicep.

"Idiot." Abbie throws an olive at Lloyd's forehead, and it hits accurately, bouncing off.

"You told him even though you knew you were meeting me *and* Jude?" I ask in disbelief.

"Like I said, I was talking for the sake of it."

"He's seen you," Charley says. "He's coming over."

I send a mental prayer to the gods to keep Jude in the men's for a while longer, hope and pray it takes him time to cool his temper before he walks out and finds something else to explode over. "If Jude comes out before I can get rid of Nick, you can deal with the hurricane." I quickly pull Jude's untouched dinner my way and push my empty plate back.

"I can't believe he's shown up like this," Lloyd mutters. "Just tell him you're seeing someone."

"Yes, just shatter his heart." Charley rolls her eyes at Lloyd.

"Hi," Nick says.

I take a forkful of rice off Jude's plate and eat it as I look up at him. "Nick, what a surprise."

Lloyd chokes on nothing, coughs, then loses himself in his beer as everyone scowls at him.

Nick laughs, uneasy. Guilty. "How are you, Amelia?"

"I'm fine." My eyes constantly dart to the men's, praying.

"The kids are getting big," he says, and Lloyd and Charley murmur their agreement.

"Good to see you, Nick." Lloyd smiles. It's more of a grimace, actually, and I notice his gaze keeps moving to the men's too. "Again."

Nick ignores the sarcasm, his eyes flicking to my friends. "Charley, Abbie."

"Nick," they murmur together over their mouthfuls.

Jesus, I thought the atmosphere was horrific before. Add an ex-boyfriend to the mix, and you get a whole new level of uncomfortable. *Please go!*

"Amelia, can you give me a couple of minutes?"

Oh God. I slow my chewing, hating this, wishing he would just stop loving me. "Not now, Nick."

"Then when?"

Everyone visibly withers at the table, and I die a hundred times over, caught between that wretched guilt and absolute dread that Jude is going to leave the bathroom any moment and find Nick at the table trying to win me back. "I'll call you," I say, desperate. Anything to get him away.

"You will?"

"Yeah, I'll call you." I drop my fork, unable to eat another thing, and stand. "Excuse me, I need the ladies'." I give Lloyd a look, one he can't possibly mistake. *Get him out of here.*

He reads it well and springs to life. "Come on, Nick, I'll walk you out."

I leave the table and peek back, seeing Lloyd guiding Nick to the door. "Fucking hell," I whisper, reaching the men's. I knock on the door. "Jude?"

"Go back to the table, Amelia," he says shortly, making me recoil.

"Are you okay?"

"I'm fine. Go back to the table."

I think better than to question him, backing up, certain I wouldn't want to be within exploding distance of him right now. He needs to calm down, and I don't know what to say to help him. *God damn you, Charley.* I sheepishly return to the table. Could this be the worst dinner ever?

"Well, that was tense," Abbie says.

I can't even look at Charley. I'm fucking fuming, and she knows it, but had she not grilled Jude, he wouldn't have left the table, and I might be in a whole other load of messy right now.

Charley juts her lip out. "I'll make it up to you."

"It's not me you need to make it up to, Charley. It's my boyfriend."

"I will."

"Good." I take some wine, seeing Jude appearing. "He's coming now. Shit, where's Lloyd?"

Charley immediately stands and stops Jude before he can take his chair and asks him to go to the patio garden with her. I note Jude's eyes have paled slightly. Not completely, but a little, just enough to tell me Charley's safe from his wrath.

Jude motions the way as he takes his glass, frowning at his plate in front of me. "Still hungry?"

I grin like an idiot and shovel another forkful of rice into my mouth, feeling like I could burst I've eaten so much. Abbie snorts over her laughter. Jude frowns at her too. "Where's Lloyd?" he asks.

"He needed to take a call," Abbie blurts, smiling. "Won't be long."

Another frown from Jude as he leads Charley out the back to the patio. "God, this really is the worst dinner ever," I say, the fork clanging against the plate when I drop it.

"Oh, I don't know. I just got free spa days for life." Abbie toasts the air. "Winning over here."

Lloyd gets back to the table and shakes his head in despair as he starts cleaning the kids up. "Amelia, seriously, that man is in pieces."

"Make me feel like total crap, why don't you?"

"I wouldn't want to be the one to tell him you're now with a billionaire hotelier."

"Lloyd?" Abbie says, winning his attention. "Shut up."

I get up and help him with the kids to kill the time, wondering what's being said between Jude and Charley.

"I think he'll live," Lloyd says, seeing my concern.

"It's not Jude I'm worried about," I murmur quietly, knowing one wrong word from Charley could tip him over the edge.

"It'll be fine." Lloyd winks in the kind of way a big brother would. "She just doesn't want you to get hurt."

"I don't want to get hurt either, but you don't see me being a mega bitch." I lower to my chair when I see them come back into the restaurant, Jude holding the door open for Charley. She smiles her thanks. Short and sweet. It's probably best.

"Okay?" I ask Jude, trying not to sound too curious. I'm a joke.

"Okay." He takes the bill from the waiter and insists on paying. "This isn't me trying to buy your approval, to be clear."

Abbie laughs. "I have no objection to you buying me anything, whether approval or not."

"Abbie," I breathe.

"What?"

"We look forward to coming over to Arlington Hall," Lloyd says.

"Just let me know when."

Lloyd gives Charley excited eyes. "Maybe my mum and dad can sleep the kids. We can have a romantic weekend. When you're in a better mood, obviously."

"Fuck off, Lloyd Duke Chaytor." Charley covers Elijah's ears again as Jude covers Ena's. She stares up at him, like, *Who's this strange man?*

"Disgusting," Jude quips, taking my hand. "It was a pleasure."

"A true pleasure," I mimic, smiling sarcastically at Charley. "I'll call you."

Jude leads me out of the restaurant. "Well, that was a date I won't forget in a hurry."

"What did Charley say?"

"Sorry."

"That's it?"

"Pretty much, yes."

"Oh."

Looking at me as we wander down the street, he pulls me into his side and kisses my forehead. "You're staying the night."

"Of course I am." I smile at the pavement ahead. "I move into my new apartment this weekend. I can't stay every night then."

He hums. "Maybe I can stay at your place."

I grin, thrilled. I'd love that. "It's not as big as your place." My phone chimes, my lip curling when I see a message from Leighton Steers.

Let me know if you change your mind. Always willing to help.

"Change your mind about what?" Jude asks, obviously close enough to see the message.

I become stiff, my head scrambling. "Nothing," I say, brushing it off. "Some work thing."

"Is he still sniffing around you?"

"No, I told you, it's just some work thing." I stuff my phone in my bag, trying not to look as anxious as I feel.

Jude stops us walking, turning into me. "Change your mind about what?"

"Jude, it's nothing."

"Then tell me."

I can see the passive-aggressive-possessive beast rising. *Think, think, think.* "He had some inside information on the merger."

Jude's head tilts. "Did he want something in return for that inside information?"

I freeze, stumped. I shouldn't be surprised Jude had Leighton Steers nailed within a few seconds of clapping eyes on him. "No, of course not. I—"

"Hey, Jude!" The gruff calling of Jude's name reaches both our ears, sparing me the agony of explaining. Or lying through my teeth.

"Oh Jesus," Jude breathes.

"What?"

"My brother."

"Casey?"

"No, the other one."

"Rhys?" I ask, seeing a man jogging across the road towards us. And there's no mistaking who he is. He's Jude, just a few years younger, a few inches wider, and with shorter hair. Rhys takes me in, up and down. "So is this the famous Amelia?"

"What are you doing here?" Jude asks.

"Well, when you mentioned you were having dinner with your girlfriend, I thought it would be a mighty shame to miss the opportunity to meet her." He gives me a big, dashing smile.

"You're supposed to be going back to Dublin tonight."

"One more night in the Big Smoke won't hurt."

"Won't it?" Jude asks. "Rhys, you could get yourself into trouble if you were locked in a cupboard alone."

Rhys chuckles as I smile fondly at Jude in protective-big-brother mode.

"Last night I fired your publicist," Jude goes on. "Today we hired a new one, and you booked a flight back to Dublin while Casey booked a train to Paris."

"One more night, chill it." Rhys muscles him out the way and homes in on me, taking the tops of my arms, scrutinising me. "Well, you're a surprise."

"Rhys," Jude warns.

"What?"

"Put her down." Jude claims me and pulls me close, putting some keys in my hand. "Go wait for me in the car, it's just around the corner." He scowls at Rhys. "I've just got to sort out my wayward littlest little brother."

"I don't need sorting out. Stop being such a nag. You've not even introduced us properly."

Jude laughs, but it has no humour in it. More nerves. "Amelia, meet Rhys. Rhys, this is Amelia."

"I've heard a lot about you."

"Oh yeah?" I ask, head tilted. "Like?"

"You're brilliant, gorgeous, witty, strong, resilient, smart."

My lips twist, trying not to smile, and Jude rolls his eyes, turning to his brother. "Where are you going now?"

"Meeting someone."

"Who?"

"You don't know them."

"That doesn't ease me, Rhys," Jude retorts, getting irritated. "Who is it?"

"A woman, alright? You don't see me interfering in your relationships."

"*Ship,*" Jude says. "Relation*ship.*"

"Will you chill the fuck out?" A surprising flash of anger passes across Rhys's face. "You've been like a bear with a sore head since—"

"Shut up, Rhys," Jude warns, moving in closer.

"Since Mum died. There you go—I said it. Finally. Are you going to punch me now?" Holding his hands out, Rhys invites the hit, and I nervously glance between the brothers, wondering if Jude will accept his offer. He certainly looks like he wants to, his jaw rolling.

Since their mum died? Not their dad? I'm confused. Jude talks with such fondness about his mother, but when it comes to his father, I see the anger he tries and fails to keep buried. But he's only been angry since his mum died?

"Rhys." Jude visibly takes in air, working his temper down. "There's a supposed sex tape out there just waiting to surface and cause a PR shitstorm for you."

I blink, surprised at Jude's one-eighty on the topic of conversation, but Rhys is obviously wary, backing off. "You said you didn't think it existed."

"Is there a sex tape?"

Rhys rolls his eyes. "Yeah, there's a sex tape."

"Haven't you risked your career enough?"

"Jesus, alright, *Dad.*"

Something switches in Jude, every drop of green falling from his eyes, his temper rising again. I step back, cautious.

But not Rhys. So much for backing off. "Look at you," he says. "One mention of him and you become the Hulk. For fuck's sake, Jude. He's dead. No one can bring him back. Just like they can't bring Mum back. Get on with your life."

"What the fuck do you think I'm trying to do?"

Rhys smiles at me. I don't know where he finds it, because I'm struggling myself. Then he comes to me and gives me a hug. "Look after him, okay? He's not as tough as he lets on."

"For fuck's sake," Jude breathes, raking a stressed hand through his hair.

"Shut up and give me a hug." Rhys drops me and slams Jude into his chest. "I'll be a good boy," he says, planting a smacker of a kiss on Jude's cheek before breaking away and leaving us, weaving through the built-up traffic as he crosses the road.

I let Jude take the keys and put me back in his side, walking us on. "You're protective of them," I say.

"Maybe," he murmurs.

I hum, resting my head on his chest, listening to his heart. "Mr. Big Tough Guy."

He laughs, poking me in my ribs in warning. "I'll show you big when we get home. All eight inches of it."

I laugh, but it's light. Uneasy. I've seen anger on Jude about his father. Not so much his mother. And yet Rhys likened Jude to the Hulk over his father—I get that—and a bear with a sore head since his mother passed. Does this mean he's only expressed anger over his father *since* his mother died? More questions mount. The rage inside Jude is very real. Very destructive.

Very worrying.

Chapter 14

I got precisely no sleep last night, but I did get the full, delicious eight inches numerous times, with pillow talk interludes between each session. Every time we took a break from each other, the questions about his anger over his father hung on my tongue, as well as Rhys's statement. *Since Mum died.* But I thought better than to ask, and it was as if Jude sensed my curiosity, because the instant one of those small silences fell, he'd roll on top of me and we'd go again. He finally drifted off at gone five with me curled in his side, and by six I still hadn't found sleep. So I got up, showered, and arranged for Humphrey to take me back to London.

Abbie was leaving as we pulled up, sipping from a travel mug of coffee. She looked at my exhausted form, tried not to smile, dropped a kiss on my cheek, and said she'd call me later. I showered, skipped the gym—I worked out enough last night—and got my arse to work.

Yawning, I rest back in my chair and click send on multiple emails, my mind naturally straying to Jude. His father. And then, of course, the pills. I'm no expert, but I'd say he still needs to be taking them, especially given the fury I got a glimpse of last night that he was obviously trying to keep a lid on. Jude's temper has always seemed extreme. It's always been a concern. Maybe he needs therapy, not pills. I sink farther into my chair on a sigh, having a mental conversation with Jude, asking him all the questions I dare not for fear of igniting that temper. He needs help. How do I—

The door flies open, and a bunch of flowers appear, Shelley behind them. "Delivery for Amelia," she sings, dumping them on my desk. "Tell me, what does a girl have to do to get this kind of attention from a man?"

I flick a sardonic look at her as I take the card and open it. And groan.

"God, you're ungrateful," she says over a laugh.

"They're from my ex."

"Sounds like he doesn't want to be your ex."

I give her tired eyes and drop the card in the bin. *Not* my bag so it can be found. "Don't suppose you know how Leighton's meeting with Kimpton went, do you?"

Shelley's eyes sparkle, delighted, and she comes closer, looking back over her shoulder. "Kimpton emailed Gary this morning," she whispers. "He didn't like Leighton."

"No." I lean over my desk, interested.

"Yes." She pouts, gazing thoughtfully up at the ceiling. "What were his exact words? Oh, yes, that's it. Not his *cup of tea*."

I chuckle. "Wise man."

"Oh, someone's popular." Leighton slinks in, and Shelley and I bolt upright, throwing each other secret smirks. Helping himself to the flowers, he checks them out, sniffing. "I thought you'd broken up with your boyfriend."

I start tapping my pen on the edge of my desk, getting worked up. Trying not to, but still. He rubs me up the wrong way. "I have. Now, if you don't mind, I have a call." Shelley takes the hint and scarpers, but Leighton lingers. I scowl at him. "How did your meeting go with Kimpton?"

"Oh, great." He smirks so wide. So fake. "Must go, I've got a follow-up with him shortly."

"Prick," I murmur as he disappears, reaching for my phone when it rings. "Dad?" I say in answer. He never calls me in the day. Never.

"Are you talking to me yet?"

"Depends if you're going to tell me how to live my life."

"Are you coming over this evening?" he asks, completely sidestepping my statement. "I wouldn't usually need to ask, but your mother's helping Abbie at the florist, and I've been left the responsibility of sorting dinner."

"Mum's working and you're cooking dinner? What has the world come to?"

"I didn't call to get an earful of your smart mouth, Amelia. Will you come by this evening to help me?"

Dad doesn't need help. This is his olive branch, after the most recent time he's tried to convince me I love a man that I really don't. *Fuck.* "I can't come over this evening, Dad."

"Why?"

I could tell him I'm going to my new place to sort a few things, but that would be a lie. I'm a grown woman. I shouldn't have to lie about my choices. "I'm seeing Jude."

"Who?"

I sag. "I'm dating a man called Jude."

Silence. "You said you were just sleeping with him."

"Actually, Mum said that."

"Last I heard you weren't sleeping with him anymore. You weren't dating, you said so yourself. And now you're dating the man who you were or weren't sleeping with? What does this mean?"

It means I'm in love! "It means I'm dating him."

"What about Nick?"

Oh, for the love of God. I drop my head to the desk. "Dad—"

"Apparently, according to you, you ended things with Nick because your career was so important to you, and now you're *dating* another man? Not just sleeping with him, but *dating* him?"

"This is a really weird conversation to be having with my father."

"Poor Nick!"

I sit up. "I don't want you to mention this to him," I say urgently. "I'll tell him myself when the time is right."

"Of course I'm not going to tell him. I don't want to break his heart."

"Dad—"

"Do you have no compassion for the man?"

"Dad, I—"

"Poor fellow's done nothing wrong."

"I never said he did." *I just wasn't in love with him, and we wanted different things!*

"I'm disappointed in you, Amelia."

"Okay, I'm done with this conversation. I'm a grown fucking woman, Dad. Concentrate on your retirement and cooking the damn dinner tonight." I hang up and yell. Then cringe to high heaven because I just dropped the f-bomb on my father. "Shit."

"That kinda day?"

I look up and find Sue at the doorway.

"Family politics."

"Nice flowers." She closes the door but stays there, holding on to the handle. I smile my thanks, not bothering to explain who they're from. "Leo just called me."

I tilt my head. "Mr. Lombardy?"

"Yes." She smiles. "Mr. Lombardy. He said you're a breath of fresh air. Obviously, I agree."

"Well, thanks." Does this mean he's bringing his business my way? "I appreciate that."

"He also mentioned that he said we met on the golf course."

I press my lips together. "He did? I don't recall."

Sue nods mildly, obviously seeing through the dummy persona I'm feigning. I'm smart. She knows it. "He got mixed up. It was an anniversary party."

Because you play golf with your husband. "Men," I huff, rolling my eyes, and Sue laughs, loud and over the top. She came here to get her story straight?

"Anyway, he'll be in touch about getting the paperwork drafted."

"Oh, that's great."

"Look after him, okay?"

My nose scrunches, as I think about all the ways Sue looks after Leo and Leo looks after Sue. "Of course."

She closes the door behind her, and I sink deeper into my chair on an exhale. So much was said in that conversation without being said. I need caffeine.

I get up to grab my fourth coffee of the morning already, opening a message from Jude as I go. It's a picture. I smile at the empty side of his bed.

Not a fan.

I call him, needing a pick-me-up. His voice will help. It's been a long day already and it's not even ten. This isn't sustainable if my brain is going to keep functioning.

His gruff voice answers, and I shake off the shivers. "You're still in bed, aren't you?"

"Do you want me to lie?" he asks.

"Yes."

"I've been up since six, worked out, ate, showered, read a ton of maintenance reports from the groundsman, approved the summer menu, discussed the expansion of the golf course with the resort manager, and signed off on endless invoices."

"How productive."

He groans, and I just know his gorgeous, naked body is stretching out in the bed as he does. Lord have mercy.

"Shit," he breathes. "That's my list of things to do today. We need to have a chat about acceptable levels of indulgence on weekdays."

I laugh. "Happy to. Will you listen this time?"

"No."

I roll my eyes and slip a cup under the machine, hitting the button that'll give me a double espresso. "How do we manage this?" I ask. "I'm good for nothing, and I have targets to reach if I'm going to hit my goal."

"You know, you could go it alone."

I get my coffee and head back. "You mean in business? Why would I?"

"Because every penny you make would go into your pocket, not to LB&B Finance Group."

"I have a noncompete clause. I can't just walk out and take all my clients with me."

"What if you don't have to?"

"Take all my clients?"

"Yes."

"I'm not understanding."

"I know people."

I stop midstride, realization slowly falling. "No, Jude," I say firmly. "That's not how I want to do things."

"You want to work your fingers to the bone?"

"Yes."

"Okay," he says, simple as that. "What are we doing tonight?" Conversation over. He took my word and accepted it. Fuck, could I love him more?

Tonight, I plan on gently asking him about the medication I found in his cupboard. About his father. I just need to pick my moment and find the courage. "I need to be in bed at a decent hour so I can get some sleep. I missed the gym this morning too."

"You don't need to go to the gym. I'm your new personal trainer, and my way of keeping fit is much more fun."

I'm not going to argue. "I'll be finished at six."

"I'll be there."

I hang up, grinning like a fool, but it falls when I spy Leighton in the distance with Gary. They high-five. Huh? That does *not* look like a conversation where Gary just told Leighton he's not Kimpton's *cup of tea*. I sip my coffee and wince at the bitterness. "Morning," I say as I approach.

"Oh, Lazenby." Leighton holds out both hands, like he wants a hug. "Aren't you going to congratulate me?"

"Congratulate you on being a first-class creep?" I ask under my breath as I pass. What the hell have I missed? "What am I congratulating you on?" I keep moving, and Leighton falls into stride with me as Gary slips into one of the senior partners' offices.

"My new clients, the Cartwright twins."

I try so hard not to bring up my coffee. Fuck, he got the Cartwright twins from Liverpool? "Congratulations." I chew over the word, trying to sound sincere. *Shit, shit, shit.* That's a massive deal and will certainly lessen the blow of not being Kimpton's *cup of tea*. The senior partners will be thrilled. Did he sleep with them? Woo them? "I'm happy for you." I smile as I turn my back at my door, pushing my way into my office.

Unfortunately, Leighton follows me in. I've had more than my fair share of him today already. He's not done gloating. "Anything interesting to share?" he asks.

"No."

He drops into the chair opposite my desk, getting comfortable.

"Is there anything else?" Fuck, I hate him.

"Maybe we should have that lunch sometime."

"What, so you can refer some of Kimpton's friends?"

His smile falters. "You have to have a certain connection with your clients, don't you? Kimpton's not my cup of tea, so I decided against taking him on."

I cough over my coffee.

"I could share some insights," he goes on. "You could share yours. It could be"—he waggles a brow—"productive."

Is he for real? He appals me. "I'm not sure your insights are worth the price I would have to pay." *Like sleeping with you, you slimebag.* I vomit in my own mouth as I flash a sarcastic smile, and Leighton chuckles as he stands and fixes his jacket.

"My insights are gold, and I'm offering you a front-row seat to a Leighton Steers seminar." Off he trots to the door. "I'll even share how I nabbed a meeting with the owner of Arlington Hall."

Another choke. *What the hell?* "The owner of Arlington Hall?"

"Yeah, you remember him?" Pound signs ping into Leighton's eyes when he backs out. "At the convention."

"Yeah, I remember him."

"Didn't I tell you I'd get him in my client bank?" The door closes, and I stare at it, my lagging brain trying to catch up.

"Shit," I hiss, dialling Jude and standing, furious. "Are you having a meeting with Leighton Steers?" I ask abruptly when the call connects.

"Ummm . . . yeah?" He definitely sounds guarded.

"Jude!"

"What?"

I sit down and stand back up again, starting to walk circles around my office. "Why are you meeting him?"

"Ummm . . ."

"Um, um, um," I snap. "Cancel it."

"No."

My nostrils flare. I know exactly what he's going to do. So much for loving him more for taking my word and accepting it. "Do not interfere with my career, Jude. That's a hard no for me."

"I'm not interfering with your career. I'm building up the hopes of some little rat who's hitting on my girlfriend so I can dash them and send him on his way with a polite warning."

"Polite?"

"Depends how I feel after the meeting."

Or if he's taken his pills. I slam my mouth shut before I can let those words tumble out. "Jude, I beg you," I whisper.

"Oh, baby, don't beg me. It turns me on."

"Jude!"

He sighs, making a long, elaborate effort of it. "He needs telling."

"I can handle Steers."

"I have more of a presence than you."

"Hard no, Jude," I warn. "If you want to see me tonight, or any other night, for that matter, cancel your fucking meeting." I hang up and yell, slamming my phone down on my desk. "Fucking man." Dumping myself in my chair, I close my eyes and take a few moments to breathe. Calm. *Give me calm.*

My landline rings on my desk, but I don't answer, definitely not feeling very calm yet. It rings off and rings again. Then rings off and my mobile starts. I lose my breath when I see Tilda Spector's name. "Fuck," I whisper, slapping my cheeks and blowing out a few controlled breaths. "Tilda," I answer, happy.

"Amelia, I tried the office, but the receptionist couldn't get through. I'm not disturbing you, am I?"

"No, no. Sorry, I was on another call. How are you?"

"Very good. I wondered if we could meet."

My back goes ramrod straight in my chair. I feel like I've been waiting weeks for this call. "Absolutely." I bite my tongue, refraining from asking why, and she laughs a little.

"Not a vulture, are you, Amelia?"

"Hate them," I say, smiling.

"How does Wednesday next week sound?"

"Perfect. Just let me know where and when."

"I'll have my assistant make a lunch reservation and email you the details. Look forward to it, Amelia."

She cuts the call, and I sit back in my chair, my smile wide, feeling so much calmer. "Yes," I hiss, performing a ridiculous fist pump that I would *die* before doing in public.

"Fuck!" The distant curse has me looking at the door, and, curious, I get up and pull it open. Leighton's storming down the corridor, cursing his arse off.

I peek down at my phone when it dings.

Done. For future reference, threatening abstinence is a hard no
for me.

I grin and close my door, hearing my computer ping. Rounding my
desk, I smile when I see an email from Leo Lombardy.
The stars are aligning.

Chapter 15

As I walk out of my building, a call comes in from Nick, and I cringe as I reject it, wondering—and worrying—about how I'm going to tell him. And when. I can't file away that responsibility forever. Wish I could. I squint at the screen of my mobile, thoughtful. Maybe . . .

I start to type out a message to him. Stop. Delete it. Start again. Stop again. Delete it again. "Shit." I stuff my phone in my bag. I can't tell him via text. I owe him more than that.

My feet slow. *I owe him.* Do I? Do I *really* owe him? I sigh to myself. I can't let him find out how he found out last time. God damn my father; I wouldn't be in this situation if he'd kept his nose out.

I head to the corner and scan the street, looking for Jude or any of his cars. Where is he? A horn sounds, startling me, and his black Ferrari pulls up, the passenger window sliding down. I dip, seeing Jude in the driver's seat. His eyebrows are on the ceiling of the car. I won't thank him for actually listening to me. He shouldn't have accepted that meeting in the first place.

"How was your day?" he asks.

"After dealing with the wayward man in my life, it was a good day."

He pats the passenger seat next to him. "Come tell me about it."

I get in and settle beside him in the leather sports seat, but before I can even think to open my mouth and share my work news, Jude's dragging me across the car.

"Whoa." I laugh, my legs getting bent at all kinds of uncomfortable angles, my dress hampering my already limited movement.

I land on his lap, my back pressed up against his steering wheel, blowing my hair out of my face. Intent swirls in his eyes as he slips his hand onto my nape and pulls me onto his mouth. I'm all in, straddling his thighs, pushing my chest into his, feeling his hands stroke across my backside. I ignore the various car parts poking me in various places and hum my happiness, running my hands across his rough face, letting my tongue lap gently with his.

It takes everything in me and more not to haul him back onto my lips when he slows our kiss, eventually breaking it. I lick my lips and lean back, spending a few moments absorbing his face.

"What?" he asks, squeezing my arse.

"I think I fancy you more each time I see you."

"Same." He gives me a chaste kiss. "How's your hand?"

I flex it, the bandage starting to annoy me. "A little sore."

He helps me back across the car to my seat. "Alright?"

"Yeah," I grunt, my leg at an obscene angle. "This car is really sexy, but it's not built for sex." I drop into my seat and blow my hair out of my face again.

I look at Jude. He's smiling brightly. "So, tell me about your day."

"Tilda Spector wants to meet me for lunch next Wednesday." I bite my lip, my eyes surely dancing.

"And she's the woman who's retiring and off-loading clients, right?" He listens. "That's right."

"That's fucking great, baby."

"I know!" I pull him over to me by the lapels of his jacket, ignoring the flash of pain in my hand, and finally let my excitement leave my body, slamming a hard kiss on his lips. "If she passes her clients over, there will be nothing Leighton can do to match me. Nothing. Plus, Leo Lombardy emailed to accept my services and—"

"Services?"

"Financial services."

"And who is Leo Lombardy?"

"The guy I had dinner with at Nonna's."

"The older guy?"

"Yes. I think one of the senior partners is having an affair with him, hence she can't take his file."

"Scandalous."

"It really is."

Jude's nose scrunches to match mine. "I got you something." Pulling away, he dips and retrieves a bag from the floor by my feet.

Nervous, I eye it. "What is it?"

"Open it."

The box is long. A necklace? "Why have you brought me a gift?"

"Because I wanted to. Open it."

I tentatively peel the gift wrap open under Jude's watchful eyes, my smile unsure, and, on an inhale, pull the box out, lifting the lid. "A pen," I say, surprised, taking in the silver ballpoint.

"It's more what it says on the pen." Jude takes it out of the box and rolls it to show me.

"It's engraved," I breathe, taking it from him and reading. I feel my lip wobble, and my eyes fill, making the engraving blur.

I've got you. Jude xxx

"In every aspect of your life," he says quietly.

And my heart melts to nothing. It's the most thoughtful gift I've ever received, because it truly means something, and that's his whole point. "I love it," I say, reaching over and hugging him hard. "Thank you."

"I've got you," he repeats, injecting so much strength into his cuddle. "And I love you."

I feel so overwhelmed. So fulfilled. It's a new feeling, and I'm a fan of it. I move my lips onto his cheek and inhale as I kiss him. "I love you more."

"I doubt it." Jude turns his mouth onto mine and nibbles at my lip. "I could do something very explicit to you right now."

"There's no room." I return to my seat as Jude lifts his arse from his, adjusting his trousers. "Okay?" I ask on a sideways smile.

"No."

I click my pen a few times as my mobile ringing fills the car, and I dip to my bag, slipping my new pen into the side pocket and pulling out my phone.

"Who is it?" Jude asks.

"My mum." I look at him in apology. "Do you mind?" I can't not answer, she'll only worry, and I bet she's in a spin after Dad's given her a rundown on our earlier row. Jude waves a hand flippantly and pulls away slowly, probably being considerate. But this is a Ferrari, and it's got a screamer of an engine. "Mum." I wince.

"Oh, Amelia, I do hate this. Your father's in a terrible mood, he won't talk to anyone, and he and Grandma have had words."

If only I could be happy that Grandma has my back. "He'll come round." He always does. He'll sulk for a few days, and then I'll go for dinner, he'll give me a silent hug, and it'll be like nothing happened.

"And you're seeing that man again? I can't keep up!"

I look at Jude across the car, worried about having to make introductions. Can I avoid it? Keep him away from my family?

"I can't stand the tension," she rambles on. "And since when do you swear, Amelia Gracie Lazenby? And at your father!"

"I was frustrated." I see Jude look out the corner of his eye. I roll mine.

"You must come immediately and make peace with him."

"I'm always making peace with him. Why can't he make peace with me?"

"Because you swore!" The engine continues to roar. "Where are you?"

I swallow and relax back. "Jude's just picked me up from work. I'm going to his place." I laugh on the inside. *His place.* I make it sound like a two-bed semi.

"In the Rolls-Royce?" Mum whispers, saving Dad's ears.

"Not today, Mum."

"Oh." She sounds disappointed. "Clark says he's richer than God."

Jude chuckles beside me, and I narrow my eyes on him. "I'll pop in tomorrow, okay?" Test the temperature and decide if Dad's had enough time to sulk.

"Okay, darling. Grandma and Grandpa will be here. We'll go for a walk in the garden."

"See you." I drop my phone in my bag and look at Jude. He's grinning at the road. "What?"

"Nothing."

"It's not my mother you should be worried about, it's my father."

He nods mildly, eyes on the road. "So they know you're *seeing that man* again?"

I settle back, uncomfortable with the conversation. "Yes, they know."

"Sounds like they've taken it well," he says, a definite sardonic edge to his tone.

"Don't take it personally."

"I'm not. And why were you frustrated?"

"What?"

"You said you were frustrated."

I don't like this. Talking about exes never goes down well. "I dropped the f-bomb on him."

"Why?"

"Because I was frustrated."

"And . . . why were you frustrated?"

"Jude," I breathe, dropping my head back. "What is this?"

"Just trying to understand the level of disapproval I'm going to face."

I'm not imagining his car getting faster. "I said don't take it personally."

"Is your father still trying to get you back together with Nick?"

"No." Total lie. "Will you slow down?" The car immediately decelerates, and I watch out the corner of my eye as Jude flexes his hands around the wheel. "You're as unexpected to them as you were to me." My voice is soft. Almost pleading. "It just needs some time."

"And they don't know why we split up?"

"No. They don't need to."

"And will your dad tell Nick about us?"

"I've asked him not to. I should do that myself, but it's still raw. I want to give it some time for him to—"

"Fall out of love with you?"

"I don't love him," I say, making that clear. "Can we stop talking about my ex and my dysfunctional family now?"

Jude seems to take a breath, reaching for my knee and squeezing. "I'm sorry. You're right, best to leave things to settle."

And how long will *that* take?

As Jude helps me out of the Ferrari, Anouska comes running out of Arlington Hall, her silky black hair wafting behind her, and practically drags Jude away, leaning up to talk quietly in his ear. I slowly pull my bag onto my shoulder, inevitably interested. She passes him something and then waves at me fleetingly before hurrying back inside.

"Is everything okay?" I ask. Jude doesn't answer. Instead, he takes my hand and pulls me along the line of parked cars. "Where are we going?" I want to kick my heels off and splatter on his bed, hopefully with him on top of me. "Jude," I breathe when he remains silent.

He eventually stops and takes me by the shoulders, turning me to face him. I give him an expectant look. He gives me a shy smile. "I got you another gift." He holds something up, and it takes me a moment to register what. A key fob. And I'm not exactly in the know about cars, but I do recognise the logo on it.

I move my eyes to his, my disbelief real. "You bought me a car?"

He sweeps his arm out, indicating the shiny grey car next to us.

"Oh my God," I whisper, staring at the Jaguar. "You bought me *this* car?"

"It's nothing."

"Nothing?" I look at the registration plate. "Jude, it's a brand-new Jaguar F-Type!"

"Do you like it?" he asks, clicking the fob, making it flash and beep. He goes to the driver's door and opens it, revealing crisp new black leather.

"It's gorgeous," I breathe, at a loss. "But I can't accept this."

His face falls, and I hate myself for it. "Why?"

"Because . . . because . . ."

"Because, because, because?"

"Because . . ."

"See, there's no reason." He directs me to the driver's seat and helps me down. "Suits you."

I stare at the wheel, smell the new interior. "Jude, I don't *not* have a car because I can't afford one," I say, looking up at him leaning on the door. "I just don't need one. I live in the city. I get the Tube or walk."

"But now you have a boyfriend who lives in a different county, and I'm getting nagged by the transport manager for constantly reserving one of the cars for you."

"But . . ." I look around me. "But . . ."

He crouches by the side of the car, taking my hand, and I pout at him, knowing I'm not going to convince him that I don't need this car. "It's just a car, Amelia. Besides, you can't be a top financial planner and ride the Tube. Look at it as a belated birthday gift."

I laugh, letting him guide my hands to the wheel. "The pen was enough."

"Come on, you can take me for a spin." He shuts my door and rounds the front, slipping his shades on and getting in the passenger seat. I watch him as he pulls his belt on, wondering how I got so lucky. "What?" he asks, faltering while fastening it.

I lean over and smother him with my mouth, and he lets me at him, his face bunched, his laugh light. "Thank you."

"Shut up and start the engine."

A flutter of excitement erupts in my tummy as I press the button to start the engine, the gorgeous thing purring to life.

"It's an automatic, so you don't have to worry about—"

"Gears?" I ask.

"I was going to say you don't have to worry about your hand."

"Oh. I haven't driven for over a year." Scanning the various panels, I familiarise myself with the controls and displays. "Ready?" I ask, slipping it into drive and pulling off, the engine humming beautifully. "Where am I going?"

"I want to take you somewhere. Turn left out of the gates."

I do as I'm bid and follow Jude's directions, my smile unstoppable.

"Like riding a bike, huh?" He reaches into my bag. "Where's your phone? I'll hook it up to Bluetooth."

"The inside pocket." I slow at the barrier before the gates, waiting for Nelson to raise it.

"I'm just going to ignore that text notification from your ex asking why you've not called him."

I feel my cheeks burning with guilt. *Fuck.* "He was at the restaurant last night," I blurt, releasing the wheel and throwing my hands up. "When you were in the bathroom cooling off after Charley went at you. I saw him and he came over and I panicked because I didn't want him finding out about you by actually bumping into you and I was worried because you can't seem to control your temper when it comes to me and other men, and so I told Nick I'd call him to get rid of him before you came out of the bathroom." I take a breath. "Obviously I had no intention of calling him, so now he's asking why I haven't, and I don't know what to say."

"Fucking hell, Amelia, breathe."

I flop in my seat, exhausted. "Don't be mad with me."

"I'm not mad."

"You're not?"

"No." He takes my hands and places them on the wheel. "Drive." Then he goes to the dashboard and starts navigating the menu. "Wait."

Taking my thumb, he holds it to the pad on my phone to open it. "Now you can drive."

I stare at him, stunned. That's it?

Peeking out the corner of his eye at me, he smiles. "Drive, Amelia."

"Right, yes. Drive." Getting back to the wheel, I pull through the barrier and do a left at the gates as instructed, accelerating smoothly.

"Done." Jude slips my phone back into my bag and gets comfortable.

It's a stunning drive, the narrow country roads winding and dipping. Each time Jude tells me we're on a straight for a while, I open her up, my smile breaking my face as Jude laughs at my excitement. He looks so casual with his elbow propped by the window, his trouser-clad legs extended. Relaxed. Content. No anger anywhere in sight.

"Slow down," he says, as I approach a curve in the road. "It's tight on this corner, and you can't see any oncoming traffic."

I ease off the accelerator, braking into the turn, and speed up again when Jude gives me the green light. He knows every bend and turn, how sharp or smooth they are. How many times has he driven this road?

"Left just past there," he says, pointing to a red pillar post box. "And go slow, it's a gravel road." He looks across at me. "We don't want to chip your new favourite thing."

"You're my favourite thing," I say, turning and wincing the second I hear a stone flick up and hit the paintwork. "Shit."

"Slow down." He laughs, placing his hand on my knee.

As a result, I push my back into the leather of my seat, clearing my throat, trying to concentrate. "Thank you for waiting until I've slowed down to do that." I glance at him, smiling out the corner of my mouth.

"Oh, does it affect your driving?" His hand starts to drift under my dress.

"Jude," I breathe, tingles chasing up my leg with his hand.

"Sorry." He releases me and slips his hands under his thighs, restraining himself, and I laugh again, loving the cheeky, easy smirk he flashes me. Today is a fine day.

"Where are we?" I ask, spotting a church up ahead.

"You'll see. Pull up over there." He points to a huge cedar tree outside the church gates, so I roll around the gravel path and gently brake, leaning forward to see the beautiful, ancient structure.

"Pretty," I muse, letting myself out and taking in the countryside, breathing in the fresh air. Meadows bursting with wildflowers blanket the surrounding fields, the sun hazy past the clouds above.

Jude holds his hand out for me, then leads me towards the church, and I can tell by his small smile that he knows I'm bursting with curiosity. He stops by the church doors, and I take in the old, cracked, heavy wood, waiting for him to clue me in as to why we're here. "I thought," he says quietly, moving in, hunkering down to get his face level with mine, "I'd show you where I want to marry you."

I jerk so much, I practically fly out of his hold. "What?" I gasp, my mind running at a mile a minute. Married? But he just made this official. "Jude, I—"

He starts laughing hysterically, and if I wasn't so relieved, I'd admire the outrageously gorgeous sight.

"That's not funny," I mutter, slapping his bicep.

"Noted." He chuckles, grabbing my hand and pulling me on. "No marriage."

I scowl at his high eyebrows as I let him lead me, my thrumming heart piping down. "I'm hardly wearing the shoes for this," I say, looking down at my heels as I tiptoe across the long grass, trying to stop my stilettos from sinking in.

Jude says nothing, just smiles down at my feet as he pushes his way through a gate. A sea of headstones come into view. "Oh," I breathe, realizing where we are.

Bringing us to a stop before a beautiful marble gravestone, he smiles across at me. "My mum and dad."

Everything in me deflates, my heart becoming heavy. This is big. *So* big.

KENT & EVELYN
IT WAS TRUE LOVE.

"It was true love," I whisper. *Oh God.*

"It really was," Jude says quietly, emotion ruling his tone too. Then he laughs under his breath and sniffs, clearing his throat. I look up at him, just catching the tail end of a rough sweep of the back of his hand across his eyes. My heavy heart cracks for him.

Stepping forward, he drops to one knee and faffs with the vase of flowers, eventually pulling them all out and resting them aside. Tipping the water out, he rises and walks across to a water barrel under a beautiful stained-glass window and fills it with fresh rainwater, returning and putting the flowers back in.

"Peonies," I say, joining him, helping to pull some wilting leaves off the stems.

"Mum's favourite. Dad used to get them for her every Friday from April to June." He cocks me a wry smile, rising and dusting off the top of the headstone. "And a bottle of Chablis."

I smile, albeit sad, when I spot a bottle of wine set to the side with two glasses. I reach for them and blow some debris from the bottom, replacing them just so.

"Wait," Jude says, taking the bottle and starting to pull the foil off from around the top. "Get the glasses."

"What?"

He nods at them. "This bottle needs to be drunk. I'll replace it."

Jude reveals the bottle's cork, then rummages through the grass and pulls out a corkscrew. "Ta-da," he says quietly, getting to work.

Laughing, I get the glasses, watching him, wondering how many bottles he's drunk while sitting here with his parents. *God damn you, Jude Harrison, you just keep giving me more reasons to love you.* He pours us each an inch while I hold out the glasses and puts the bottle back by the headstone. Handing one over to him, I link an arm through his and rest my head on his upper arm, smiling when I see him lift his wine a little in toast to his mum and dad. I follow his lead, giving my own silent thanks to them. People I don't even know, and yet feel like I do. Or, at least, his mother.

I take a breath and take the plunge. "You've never really talked about your dad."

"It's hard," he says, after a few moments of silence, staring ahead at the gravestone, his jaw definitely pulsing a touch. Naturally, I want to ask why, and inevitably, I think about the pills again. And what Rhys said. I can see that anger now, just from mentioning his father. "He died suddenly," he goes on. "Heart attack." Another clear of his throat. "He suffered with angina, but it was controlled with medication. I found him."

"Jude." I remove my head from his arm and tighten my hold. "I'm so sorry."

He smiles down at me, then slides his hand into mine, leading me to a bench under a willow tree. "Sit," he says. The gold plaque on the back of the bench catches my eye.

EVELYN'S BENCH

"I had it put here for Mum to sit on when she visited." He lowers next to me, keeping hold of my hand. But now Jude sits here. "She used to wear heels." He peeks down at mine. "All the time. Even her slippers clicked the wooden floors around the house. It was her thing. Shoes. Dad used to say she'd put Imelda Marcos to shame."

I laugh lightly, moving in closer, resting into his side as we sit on his mum's bench and sip wine.

"She visited him every week. At least, that's what she told me. I think she came most days."

"She was lost without him," I murmur, remembering Jude telling me that.

"She died in her sleep."

"What?"

"She wasn't taking my calls," he says quietly. "So I went round and found her in her bed." His voice cracks. "She was perfectly healthy. There was no explanation. Sudden Adult Death Syndrome, I think they call it." I know what he's going to say next, and I'm not sure I can hear it. "But I think she died of a broken heart."

"Oh, Jude," I whisper, looking up at him.

"I didn't have a chance to miss Dad." He stares forward, that jaw starting to pulse again, as if he's biting down on his back teeth. "I was the eldest boy. I had to make sure everyone was okay. But Mum? All I've done since she's been gone is miss her."

I chew at my lip, once again seeing those pills in Jude's bathroom cupboard. Will he use this opportunity to tell me he might have struggled in the past? But I feel like he's still struggling. So why isn't he taking the pills? This enlightenment does, however, explain his anger since she died. He was so focused on being strong for his family after his dad passed away, he didn't have room for grief until Evelyn died. And now it seems like he's dealing with a tsunami.

Laughing under his breath, Jude peeks down at me. Smiles. Dips and presses his lips in my hair. "I ended things with Katherine a year after Dad died."

Every muscle in my face aches to screw up. I don't want to think that he was going to marry someone. "Why?"

"She was needy."

I release an unattractive snort of laughter, and Jude looks down at me with another grin.

"And jealous," he says, wiping away my amusement.

Well, that makes sense. I've definitely detected a touch of the green-eyed monster. A touch? But . . . "Jealous of who?" *God, please don't hit me with a past of cheating and betrayal.*

"Of my relationship with Mum," he replies. I don't do a very good job of hiding my recoil. "Katie hated—"

"Wait, Katie?"

"Katherine. She was known as Katie until she got married and decided it wasn't grown-up enough for her. Anyway, Katherine hated that I put my mum first. Hated that I would change our plans so I could have dinner with Mum instead. I just . . . I don't know. I didn't have the energy or patience for her. She was always pleasant to Mum, but I sensed the underlying resentment. Mum was oblivious, though."

"I don't like Katherine," I declare, not that he needs to hear it. He knows. And I hate that he still slept with her. *Hate it.*

"But most of all, I called it off because what I had with her wasn't a patch on my parents' love. Seeing them together made my heart so happy. Then seeing how devastated Mum was when Dad died made my heart break. I didn't feel like that about Katherine. I want what Mum and Dad had."

I stare forward, feeling like a swarm of butterflies have been released inside me, as Jude gets up, places his wine on the ground, and crouches in front of me. Relieving me of my glass, he sets that down too and takes my hands gently. "The way Mum looked at Dad," he says, his eyes pouring with sincerity. "I see you looking at me like that, Amelia." His gaze searches mine, waiting for me to speak. I have no words. My heart is speeding. "And I know for fucking sure I look at you like I adore you, because I really fucking do."

I'm not sure it's acceptable to swoon in a graveyard, but here I am swooning in a graveyard. And I know, right in this moment, I'm looking at Jude like I adore him. Because I do. I can deal with his . . . quirks. And maybe now, after years of grief and no direction, only Arlington Hall to keep him going, he sees a future.

With me.

I cannot believe I'm thinking this. I've been well and truly swept off my feet, and it isn't just all-out crazy chemistry that's blindsided me. It's Jude Harrison in his entirety. Including his vulnerabilities. Including his quirks.

I reach for his wide shoulders and pull him into my seated body, and he drops to his knees between my legs. "I really fucking do too."

He holds me tightly, and it feels so poignant. I wasn't prepared for him. He wasn't prepared for me. "Promise me you'll always listen to me when I talk," he whispers. "See me when I'm in front of you. Take my hand when I give it to you."

I pull out of his hold with some effort, finding his face. I hate the despondency I see. "What's wrong?" I ask, holding his cheeks.

"You overwhelm me."

I want to laugh. Don't.

"Promise me," he demands.

My forehead furrows, wondering why this is so important to him, thinking perhaps it's connected to his parents. "I promise."

He nods. "Okay," he breathes. "Okay."

"Can I ask you something?" I immediately bite down on my lip, wondering if I'm making a monumental mistake.

"I don't know." He leans back, his expression questioning. "The look on your face tells me you don't want to ask, so I'm a bit nervous about what you're going to say."

I smile. It's small and guilty. "I found the antidepressants in your bathroom cupboard." I blurt it all out quickly and hold my breath, watching with unease as his eyes slowly widen. And darken. They definitely darken.

"Oh."

"I wasn't snooping. I was looking for eye drops because it was the morning after the night I got a bit drunk and you wanted me to meet Casey."

"You were more than a bit drunk."

I shrug. "You were depressed."

"Apparently."

My recoil is unstoppable. "That sounds like you don't think you were."

"I don't know what I was."

"Well, did they help? The pills, I mean."

"Yes, they helped." He tilts his head at me when I squint. "What?"

"You don't take them anymore?"

"No. Why?"

"Well, I don't know. Sometimes I wonder if you should."

It's Jude's turn to recoil. "I'm not depressed. Do you think I'm depressed?"

"Maybe more angry than depressed."

"You think I'm angry?"

"You *don't*?" I didn't mean to sound astounded.

"I assume you're talking about the occasions when—"

"You had my brother by the throat, a member of staff thrust up against a wall, a colleague of mine on the floor after you booted his chair out from under him? Yes. Yes, I'm talking about those occasions." And more.

His eyes narrow, unimpressed. "Isn't a man allowed to be pissy if another man tries to come on to his woman?"

I laugh, leaning forward, getting my nose close to his. "Only one of those men was trying to come on to me. The other two were innocent bystanders."

"So I act first, think later."

"And your dad," I continue, taking this opportunity and running with it. "Rhys is right. Every time he's mentioned, I see something change in you." Chewing his lip, Jude studies me closely as I watch his irises change colour before my eyes. "Like now. Your eyes change colour when you're angry."

He blinks, as if he can change that. "My eyes?"

"Yes, they're darker when something's bothering you. Bluer."

"What colour are they when I'm horny for you?" he whispers, coaxing my mouth open, combing his fingers through my hair and gripping.

"Greener," I mumble around his kiss.

"You make me less angry." His tongue circles mine so slowly and delicately, his head tilting and turning to go deeper.

"Are you sure?"

"Oh, baby, trust me, I'm sure."

I retreat slowly, holding his wrist. "Don't be angry," I whisper, feeling at his face, my eyes searching his.

"I just need to forgive him for dying," he says quietly. Because if his dad hadn't died, neither would've his mother. And that explains his anger perfectly. Doesn't it? "I'm getting there. And that's all down to you, Amelia."

And he's shown me I can have it all. Love *and* a career. "I love you," I whisper, feeling at his rough cheeks.

"I'm grateful."

"Thank you for sharing this with me."

Jude nods, taking a deep breath, looking up to the sky. "We'd better move." Getting to his feet, he pulls me up, and I glance up too, seeing a huge black cloud rolling above us. The sun disappears behind it, dimming the light. "Come on," he says, putting the glasses and bottle back by the graveside and reclaiming me, just as the cloud seems to burst directly above us, pounding us with bullets of rain.

"Shit!" I yelp, as Jude starts jogging, tugging me along. "Fuck!" My heels sink into the ground, and a foot slips right out, leaving one shoe behind. I start a wonky hobble, Jude's hand tight around mine. "Wait!" I yell, laughing. "My shoe!"

He stops and looks back, his face, hair, body, all drenched. My gaze drops down to my front. I'm soaked too, rain hammering my body. And I smile, feeling so fucking alive. In a graveyard. I laugh, my eyes on Jude's body. His shirt stuck to his chest, his nipples visible. His hair plastered across his face. Christ knows what I must look like.

His smile stretches into a grin, his hand raking through his wet hair, as he diverts us back and dips to pick up my shoe, removing the other one from my foot as he does. Then he slowly walks us out of the graveyard, in no rush at all.

Both of us drenched.

Both of us not giving a shit.

Because nothing could ruin the feeling inside right now.

Chapter 16

Pure white with the Arlington Hall crest on the breast, the robe skims my ankles, and the sleeves reach my knuckles. I feel like I'm wrapped in fluffy clouds.

Jude's tossing something in a pan when I walk into the kitchen towel-drying my hair, and the waft of something delicious—not Jude—invades my senses. He's in grey sweatpants. Bare-chested. His wet hair is a mess of waves falling around his ears. I've never had a type. I do now. Him.

"Smells good," I say, perching on a stool and flicking my head down, wrapping my hair in the towel and making a turban. When I lift my head again, Jude's serving up two plates.

"Spaghetti à la Jude," he says, sprinkling some basil leaves over the top before sliding my plate across to me.

My mouth waters as I collect my fork, and Jude sets a glass of wine by my plate. "I could get used to this."

"Do," he says, joining me, kicking his foot up on the footrest of his stool. "It's not going anywhere." He nods at my damp dressing. "That needs changing."

I smile as I spin my fork in the pile of spaghetti and pop it in my mouth, humming my approval. "You're good at this."

"Better than Nonna's?" he asks coyly, digging into his own plate. I don't answer, not because it isn't. "Casey's the master chef of the family."

"Where does he chef?"

"On yachts, mainly. Private dining. It's insane how much people pay for him to feed them."

"Sounds like an incredible job."

"He loves it. He was named in an article in *The Times* when he was twenty-two. Things to do before you die: Have Casey Harrison cook for you. Since then, he's travelled the world, cooked for the rich and famous."

"Wow."

"It's made him a millionaire."

"Double wow."

Jude nods. "I asked him to take charge of the Orangery here when we opened, but he has far more fun on superyachts." He quirks a brow as he takes a mouthful and chews. "It was probably wise. We'd clash."

Interested, I turn into him more, taking a break from the spaghetti for some wine. "Why would you clash?"

"We're different. We all are. Apparently, I'm sensible and strategic."

"Yes." I laugh. "You were *very* strategic when you pursued me."

Jude's fork falters as he plunges it into his pasta, a wave of something passing across his face. Then he smiles. "Casey is more mañana mañana. He's irritatingly laid-back."

"And Rhys?"

He blows his cheeks out. "Rhys is a bit of a loose cannon, as you've probably gathered."

"You worry about him."

"He's successful, good-looking, charming, but he's always had a problem with restraint."

"The sex tape."

"He's a sportsman." He tilts a wry smile my way. "Gets lots of attention, if you know what I mean."

I scoff. And Jude doesn't? They are three very handsome, successful, charming brothers. "I know what you mean."

"You look good in the robe." His voice has dropped a few octaves. "Very good."

I purse my lips around another bite, seeing the intent in his gaze. "This pasta is too good to abandon."

"You think?" He turns farther towards me and drops his fork, plucking out a piece of spaghetti and popping one end past his lips. My swallow is lumpy, my pulse picking up, as he leans towards me and pops the other end into my mouth. Then he slowly creeps forward, doing all the sucking, his eyes shining and stuck to mine. I drop my fork, brace myself, and when our lips meet, I groan, slipping off the stool and putting myself between his open thighs, deepening our kiss. "Think I've found something tastier," he mumbles, pulling the robe open and having a thorough inspection. It hits the floor, and his hands rest on my hips, sending a flurry of shudders through me. My head drops back, the towel falling away, my wet hair tumbling all over my back and shoulders. Every inch of me calls for him, my breasts aching, my nipples hardening, a deep, intense throb hitting me between my thighs. "Come here." He pulls my head up and reclaims my mouth, lifting me from my feet and sitting me on the counter. Plates clatter across the wood, being knocked aside. Tearing his mouth off mine briefly, Jude moves the wine, then pushes me down to my back, bending over me, returning to my mouth and kissing me hungrily.

He shoves his sweatpants down, then hooks his arms under my knees and pulls me farther to the edge, his hips at the perfect height to enter me. My spine bends, my eyes close, and I exhale as he slides in, his hands shaking where they rest on my thighs. He doesn't hang around— I'm more than wet enough. He starts to pump, the penetration deep and oh-so-mind-bendingly high. I moan, writhe on the wood, reaching for his hand on my leg and gripping it.

"God damn." He hisses, increasing his momentum, the sounds of his gratification in my darkness forcing me to open my eyes and watch him unravel. The strain on his face is one of my favourite expressions on him. The pleasure. The greed.

"Yes," I whisper, releasing his hand when he flexes it, taking my feet to his shoulders, holding them there, his tempo never faltering. Every advance has me crying out, every withdrawal makes me moan. "Yes, yes, yes," I breathe, floating away, feeling the pressure build.

Jude's head drops back, his eyes close, his hands lying over the tops of my feet. Ripples roll across his torso, the skin of his stomach taut. "Fuck, Amelia," he yells at the ceiling.

My arms reach out above my head, frantically searching for something to hang on to, because I feel like I could take off, the power of the pleasure gushing through me so strong. "Jude," I say in warning, feeling it steaming forward. "Jude!"

His hands clamp down over my feet harder, his head drops, and I watch in rapt fascination as his eyes turn wild, his neck veins bulging. Then his body folds in, he hisses, and a palm slams into the wooden counter to hold himself up. I feel the wet heat of his release fill me, and with that, my body releases too, the power of it locking me in position, before I start to convulse. He gasps, I yell, and he collapses over me, both of us breathless, our bodies vibrating violently.

"Fucking . . . hell." His forearms rest on the wood either side of me, his head hanging low. Beads of sweat drip from his face onto my boobs. "I could be inside you twenty-four seven." Exhausted, I look up at the ceiling, recovering, as Jude takes a nipple into his mouth and sucks and licks softly for a while. "Definitely tastier," he whispers, kissing in between my breasts and licking his way up my body to my neck, onto my chin.

My lips.

Content.

I'm so fucking content. And for the first time, in *every* aspect of my life.

I let him kiss the daylights out of me, my hands on a mission through his hair. "Watch your hand," he says, gruff.

"It's fine."

"Still hungry?" He rests his head on my chest, feeding his fingers through mine.

"Not really," I say with effort, wincing as he slips out of me. After getting his sweatpants in place, he pulls me up, smiling at my mess of wet hair. He looks so content too. No stormy clouds hanging over him, his temper tamed.

"How were your brothers when you lost your parents?" I ask, the question falling out without warning, surprising us both. I wonder for a moment if he'll answer. I'm sure he thinks he's talked enough about his parents today, but he finally smiles a little and drags a light fingertip down my cheek.

"They dealt with it in their own way. Casey escaped into a kitchen, Rhys escaped in women, booze, and rugby." He pushes his lips to my forehead. "Never be at odds with your parents, Amelia. You never know when will be the last time you see them."

I want to cry for him. *Could* cry for him. Nodding, I let him get me down. He helps me into my robe and puts me on my stool, before sorting himself.

"Need a tissue?" he asks as I have some wine, what he just said about parents sitting heavy on my mind.

"Yeah, give me a second."

"Of course," he says, starting to collect the plates.

I leave the room and go to his bathroom, cleaning myself up before calling Dad.

"Darling?" he answers, sounding worried. "Are you okay?"

"Yes, why?"

"You're calling me when you're not talking to me. This isn't how we do it. You come round for dinner, make me a cuppa, I give you a hug, and that's that."

I sit on the edge of the bed and fall to my back. "Aren't you fed up with doing that?"

"No, I like it when we make peace."

"That's not making peace, Dad. That's me letting things slide because I hate being at odds with you."

"I just want what's best for you."

"What *is* best for me?"

"Well, security. A decent, strong man who can look after you."

"Any decent, strong man? Or just Nick?" And I don't need looking after, but I won't get into that.

"He fits in," Dad grumbles.

"Yes, with you, Dad. He fits in with you. He didn't fit in with me, and since you're talking about what's best for me, I think I'm qualified to let you know, it isn't Nick."

"Oh." If I could see him, I know he'd be pouting. "And this new man, might he fit in with you?"

I suck my bottom lip in, daring myself to say it. "I think he could," I whisper, almost reluctantly. "I really think he could."

"Then I should meet him."

I snort. "You'll meet him when I decide you've had a suitable amount of time to control your urges to stick your nose into my business."

"You're my little girl!" he huffs, outraged. "It's my business to be in your business."

"I'm a woman."

"You'll always be my little girl."

I sigh, but I smile. "I love you, Dad. Even though you're trapped in the Middle Ages."

"And I love you, darling, even though you're a headstrong pain in my backside who swore at me." He pauses a beat. Sighs too. "But I wouldn't have you any other way. Keeps me on my toes. I hope this new guy knows what he's signing up for."

I grin like an idiot. "I've got to go. Jude's made me dinner, and I've got to help him clean up."

"Oh?" Dad says, quiet and interested. "Jude, eh? Where does he live?"

"Oxfordshire."

"How the flaming heck are you getting home from Oxfordshire?"

"Driving."

"What?"

"I have a car now."

"You do?"

"A Jaguar."

"Well," he says, kind of surprised, kind of impressed. "You really are doing well, aren't you?"

"I am, but I didn't buy it."

"What?"

"It was a gift from Jude. Bye!" I hang up and leave that with him, smiling at the thought of him yelling Mum's name, stalking around the house looking for her so he can tell her. I quickly put a call in to Abbie. "Hey."

"Evening."

"Where are you?" I ask, hearing a busy background, guessing she's in a restaurant.

"On a date."

I scramble up, shocked to my core. "Who with?"

"Vince Hightower."

"You know I don't know who that is. Wait." I quickly go to my screen and hook Charley in, even though I'm technically not speaking to her. "Did you know she's on a date?" I ask when her face appears.

"Shhh," Charley hisses, directing her camera down. Ena is asleep in her arms. "A date?" she whispers.

"Yes," I whisper back.

"Who with?"

"Vince Hightower."

"Is that a superhero's alias?"

I snort.

"Fuck off," Abbie whisper hisses. "He came into the florist earlier and ordered some flowers."

"Who for?" Charley asks.

"His mother."

"Awww," we both coo.

"He asked me out, I said yes, and here I am." Abbie shrugs. "Girls, I have *got* to get out of this rut. Maybe I just need to accept I'm never going to have that kind of explosive passion again." Another shrug plus a grimace. "Manage my expectations, you know what I mean?"

We both nod.

"Jude bought me a car."

Both of my friends go bog-eyed. "A car?" Abbie asks. "What kind of car?"

"One that drives."

"Dickhead."

"It's a Jaguar." I give them wide eyes too. "And he gave me an engraved pen."

Abbie swoons. It makes me smile. "What did it say?"

"I've got you."

"Oh my God," she breathes. "I might faint."

"As in, you're his?" Charley asks, frowning. "I've. Got. You. Possessive?"

"No," I say, the word drawn out, sounding like a warning. She better not kick off again. "As in, he's got me. Holding me. Is there for me."

"So cute!" Abbie sings.

"He took me to see his parents' graves earlier. Told me about them. It's so sad. Jude found his dad. Heart attack." Both girls jut their bottom lip out. "And his mum died in her sleep. She was perfectly healthy. Jude said it was a broken heart. He found her too."

"Oh my God," Charley whispers. "It's hard to hate someone who found both his parents dead and suffered grief like that."

I could never hate Jude. "Are we friends again?"

"Yes, we're friends," Charley says.

"And in future, will you be nice to my boyfriend?"

"So long as he treats you right."

"Look, girls." Abbie flaps an impatient hand at the screen. "I appreciate the update on all things, but my date is going to think I've bailed if I don't get back to the table."

"What does he look like?" I ask.

"How old?" Charley pipes in.

"Is he tall like his name?"

"What does he do for a living?"

"When can we meet him?"

"Bye!" Abbie hangs up, leaving me and Charley chuckling.

"I've got to go too. Ena's had a sleepy poo, and I need to try and change her without waking her up. Are you around this weekend?"

"Yeah, I'm getting the keys to my new place tomorrow. We're doing an IKEA trip Sunday. I need to buy some furniture. Especially a bed. I need a bed."

"Even though you stay at Jude's every night?"

"It'll be over an hour to Jude's from my new place. I can't sustain that during the week. I'll call you tomorrow." I hang up and smile down at my phone, happy things are back on track with the girls. And my dad.

I look up when Jude appears at the bedroom door. "Everything okay with your dad?"

I tilt my head. He wasn't listening. He just knows, and once again I'm adding something to the list of things I love about Jude. It's far outweighing the list of things I don't like. "I better think about getting myself home in my new car."

Remaining where he is in the doorway, Jude considers me for a few seconds, and I just know he's plotting to keep me here. "Grant me one wish," he eventually says.

"Just one?"

He cocks his head, slightly amused. "For today."

"What?"

"Let me be overprotective and controlling for a moment."

My eyebrows shoot up. "Go on."

"I'd rather you didn't drive these roads in the dark. At least, not until you're familiar with them. Let me drive you."

I bite at my lip, pondering that. Only for a second. "Okay."

"Oh, well, that was cleaner than I expected." He comes to the bed and lays himself all over me, kissing me in thanks. And I'm his again.

"I love my car," I mumble in between the swirls of our tongues. "I love my pen." Another swirl. "But the best gift you gave me today was you." Everything he's shared, I'm so grateful for it. For *him*.

"Mum would have loved you," he says quietly, pecking his way to my ear.

"She's famous for being a lady of exquisite taste." I inhale and absorb the feel of his tongue dragging lightly up the shell of my ear, his arousal growing against me. "Of course she would." *Oh God, I just can't get enough of him.*

He chuckles and kisses his way to my nose, biting it. He looks deep into my eyes. Lets his mouth fall to mine again.

"You know," I mumble around his slippery-soft tongue teasing mine, "it's light at five a.m., so I could drive home then."

Jude pulls back, his eyes sparkling happily. "You know how to please your man." And then he resumes our kiss, rolling us so he's on the bottom. "You're staying the night." He rips my robe open, stroking over my breasts as I lift and get him positioned at my entrance before slowly sinking down. His eyes squeeze shut, and I watch his face contort as I ride him unhurriedly, circling and grinding, feeling every inch of his prime chest.

Beautiful.

Just . . . beautiful.

Chapter 17

Leighton appears from his office as I'm wandering down the corridor. I bite my tongue, mentally repeating to myself to keep my mouth shut. "How'd your meeting with Mr. Harrison go?" *Fuck it.*

He sneers at me, an eye narrowing. He can't possibly know it was me who stuck a spanner in his works, but still. I feel like he's looking at me accusingly. "Momentarily deferred." His pace slows, indicating he's about to stop and try to chat. So I keep mine up, passing him. Postponed? *Idiot.* "Lunch?"

"Busy," I say, smiling sarcastically over my shoulder. As soon as I'm in my office, I roll my eyes. "Creep." Going to my desk, I drop to my chair, dump my files down, and work my way through some client approvals so I can start actioning the movement of some funds. I must carve out time to make notes for my meeting with Tilda Spector too. I smile to myself. Leighton will have a hernia.

"Amelia," Gary says, breezing in. "How's it going?" He lowers to a chair and reaches for my glass paperweight, tweaking it.

"Great."

"A little birdie told me you have a certain lunch meeting with a certain semi-retiring adviser that goes by the name of Spector."

"How do you know?" I ask, taken aback. I've not mentioned it. I don't want to jump the gun; nothing may come of it, and I certainly don't want Steers knowing.

"A certain birdie was Spector." Gary jiggles his eyebrows.

"Wednesday," I confirm.

"Interesting."

"I know," I agree. "Any tips?"

"She likes you. I think she sees herself in you when she was starting out. You know, if you secure that agreement, you're going to smash your year target by quarter two."

"No pressure, eh?"

"And what about Harrison?"

I freeze in my seat, coming over excruciatingly hot. "Mr. Harrison?" I more or less squeak. "What about him?" I clear my throat, trying to tamp down the blood rising to my cheeks.

"He's changed his mind on Steers."

Fuck, fuck, fuck. "I didn't know he had a meeting with Steers."

"Leighton didn't brag?" Gary laughs, and I become increasingly uncomfortable. "Well, he had a meeting scheduled with Harrison, but he cancelled."

"Shame."

"And requested you."

My jaw drops. "What?"

He smiles and stands. "Why'd you look so surprised?"

Because I am. *God damn you, Jude.* "I've never really spoken to him." What the hell am I saying? I need to be up front. Except I can't. Not now. If I tell my boss I'm involved with Jude, God knows what he'll think. I glance at my phone, dying to grab it and call my unruly boyfriend. Yell at him.

"Well, you're making a name for yourself, Amelia. And if you have the likes of Tilda Spector championing you, people listen." He stands, and my dazed gaze rises with him. My face must be spelling out a whole lot of panic.

"I'll call Mr. Harrison," I murmur, at a loss.

"No need." Gary heads for the door, glancing at his watch. "He's here."

I push back into my chair, my stomach bottoming out. "Here?" I whisper. "Mr. Harrison is here?"

"I'll tell them to let him up." The door closes, and I sit in my chair, staring at the wood, my brain short-circuiting. Cognitive thought finds me way too late. I grab my phone and dial Jude, going to the door and peeking out. Jesus, where the fuck is Leighton? Jude's phone goes straight to voicemail.

"Shit." I hurry to the elevators, walking fast, one gear off breaking into a run, constantly checking around me. The lift dings, just as I land in front of the doors, and I brace myself to push Jude back in. *The fucker.* What's he playing at? Except when the doors open, the cart's empty.

"Amelia." Shelley's voice has me turning around, finding her walking down the corridor towards me with a shit-eating grin on her face.

And Jude's behind her.

"Look who's here," she practically sings, her eyes wide and delighted.

"Yes, look," I murmur, annoyingly dizzy at the sight of my newly acquired boyfriend. Suited. Booted. Stubbly. Eyes dancing, his hair sexed up. "God help me," I whisper, slapping a smile on my face, peeking around for any signs of Leighton.

"Miss Lazenby." Jude stops, his stance wide, his hands in his pockets.

"Mr. Harrison." I'm going to fucking kill him. "Step into my office." I sweep an arm out to the door behind him, and he looks back.

"Now there's an offer a man could never refuse." He smirks. I'm going to kill him *twice.*

Slowly.

Shelley chuckles, flustered, and I give Jude a glare I know he'll read well. *Yes, you're in trouble.* I pass him, and he falls in line behind me. Close. "This morning was fun," he says quietly. "I think reverse cowgirl is a new favourite."

"Pack it in," I hiss, pushing my way into my office and holding the door open for him.

He steps in, takes in my workspace. "You didn't enjoy riding me?"

"Jude," I breathe, closing the door. "What the hell are you doing?"

"I'm here on business." He helps himself to a seat in front of my desk. "And I was missing you."

My eyes are daggers on him as I lower to my chair.

"I thought I'd kill two birds with one stone."

"Are you insane?" My gaze constantly flicks from him to my door, praying I can get him out of the building before Steers finds out he's here.

"This is a really great desk." He leans forward and strokes his hand across the glossy wood, a small smirk tickling the corner of his lips. "We should christen it."

"You're assuming it hasn't already been christened."

The smirk drops like a rock, his expression darkening. "That's not funny."

"Neither is you being here, Jude." I slap my palm down and lean forward. "Explain."

"I want you to take over my financial affairs."

He's crazy. Confirmed. My God, someone find me some patience. I pick up my new pen and start clicking the end, apprehensive, eyes still bouncing back and forth from Jude to the door.

"Nice pen."

I drop it immediately. "Do you want to be my boyfriend or a client?"

"That's a ridiculous question."

"You can't be both. It's one or the other."

"I'm trying to help."

"This isn't helping me; it's stressing me the hell out."

"Why? If I give you my money to invest, it guarantees you'll smash your numbers, and then you'll make partner. You won't have to depend on winning Tilda Spector's business or on Leighton Steers failing."

I groan, dropping back in my chair and looking at the ceiling. "That's not how I do things."

"What, easily?" He scoffs. "I guess I should have known that. You made it really fucking hard to nail you." I stare at him, flummoxed, and he gives me a boyish grin. "I love you," he murmurs.

"Well, I don't like you at this particular moment of time, Jude." I get up, needing to walk off some of this annoyance. "I want to earn my way, not have my rich-as-sin boyfriend buy it for me." I walk a few laps of my desk, Jude's eyes following me.

"You're making me dizzy," he grumbles, reaching for my wrist as I pass him and pulling me onto his lap.

"Jude!"

"Stop complaining." His mouth is on mine before I can protest, and I momentarily loosen, reciprocating, kissing him back. Until I manage to seize the small scrap of sense I still have.

Wriggling out of his hold, I escape him and fix my hair, ignoring his sigh of exasperation as I go back to my chair, making sure the desk stays between us.

"You said I couldn't meet with Steers," Jude drones. "So I thought I'd meet with you."

"You didn't want to meet with Steers. You wanted to be an ape and subtly mark your territory." I won't tell Jude that Steers is still being suggestive, maybe a little touchy-feely too. It would be fatal. "Look"—I lean over my desk—"do you want to go public?"

He waves a finger between us. "What, like me and you?"

"Yes."

"We're not public?"

"Not at my workplace, no." Nor with my ex, but, surprisingly, we're both in agreement on that.

"Well, that's becoming obvious," he mutters. "Why haven't you shared our relationship with anyone here?"

"My private life is my private life. No one here needs to know about it. Or they *didn't* need to know. I can't take your portfolio on, Jude. It's a conflict and would be frowned upon."

"That's stupid."

"It's just how it is."

"Well, I'm here now."

"Yes, you are," I say shortly. "And now I have to figure out how to handle this so no one thinks I'm sleeping with you for your money." I flash him a sarcastic smile. "Ironic, huh?"

He gives me a tired expression. "Quite."

"Why can't you stay with your current adviser?"

"He's moving abroad and has passed me off to one of his replacements. We don't jell."

"Then I'll recommend to Gary that one of the senior partners takes you on."

"Fine."

"Good."

"Can I have a kiss?"

"No. Leave."

He blinks, injured. "This isn't going how I expected."

"What do you want me to do, Jude? You've put me in a really difficult situation, and now I have to figure out how I'm going to get out of it with my integrity intact."

"Are you saying no one can ever know about us?"

"Did you hear me say that? Until you stormed my workplace, people knowing about us wouldn't have been an issue, but then you went and arranged a meeting with me to discuss your financial affairs, and suddenly I find myself in a situation where my integrity and business practice could be put under the microscope." I lean closer, getting more and more worked up. "I'm on the cusp of making partner, Jude. I've worked my arse off for this, and you've just swooped in and potentially shat all over my progress because you had a large dose of possessiveness."

He's silent, clearly thinking of what he should say to that. There's nothing he can say.

"Just go," I breathe, motioning to the door. I'm surprised when he slowly rises, no question.

"I'll see you after work." It's not a statement, more a question. I don't like this uncertainty on him, but I need him to know that any interference with my career is a hard no.

"I have things to do."

He withdraws, stung. "Like . . . ?"

"Apartment stuff." *Translated: I need some breathing space from you.* And I know Jude's concluded that too.

"Right," he says, nodding mildly, chewing the corner of his lip in contemplation as I look at him with an unwavering, steely gaze. He reads that well too. "So when am I seeing you next?"

"I'll call you."

"Right." He walks slowly to the door, looking heavy, as I pick up my phone and dial Leighton, hoping to keep him at his desk while Jude makes his exit.

"Lazenby," Steers drawls. "Changed your mind on lunch?"

Jude looks back, disgusted, his sheepish demeanour disappearing in a heartbeat. I tilt my head at him. "No lunch for you, Steers. *Ever.* But your thoughts on the midday drop on the FTSE would be welcomed." I point to the door where Jude's hovering, silently ordering him to go. This is a problem of his own making. He can deal with it.

Yanking the door open aggressively, he stalks out, pissy, and I sigh, falling back in my chair, not listening to Steers bang on about the minuscule drop and what's spiked it. "I thought the same," I say when I know Jude's had enough time to leave, hanging up. "Bloody man," I mutter, getting up to go in search of Gary. I can't sit on this. I tap his door and poke my head round. "Got a minute?" I ask.

"Sure."

I step in, closing the door behind me. "Please don't tell Leighton that Mr. Harrison was here to see me. He'll think I'm conspiring."

"Why would he think that?"

"Well, Mr. Harrison cancelled his meeting with Leighton and then requested to see me. You appreciate how that might look."

Gary's mouth tilts down, his expression telling me he's not getting it. "Happens all the time, Amelia. Some clients just don't jell with certain advisers and request another."

What do I say? That Jude thinks Leighton's a douche and is after his girlfriend? That *I'm* Jude's girlfriend? "Here's the thing, Gary." I've got to be open, tell him who Jude is to me and that I propose recommending him to one of the senior partners. Maybe even Gary himself. The board will be over the moon to obtain such a high-wealth client, whoever he is. "Mr. Harrison and I—"

The door swings open, and Leighton falls in, appearing a bit flustered. *Shit.* Did he see Jude? Ask him questions? *Shit, shit, shit.* I frantically search my brain for the words I might need to get myself out of this mess.

"Gary," Leighton puffs, out of breath. He's run here. "News flash. I've got it on in the boardroom."

Gary's up like a shot, hotfooting it out of his office. "Can we pick this up?" he calls, following Leighton. "We've been waiting for news on a bailout; we've got plans riding on it."

"A bailout? Anything I should know?"

"Not unless you have IDF Telecoms on your radar."

He's gone before I can answer. "I don't," I murmur.

Fuck it all to hell.

Chapter 18

Gary didn't emerge from the boardroom for the rest of the day. I walked past a couple of times, and it looked tense in there, all the senior partners huddled around the table with Gary and Leighton, so I didn't disturb them, cracking on with preparations for my meeting next week with Tilda Spector. I'll talk to Gary on Monday.

Abbie and Charley were both up for bringing our trip to IKEA forward, so after I've collected the keys for my new apartment, I head there to meet them. In my new car. Which, right now, I feel guilty for driving.

I pull up and get two sets of high brows as I step out of the brand-spanking-new F-Type and hit the fob to lock it.

"Wow," Abbie breathes as I stand before them, me and the car under close scrutiny. It was a novelty driving to work. The parking, not so much. I didn't realise how much I've missed being on the roads. And yet it's not sustainable; the parking is expensive and the traffic horrendous.

"Are you two done drooling over my new wheels?" I ask, tossing my handbag onto my shoulder and heading to the entrance.

"So what are we shopping for?" Abbie asks, joining me on one side, Charley on the other.

I laugh. "Everything. But let's start with a bed. Do you think I'll fit a bed in my car?"

"I came in Lloyd's wardrobe on wheels," Charley says, pointing back at his A7 estate. "I knew you'd need a lot, and you could get a whole apartment in the back of that thing. We'll have a flatpack party at your new place." She links arms with me. "Lloyd's taken the kids to his parents for dinner, so I'm all yours."

"And me." Abbie nudges me in the side. "Although you won't be doing much DIY with that. Isn't it healing?"

I look down at my bandaged hand. "It's still a bit weepy. It just feels safer covered. I'm scared of knocking it."

"You should have it checked if you're worried."

I nod my agreement and let them flank me into IKEA.

In a convoy of three cars, we drive back to my new place packed to the rafters with home essentials. It was a productive trip and great to spend time with the girls, chatting as we all steered trollies around the store, browsing, throwing things in, discussing the merits of leather versus fabric couches. A headboard? Wood or velvet? King-size or super-king?

Nothing was mentioned about Jude, and I didn't volunteer anything either. Abbie's date, however, was a hot topic. She likes him. I can tell. She's never been on a second date with anyone, and they have one planned for next week.

I let us in through my own personal front door and kick my way through some post, passing the bedroom on the left before emerging into the kitchen that opens up onto the secluded courtyard.

"Oh, I love it," Abbie says, poking in and out of cupboards.

"Jesus, the height of the ceilings," Charley breathes, her head craned as she drops a few blue bags in the corner. "It smells like paint."

I draw the curtains at the bay window in the lounge area. "The landlord recently gave it an overhaul. New kitchen, new bathroom, a lick of paint." Walking through to the kitchen, I go to the double doors that lead onto the courtyard and push them open. "New patio."

"Oh, Amelia, it's perfect."

"Isn't it?" I gaze around, totally enchanted. When I viewed it almost two weeks ago, I was not in the best headspace, was finding it hard to appreciate how perfect it was for me when I felt like I was in total turmoil. Now, though, I can see. I'm glad I didn't let it pass me by.

"I bought supplies." Abbie magics a bottle of prosecco from her bag. "We can't build furniture without some fizz."

"Just a small one for me," Charley says, producing a toolbox. "I brought supplies too."

I pout, feeling a little emotional. "What would I do without you two?"

"Sleep in any of the dozens of swanky suites at your stinking-rich boyfriend's luxury hotel?" Abbie says. "Where is he tonight, anyway?"

"We're not joined at the hip, you know," I retort, evasive, going to one of the IKEA bags and finding the box of mugs. "So where's the next date with Hightower?"

Charley snorts as Abbie works the cork on the prosecco. "There's one thing bothering me that I've not mentioned." The cork flies out and hits the ceiling. "He still lives with his mum." She pours into the mugs.

"I did until a few weeks ago," I say. "Don't be judgy. Did he give you any context?"

"No."

"Did you ask?"

"No. Maybe on our next date. Cheers!" She toasts the air, going off to explore.

"Okay, what's the priority?" Charley asks.

"The bed."

She whips out an electric screwdriver and aims it at me. "Let's do this."

◆ ◆ ◆

A few hours later, I have a bed, a bedside table, and a rail to hang some clothes on. We've stocked the kitchen drawers and cupboards with various kitchenware, and I even managed to get a Tesco Whoosh delivery for some essentials—tea, coffee, milk.

Charley's made my bed, and Abbie's hung some of my dresses up. It's sparse, but it's a start. "Thank you," I say, so grateful, pulling them in for a group hug.

"I should get back." Charley checks her phone. "It's nearly ten."

"Yeah, I have a trip to the wholesalers at the arse crack of dawn, so I'm going to shoot too." Abbie pushes a box into the corner with her foot as Charley collects her tools. "Will you be okay on your own?"

"Sure," I say, confident. Truth is, I've never lived alone. Before Nick, I was with my parents, and after Nick, I split between my parents', Abbie's, and Jude's. This is new. A novelty. "I'm going to make a cuppa and snuggle up in my new bed." *Alone.*

I see the girls out and spend a few minutes collecting bits of cardboard and stuffing them in a box before heading back into the kitchen to make that cuppa. "Fuck," I mutter, realizing I'm missing something quite essential. A kettle. Pouting, I pick up the bottle of prosecco and hold it up to the light, seeing an inch left in the bottle. I shrug and tip it into my mug, sipping as I riffle through my bag for a fresh dressing before getting some warm, salty water. Then I spend the next fifteen minutes holding my breath as I clean around the wound. It's red. Too red? I ponder that as I redress it, deciding I'll give it a couple of days and get it checked out if it doesn't improve.

Flicking all the lights off and following my feet to my bedroom, I strip to my underwear, pull on a tee, finish the last of my fizz, and go to the bathroom to brush my teeth.

I'm spitting and rinsing when I hear a knock at the door. I frown and pop my brush in the holder, wiping my mouth on the towel before I go to the window, peeking past the blind.

Jude's on the doorstep, hands stuffed in his pockets, his shoulders slumped, his head hanging. I feel my shoulders drop too, as I watch him waiting for me to answer the door. It doesn't even cross my mind not to. Kicking a few bags out of the way, I go to the door and open it, and he looks up. Silent. Waiting for me to invite him in. I breathe in deeply and exhale, releasing the door handle and making my way back to my room, hearing him close it behind him. I'm too tired to debate his transgressions.

I climb into bed and listen as he moves around the bedroom, undressing, and a few moments later, the bed dips and he's curling himself around my body. "I'm sorry," he whispers, kissing my shoulder and slipping his hand under my T-shirt onto my stomach.

"You exhaust me."

"I'm staying the night." Pushing his lips into my hair, he breathes in long, his chest inflating against my back. And then he settles. And because he's here, wrapped around me, I do too.

Chapter 19

Light floods into the bedroom through the slatted blinds, making me squint as I sit up and look around. I can hear noise coming from the kitchen, so I pull my hair into a ponytail as I follow the sound, finding Jude in his boxers opening and closing cupboards. He sees me by the door and smiles timidly. "I was going to make coffee, but I can't find a kettle."

"I don't have one yet." I pass him on my way to get a glass of water, but don't make it. He seizes my arm and gently pulls me into his front, kissing me soft and slow. The smell of him and feel of him against me wakes up my senses, and I succumb to the energy between us, accepting his tongue in my mouth, pushing my front into his. "I'm not talking to you," I mumble, my hands disappearing past the waistband of his boxers.

"I'm not asking you to." He lifts me to his body, and every limb curls around him as he walks us back to my bedroom. He sits me down on the edge and kneels on the floor, putting his hands on my thighs and spreading them.

"Shit," I whisper, as he kisses the insides of my knees, sending ripples of need through me. He peeks up at me, his lips moving agonisingly slowly, his eyes telling me he's enjoying my building condition. I lift my T-shirt over my head and throw it aside, dropping to my elbows and looking down my body into his hungry gaze as he dots kisses up the insides of my thighs, alternating between legs, each press of his lips into my flesh having me tense a little bit more in anticipation. Then when he reaches the sensitive, delicate skin just shy of my entrance, he nibbles and sucks, and I groan, my head rolling. The tip of his tongue skims the tip of my clit, making me convulse, and then swirls deep, making me shake.

"Jude," I murmur, and he hums against me, lapping greedily through my wetness, sucking me into his mouth, pushing his tongue inside me. My shoulders start to ache from holding myself up, but I don't tumble to my back. I want to see him. I sit up, spread my legs more, hold his hair in my fists, and look down at his face buried in my pussy. It's the most erotic vision, his lips wet, his eyes sparkling, his fingers clawing into my thighs as he licks me out, feasts on me, his hot mouth encasing me, kissing, biting, sucking, swirling. The fingertips of one hand un-claw, and he reaches between his legs, groaning when he takes himself in a fist. "Oh God," I whisper, my pleasure pushed into a whole new frenzy. "Jude."

He works himself as he works me, taking us higher, my fists in his hair brutal, making him hiss when I yank.

"I'm coming," I yell, out of my mind, dizzy, every inch of me burning. "I'm coming!" I feel myself reach the point of no return, my breath held to take the hit, but suddenly his mouth is gone. "Jude!" He yanks me off the bed onto his lap, and I sink down on a yell, my build revived. My mouth homes in on his shoulder, clamping down as he fills me to the absolute brim. "I won't be long," I warn, knowing the moment we start moving I'm going to be flung into delirium. I kiss the spot I've just bitten and across his neck to his jaw, onto his lips.

"Me either." He lifts his arse from his heels, raising to his knees and then his feet, all the while keeping us connected. My back meets a wall. His eyes explode with intent. "Ready?"

"No." The word is pure air. "I'm never ready for you, Jude Harrison."

He groans and swoops in, taking my mouth hard and pushing me up the wall with a swivel of his hips, kissing me violently.

And it's glorious.

The sweat is instant. The shock waves relentless. His control and accuracy are faultless, every drive measured. I slide up and down the wall on constant yells, fighting with his hair, pulling, biting at his lip, the deepness he's achieving sending me wild.

"Still not talking to me?" he grunts, following up his question with a particularly brutal pound.

"No." I fist his hair at his temples and hold tight, making him face me. I look into his eyes, enduring his power and pace, taking it all. "Fucking hell, Jude," I gasp, slamming my head back, the friction of the plaster rubbing against my spine becoming sore, my hand throbbing. "Oh God." I puff and pant, my stomach muscles in pieces, enduring his power.

"Keep making those noises, baby."

"Oh, Jesus." I can feel it threatening, slithering through my body. "Oh God."

"Fuck, yes."

"Jude!"

"I've got you, baby."

"Oh God!"

"Come on!"

"Oh, yes!"

"Fuck, you look incredible."

"I'm coming!"

He growls and hammers on, faster. Harder.

"Jude!"

"Yes!"

I bury my face in his neck on a yell, my throat instantly raw, my body out of control, shaking against him as he spills himself into me, cursing to high heaven. It goes on forever, our shouts, the pleasure, my world spinning out of control, until he convulses, his fist smashes into the wall, and he crumples to the floor, cushioning my landing.

I lay, spattered all over his sprawled body, panting, replete.

Tingling everywhere.

"I take it I'm forgiven," he wheezes.

"I take it that means you're sorry," I puff back, beat, but somehow finding the energy to lick my way across his chest, up to his salty neck.

"I'm very sorry." He tilts his head back, lengthening his neck for me, giving me more licking space. "And I forgive you too."

"What did I do?" I ask, making it to his chin. His cheek. His eyes. His forehead.

"Threatened abstinence. I told you, that's a hard no for me."

"And interfering with my career is a hard no for me."

"Are we establishing boundaries?"

I smile despite myself, sitting on his hips and admiring his sweaty, shiny chest, my palms on a feeling mission.

Jude rests his hands over mine, stilling them, and checks my dressing. "Really, Amelia?" There's some blood on the edges. Not a lot, but still. It shouldn't be bleeding.

"I needed to put my bed together."

"You didn't, though. You could have laid off on the stubbornness and stayed at my place."

"I wasn't talking to you."

"But you are now?"

"Since you apologised, yes."

"I love you."

"I love you too."

The smile that breaks his face could break *me*, and he sits up, tackling my mouth again. "I love your new place."

"Me too."

"Can we have sleepovers?"

I laugh into his mouth, holding him in a firm hug as I devour him. "Whatever you want, baby," I say with an edge of sarcasm, giving him one last peck before lifting from his body. "I have to go to the gym."

"It's Saturday. You're on my time."

I snort unattractively in amusement. "I've been on your time all week."

He scowls. It's quite endearing. "You can go to the gym at Arlington Hall. In fact, you should cancel your membership. It's a waste when you have a gym at your disposal. It's better too."

"I'm not cancelling my membership, Jude."

"Fine. Are you driving?" he asks, falling to his back, his eyes following me into the bathroom.

"I was going to take the Tube."

"That would be silly because you'd have to come back here to get your car so you can come to see me."

"Why can't you come to see me here?"

"Because I stayed at your place last night," he calls.

I flip on the shower, smiling to myself. My place. It sounds good. I drape a towel over the top of the door and step in the stall. "Fine, I'll drive to the gym."

Jude appears in the doorway, beautifully bare, his semi-erect cock still twitching. My God, he's just too beautiful for words, and he knows it.

"I need some help," I say, coy, opening the door for him while holding up my injured hand.

He smiles—it's wildly stunning—and saunters over, casual. He's firming up again, a little more with each step. "Keep your hand out of the spray." He places it on the pane of glass, eyebrows high, and eases me back against the tiles. The cold has me inhaling sharply. And when he slowly falls to his knees, I brace myself for another Jude Harrison Special.

"Greedy," I murmur, as he reaches forward and forces my legs apart.

"Then you'd better keep feeding me." His hot mouth is on me in a second, and my knees instantly give, sending me sliding down the wall on a broken groan, my eyes crossing with pleasure.

◆ ◆ ◆

Pulling the door closed behind me, a travel cup of coffee in my hand, I aim my fob at my car, thoughtful. New apartment, new car.

New boyfriend.

"What are you thinking?" Jude says, taking my freshly dressed hand gently and walking us down the path to the road.

"Nothing," I say, hearing another door close. I look back and see a man leaving the door next to mine that leads up to the apartment above. Mid-twenties, I'd say. Smart in a creative's type of way, his jeans too tight and too short, his duster coat definitely from a vintage store. He spots us, and I sense a wariness I'm not sure I should like. "Hi." I pull Jude to a stop. "I'm Amelia. I just moved in."

He looks between me and Jude. "Jasper," he says, getting his rucksack on his back. "Welcome." He eyes Jude.

"Boyfriend," Jude pipes up, moving closer.

I roll my eyes at his blatant claim on me.

"Do you live here too?" Jasper asks, making me laugh out loud.

"No, Jude lives in Oxfordshire." In a hotel on grounds probably bigger than this district. "He stayed the night."

"Yes, I heard." Jasper holds his hand out to Jude, his eyebrows brushing his hairline. "Or at least I heard this morning."

I die on the spot as Jude chuckles, accepting Jasper's hand. "Nice to meet you."

"Pleasure," Jasper says.

"For Amelia, yes," Jude quips.

I shrink, elbowing him in the ribs, making him laugh more. "It was nice to meet you, Jasper." I pull Jude on, seeing his black Ferrari parked in front of my Jaguar, and I'm soon pressed into the side by his big body. I semi-scowl at the further blatant display of ownership.

"Looks like I might have to invest in some gags if you can't keep your screams for me under control, baby." He nuzzles into my face, biting at my cheek. "We don't want to upset the neighbours."

"Or I just resist you when we're at my place."

He lets out a sharp bark of laughter, and I laugh too. Because that statement was truly laughable. I can't resist the irresistible. Proven.

"Have a wonderful time at the gym missing me."

I shove him away and go to my car, dropping into the seat and watching him as he walks backwards to his Ferrari, a stupid, shit-eating grin on his face.

God, he's maddening.

Adorable.

Mine.

Chapter 20

After working out, I make my way to the car park around the back of the gym, smiling when I press the button on my fob, making my Jaguar beep.

"Is this your car, miss?"

I slow, seeing a man standing on the other side of my Jaguar. The attendant. "Yes, it's mine."

He appears regretful. "You might want to call the police."

"Why?" My heart starts to slow, uncertainty plaguing me as I approach him. He's looking at the side of my car, a massive frown on his face.

And my stomach falls to the concrete when I see what he's looking at. "Oh my God," I whisper, my eyes running up and down the paintwork.

"Looks like someone's got it in for you."

I stare at the words scratched into the doors of my brand-new car.

Gold-Digging Bitch

"Any idea who?"

"No." My mind isn't allowing me to consider that. The words stretch over the driver's door, onto the wing, big bold letters that could be read from the other side of fucking town. I blink and look at the guy, dazed. But I can see what he's thinking. *Gold digger.*

"Brand new too, huh?" He heads across the car park, pulling his mobile from his pocket. My eyes bat back and forth between him and my car. Do I need to call the police? I don't know. My brain finally clears for me to contemplate who'd do this. *Gold-digging bitch?* Naturally, Katherine springs to mind first. But she doesn't even know I have a car to vandalise. No one knows I have a car.

I look up and around, seeing a camera mounted on a nearby pillar. "Can you check the footage?" I ask, going after him as he heads to a cabin on the far side of the car park.

"All recordings are stored at our main office, love. I've let my boss know, but it's company policy to only release footage on police request."

I recoil, chasing his heels. "But what if I don't want to involve the police?"

He goes into the cabin and plonks himself on an old, threadbare swivel chair, hitching a brow. I can't say I appreciate the conclusion he's obviously drawing. *I'm not a gold-digging bitch!* "Then I guess you get your car fixed and get on with life."

"And what about your company? This is supposed to be a secure car park."

He points his pen to a sign on the pinboard, and I roll my eyes at the large print informing me that my car is left at my own risk. "No one can steal your car, miss, but we have a pedestrian gate."

"Well, I didn't consider that someone would purposely target me for a hate campaign today," I grumble, turning on my trainers and leaving. I'm obviously getting nowhere. I've not even had my new car for forty-eight hours. I open the door, refusing to look at the handiwork someone's made of my new pride and joy, and throw my bags on the passenger seat, slipping in.

The barrier rises when I pull up, and Jude's ringing me before I've turned onto the main road. I feel a wretched lump grow in my throat, my face screwing up. I absolutely do not want to tell him about this, but it's not like I can hide it. So I take a breath and answer his call, bracing myself.

◆ ◆ ◆

The burning rage emanating from him as he stares at the scratched-in words is ripe, forcing me to keep my distance to avoid the heat. He looks fit to burst. "And they wouldn't show you the CCTV footage?" he says to my car.

"Only the police."

Jude reaches for his cheek and wipes roughly. An angry sweat? "Gold-digging bitch," he breathes, and I flinch.

I am not asking him who he thinks did this. Do I even need to? I'll leave this for him to deal with, because I'm truly fearful of what I'm capable of when it comes to Katherine Jenkins.

On a weighted sigh, Jude comes to me and cups my cheeks, dropping a lingering kiss onto my forehead. "Why don't you head upstairs and take a shower. I'll be up soon."

"Why? Where are you going?"

"I've got a few calls to make." He encourages me onwards, pulling his phone out and wandering off towards the rose gardens. I watch him go, his pace slow, one hand in the pocket of his jeans.

"A few calls to make," I muse, taking backwards steps towards Arlington Hall. Did he have those calls to make before I arrived with my vandalised car? My cheeks balloon with my exasperated exhale as I turn and pass through the glass doors. Evelyn Harrison brings a needed smile to my face, and I take her in with new eyes, appreciating her more than ever.

"Amelia," Anouska says, smiling from where she's perched on the pedestal desk. "Going upstairs?"

"You know, I think I need a drink." I motion towards the Library Bar as I head that way. "Mind?"

"Of course," she says, laughing, like, why am I asking?

I point back outside. "Will you let Jude know I'm in here when he's done on his call?"

"Absolutely. Enjoy."

"Thanks, Anouska."

When I enter, I find Clinton's showing off his cocktail-making skills to a couple sitting at the bar, delighting them. A few stools in between them and another couple are free, so I hop on, plucking the menu from the gold stand, browsing. At the very top, taking first position from Hey Jude, is the Amelia. I still can't believe he named a cocktail after me.

"The Amelia is officially our most popular to date," Clinton calls, pouring.

The couple claim their glasses and sip, and the woman smiles at me. "You should try it." She looks to the heavens. "Divine."

Clinton chuckles, placing a napkin down for each of them, then a small bowl of olives. No nuts. "Do you want one?" he asks. "I'm told it packs a punch."

"Ha ha," I drone, closing the menu and waving a hand in playful order. It's hardly past noon, but it's the weekend. I'll cut myself some slack. Besides, I'm in shock. "Get me the Amelia."

"Oh, you won't regret it," the lady says, giggling. "This is my third. It's our anniversary weekend."

"Aww, congratulations." I smile as she places her hand on her husband's knee, and he clasps it. "You've come to the best place."

"Right?" she says, gushing. "Isn't it incredible? It's been on my bucket list since it opened!" She offers her hand. "I'm Denise. This is my husband, Leroy."

"Pleasure," I say, accepting. "I'm . . ."

"This is Amelia," Clinton says, smiling at the shaker as he prepares my drink.

"Oh, like the drink!" Denise laughs. "How funny!"

I smile, awkward. "Yeah, like the drink."

"Not *like* the drink," Clinton pipes up. "She *is* the drink."

I look at his grinning face tiredly. "What's taking you so long?"

He lets out a bark of laughter, shaking vigorously, and poor Denise falls into a state of total confusion.

"I hope you have the best weekend," I say, making her smile again.

"Thank you." She turns to her husband and some hushed whispers go down.

"Anytime today," I call, increasing Clinton's amusement, and on a dramatic pour and over-the-top twirl, he slides my drink towards me. I waste no time taking my first sip, sighing. I hate how good it is, especially at this time of day.

"You look like you've had a rough day, and it's only just afternoon." Clinton gets on with polishing some glasses. "Come on, get it off your chest."

"Well, yesterday, the man I'm seeing turned up at my office and has put me in a bit of a sticky situation."

"The man you're seeing?" he asks. "I heard he was your boyfriend."

"And who told you that?"

"Jude."

I laugh. "Was he growling when he put that out there?"

"I wondered what the low rumble was. I thought the ice machine was about to blow up."

I smile around the rim of my glass. "He's very aware of his passive-aggressive possessiveness," I muse.

"And what about you?"

"Oh, so you heard about my run-in with Katherine?"

"May have."

Brilliant. I peek over my shoulder, checking the bar entrance. "How much do you know?" I ask, testing the water.

The look on his face alone tells me Clinton knows a lot.

"Don't you think it's weird?" I ask.

"Totally." He spots someone at the end of the bar. "Just be careful, okay? The last woman Jude was seeing disappeared."

I recoil, not knowing what part of that statement to process first. "Disappeared?" He was seeing someone?

"She was a rep for one of the beverage companies that supplies Arlington Hall. Jude was seeing her." He falters. "Sleeping with her. Whatever, I've already said too much. I'm just saying, Jude called it off and suddenly we had a new rep. I like you. I don't want Katherine and her misplaced sense of ownership to chase you out of town." Clinton places his finger over his lips as he leaves me.

Well, damn. Ownership? She's deluded. And why didn't I ever wonder about any other women? Maybe because Katherine filled up that space for wondering. *And, damn you, Clinton, I'm grateful for the heads-up, but I can't do much with that information since I'm not supposed to have it.*

"Huh," I murmur to myself, looking out the window onto the front, where I see Jude waving to someone. I get up and wander over, looking out. Katherine's husband, Rob, climbs out of a sports car and approaches Jude, and despite not being able to hear what's being said, the body language speaks volumes. Jude's arms come out, in the kind of way that suggests he's asking, *What the fuck is this?* Rob looks at my car. Then looks up to the heavens.

"Oh my God," I say quietly to myself. Rob obviously thinks it's his wife too. My teeth clench. So she thinks she's going to chase *me* out of town? *Never,* I vow to myself. She'll have to drag my dead body away.

Now who's passive-aggressive possessive?

I huff to myself, making my way back to the bar and slipping onto the stool, finishing my drink.

"Another?" Clinton asks.

"Yep." I slap the bar. "Keep 'em coming."

"You got it."

"And pass me some of those olives too."

Clinton sets a bowl down on a smile and gets to work on my second drink as I pluck an olive out and nibble around the stone. "Pitted or not?" I ask.

"Not," he calls.

"Me too. They're firmer when they still have the stone inside. Kind of creamier." I study the flesh of the green olive. "Black or green?"

"Green."

"Me too." I sigh and drop the stone onto the side plate. "I bet you didn't expect such a riveting bar conversation today, huh?"

Clinton laughs. "I'm a barman. It's in the job description to help take people's mind off things."

I laugh, not in amusement, and help myself to another olive. I'm on my fifth when Jude appears beside me, nodding at my empty as Clinton replaces it with a fresh new drink. "That kind of day?"

I look at him with exasperation. "Had better. What did Rob say?" I ask, making him tilt his head in question. "I saw you out there talking." It's not like he was hiding, and there's a direct view onto the front from here.

Jude glances back over his shoulder, as if reminding himself of that. "I wouldn't put it past her. But I don't want you to worry about it."

"I'm not," I say with grit, surprising Jude.

"You're not?"

"No."

"Good." He reaches for my stool and drags it closer. "Are you done?"

"I'm done."

"Then let's talk about something else."

"Like what?"

"I want to take you away."

"Okay," I agree easily, observing his slow, thoughtful nod, watching as he drifts into a daydream. "Are you alright?" Why does he seem vacant all of a sudden?

He visibly shakes himself back into the room, smiling. It's forced. "Sorry, what did you say?"

I lean back. "I asked if you're alright."

"I'm fine." He stands, collecting my hand, frowning past me. I look back to the woman, Denise. Comprehension seems to have just hit her.

"You're the guy who owns this wonderful hotel," she says, excited. "Oh my, it all makes sense now!" She lifts her drink. "The Amelia."

Jude laughs. "Yes, and just like my girlfriend, it leaves a wicked aftertaste."

Denise erupts into belly-clenching laughter. "Oh, that's funny. How romantic. Have you been dating long?"

"Long enough to get a cocktail on the menu in honour of her." Clinton chuckles, prompting a glare from Jude. "You can't fire me."

"Can't I?" Jude grumbles, taking my cocktail off the bar and dragging me away. "We're having lunch in the Piano Bar. Put Amelia's drinks on my tab."

"Yes, boss."

"He's right," Jude says. "I can't fire him."

I laugh. "So, we're going for a relaxed lunch, are we?" The Piano Bar is cool and laid-back, rather than formal and refined like the Orangery.

"We are."

"What will you do?" I ask as he guides me across the lobby. "There are no tablecloths to hide your wandering hands."

He snorts, pulling out a tub chair for me, giving me a wide, full-beam smile. It takes him from handsome to illegal. "Restrain myself."

Plucking the menu off the table, I lower and browse the options. "Burrata and risotto," I say decisively, slamming it shut.

"Are you in a rush?"

I cross my legs and relax back, taking in the busy Piano Bar. "I think we could both do with letting off some steam," I muse. His laugh is sardonic, and I sigh. "What am I going to do about my car?" I pout. "I can't drive it like that."

"I'll get it repaired," he says, making me feel guilty. The car cost him enough. "Please don't worry about it."

"I'm not worried. I'm annoyed."

"Don't be annoyed," he breathes as he pushes my cocktail towards me.

Is he for real? Don't be annoyed? Sure. Easy. And rich, coming from him.

"Thanks." I lose myself in my drink and try to push back my irritation. It's not Jude's fault. "What are you having?"

"Prawns," he answers. "You've got your meeting with Spector soon, right?"

"Wednesday."

"Ready for it?"

"As ready as I'll ever be," I sing.

"What's your strategy?"

"Patience. Listen. Don't overtalk or overwhelm her with all the reasons why I should be the chosen one." I smirk around the rim of the glass when Jude chuckles.

"You'll smash it," he says, and just that stupid little comment makes my heart swell.

"So where are you taking me away?" I ask.

"Florence?"

I'm interested. And very excited. "Really?"

"That looks like it's hit the spot."

"It's been on my list of places to visit for years."

"Mine too." He smiles. "The architecture is mind-blowing. It's what I did . . . well, before Mum found . . ."

"You were an architect?" I ask, shocked, lowering my glass. "How didn't I know that?"

"Because I've never told you."

I give him a playful, dirty look. "And how much more haven't you told me?"

He laughs lightly. "I followed in my dad's footsteps, but I was more modern than Dad's classic grand. I loved mixing old with new. Like ancient, raw bricks with frameless glass. Clean plaster with original tumbled floors." He gazes around the Piano Bar. "Dad was old, I was modern. With this place, I wanted to make sure there was plenty of his influence. For Mum."

"I think he would have loved it."

Jude smiles mildly, nodding his thanks when a bottle of beer is put in front of him. "We'll take the burrata, prawns, and risotto, please, Audrey. Make sure there's no nuts in any of those. Or anywhere near them."

"I'm pretty sure there isn't," she says, smiling.

"Well, I was pretty sure there weren't nuts in the Eton Mess, and yet there was." He hands the menu back on a tight smile and Audrey blinks. "Double-check, okay?"

"Of course." She casts a smile my way before she leaves, and I return it, feeling like a massive inconvenience.

"Do you enjoy running Arlington Hall?" I ask, because that's an entirely different ball game and out of his architectural scope. Jude was right. It's a very special place, and that's entirely down to him. The effort he's put in to making it what Evelyn Harrison imagined, the time and dedication he's given in honour of his parents. It's admirable.

"I hardly run it. Hiring the best team was essential, given I knew fuck all about running a hotel." He laughs. "I've learned along the way with their help. Honestly, they're invaluable. Especially Anouska. She was managing a hotel in Manhattan before I poached her."

"You're ruthless."

Amusement slides across his lips, stretching them. "Maybe." His hand meets my knee, and I shift in my chair, electric shocks shooting up my thigh and smacking me straight between my legs.

"*So* ruthless," I say, breathless.

"Shall we take lunch in bed?"

I'm up like a shot, Jude's gaze rising with me. I need to get him somewhere private before I make a spectacle of us both. "I'll see you upstairs," I say, hearing him chuckle as I go.

I leave the bar with haste, making my way through the lobby, my stomach fluttering madly, and I'm about to take the stairs when I see Katherine rounding the corner from the spa. She's in her gym kit, but judging from the lack of sweat and the fact her makeup is perfect, I'm guessing she's not made it there yet. I look down at my leggings. Feel at my still-warm, slightly clammy cheeks. *What the hell did you do to my car, you mad bitch?*

She falters in her pace when she sees me, her animosity instant. Why is she still kicking around here?

I mentally demand my feet to carry me up the stairs, away from her toxic energy, but for all the will in the world, they won't bloody budge.

"Amelia," she says, resting her weight on one hip. It's the kind of stance a woman takes when she's about to launch into ultra-snarky bitch mode. Call another woman she dislikes and doesn't respect *sweetheart* or something equally condescending.

I somehow manage to convince my legs to work.

"How's your new car?" she calls, quickly halting me again. Staring forward, I imagine all the ways I'd like to hurt her. But in this moment, I realise the best, most effective way is to simply be with Jude.

So I turn and smile, walking backwards up the last few steps. "My new car is as beautiful as my new boyfriend. As comfortable to ride too." Now I must shut up and move on, and yet her face, a picture of pure indignation, is like petrol on my flames. "Oh, and, Katherine, you must try the new cocktail on the menu. I hear it packs a punch. Toodle-oo." I pivot and smirk to myself as I walk, getting ready to strip the moment I'm in Jude's apartment.

"My God, you actually think you know him, don't you?"

My feet falter, but somehow, I keep walking. I don't like the sound of that at all. I make it through the door of Jude's apartment and breathe in deep, fighting back the angry increase of my heartbeats, pacing up and down, hearing her say that last thing over and over. What the hell did that mean?

Jude bursts through the door, his T-shirt half off. He screeches to a halt, looking me up and down. "Why aren't you naked?"

"I just ran into Katherine."

His shoulders drop. That pisses me off too.

"She laughed at the idea that I *think* I know you." My arms fold across my chest. Protective. Like a woman getting ready to block something damaging. I huff under my breath and unfold them. "Why would she laugh at that?" I ask. "Is there something I should know?" Or something more? And can I take it?

Jude feeds his arm back through his T-shirt and pulls it down. "She's trying to get a rise out of you."

"She's succeeding!" I cry, turning and going to the kitchen. I need water. The sound of Jude's boots follows me in, but he remains quiet behind me as I bang my way around his kitchen. After glugging back half the glass, I slam it down while Jude hovers on the threshold, as if scared to enter. "It would be easy not to give her a rise if she wasn't here." I throw it out there. "Why haven't you told her to fuck off?"

He laughs under his breath, looking at the ceiling. For patience? I'm astounded. "It's not that simple."

"It's not that simple?" I parrot on a recoil. "It's *very* simple. This is your hotel, Jude. Go tell her to find another health club to work out at."

"For fuck's sake," he breathes, daring to enter.

"Are you just going to carry on saying stupid shit?"

"Amelia." His tone is low. Pacifying. I don't appreciate it.

"Don't *Amelia* me," I warn, circling around the island, keeping myself on the other side from him. "She vandalised my car, Jude. She's making me *not* want to come here."

His eyes slightly narrow. I don't appreciate that either. "I'll talk to her," he says, calm, rounding the island towards me.

I instinctively move too, away from him. "I don't want you to talk to her."

"How the hell can I fix this if I can't talk to her?"

"First, you don't talk to her, you *tell* her, and you fix it by *telling* her to fuck off and never come back." Am I being unreasonable? Bratty? God, I don't even know. But I do know I shouldn't have to ask him to do this. I'd love to see him invite my ex into his hotel and cause a daily shitstorm. My head in my hands, I breathe into them, hating this version of myself. I'm a big girl. I can take Katherine's digs and deflect her claws. But every day? I'm already exhausted by her. And, besides that, I shouldn't bloody have to.

My wrists are suddenly wrapped in Jude's palms, and he pulls my hands away, making me face him. "I will fix this," he says, sincere. "I promise."

Have I ever been so needy? It's an odd sense of vulnerability and *very* significant. I love him enough to care. He means enough for me to feel this way. "Okay," I murmur, standing before him, heavy and tired.

"I'm going to make everything better." He strokes his hands up my bare arms, shivers following his touch over my shoulders.

"How?" I whisper, pulling my shoulder blades in to sustain the torture of his breath in my ear.

"First," he says quietly, licking the sensitive spot below my lobe as he tugs my workout top up over my head, thrusting his hips into me, "I'm going to take off all these sweaty clothes and lay you on the kitchen floor." My eyes close, my brain empties, leaving room for only Jude. "Then," he breathes, biting down on my lobe and dragging it through his teeth. My hand flies up and fists his T-shirt.

"Then what?" I ask, my head rolling on my neck as he kisses my throat.

"Then I'm going to pour champagne all over your tits and pussy and lap it all up until you're begging for penetration."

"Hmmm." A hard, distinct bang lands between my legs, making my feet tread on the spot. "Do it."

"Oh, baby, how you burn for me." His hand slips past the seam of my leggings and knickers, his fingers stroking through my soaked flesh. "Fuck," he hisses, as my torso folds and I use his T-shirt to yank his mouth onto mine, kissing all my frustration away.

"You're irresistible, Jude Harrison," I garble around his lips, pushing him back against the island.

He turns us, bending me back on the counter, bringing his chest down to mine. "You're quite irresistible yourself."

"I am?"

"And coy." He fists my hair and holds my head as he slams his lips onto mine, grinding his groin into me before reaching for my trainers and pulling them off. They hit the floor with a thud. My leggings are next, peeled down my legs, taking my knickers with them. "Let's make love, baby," he says, easing one cup of my sports bra down, his mouth encasing my nipple, sucking it to a bullet. The hard length of him past his jeans rubs into my lower stomach, sending me out of my mind, my hearing becoming distorted, along with my vision.

Ring, ring, ring.

"Ignore it," I order, as he moves to my other boob, splitting his worshipping tongue across both breasts.

"I had every intention of ignoring it."

I arch my back as he skates a palm over my hip, and as soon as his mobile rings off, it rings again.

And again.

And again.

By the fifth time, Jude slams his fist into the wood on a curse and surfaces, looking dazed, his lips swollen and wet. "Who the fuck is that?" he grumbles, leaving me on the counter and adjusting himself as he dips into his back pocket. Breathless, I peel myself up from the counter, feeling a little dizzy. And pissy.

I brush my hair off my damp cheeks, trying to catch some air and at the same time curb the powerful throb between my thighs.

"What?" Jude answers, clipped. Then he frowns. And when he looks at me, I one hundred percent do not like his frown. "Yeah, thanks for letting me know."

"What is it?" I ask when he's hung up, spinning his mobile in his grasp, thoughtful. "Jude?"

"It was the kitchen." He starts walking up and down. "There are no nuts in the Eton Mess."

"Huh?"

He stops and looks at me. "What else did you eat that evening?"

I try to cast my mind back, scratching through my mind for the answer he wants. "Nothing. I only had a few bites of the Eton Mess."

"Yeah, I thought so." He places his phone down. "Your food got contaminated, and that's not acceptable."

"Oh," I whisper, watching Jude fall into thought. "So what are you going to do?"

"Take everything off the menu that contains nuts."

I laugh. "You can't do that."

"Watch me." He crowds me, popping a kiss on the end of my nose. "Arlington Hall is now a nut-free zone."

My fingers claw into his arse and pull him closer between my thighs. "What are you doing here, then?"

"Ha. Ha." Rolling his mouth onto mine, he kisses me back down to the counter and slips his touch through my wetness. "Hmmm," he hums, pushing his fingers into me.

I moan in answer, tightening every muscle, drawing him deeper.

Ring, ring, ring.

"Ignore it," he says, as my mobile yells from my bag by the door.

"I had every intention of ignoring it." My arms slip onto the back of his head as his mouth drifts south.

Ring, ring, ring.

He removes his fingers and replaces them with his mouth. "Oh God." My back bows, and my eyes fall to the mirrored fridge doors. I can see his head buried between my bent legs.

Ring, ring, ring.

I hum, purr, writhe, savouring his hot, wet tongue slipping easily through me, hearing him undo the fly of his jeans. "I want you." I grab his hair and pull his face up. "I want you now." My insides are screaming for him to sate the burn building.

"How badly?" he whispers, placing a hand on my chest and dragging it down my body, his eyes following as he frees his raging erection.

"*So* badly."

Ring, ring, ring.

"Fuck!" he hisses, gazing up at me with a look somewhere between frustration and desire. "Who the hell is that?"

"Ignore it." I grab him and haul him down onto my mouth, shifting my hips to help him fall into place between my legs.

Ring, ring, ring.

"Jesus Christ." He pushes himself up and gasps for air, looking around the room. "Where the fuck is your phone?"

Wilting in disappointment, I throw my arms over my head. "In my bag by the door."

Jude stalks off, pulling his jeans up over his arse as he goes.

"It's your mum," he says when he's back, holding up my phone. "Ten missed calls."

My wanton state is forgotten in a heartbeat, my heart racing for an entirely different reason. I feel like the blood has just drained out of my face, and Jude suddenly looks as anxious as I feel. Bringing my phone to me, he stands between my open legs, as if worried I might fall off the counter. I try to dial Mum back, but my hands are shaking too badly, adrenaline of the unknown ruling me. She calls again before I manage to convince my fingers to work.

"Mum?" I say, my voice audibly shaky. Jude rests his hands on my bare thighs and starts to stroke, waiting. Patient.

"I don't want you to be upset, Amelia," she says.

Of course that has the reverse effect. "Why would I be upset?" I ask, my eyes on Jude's as he waits.

"It's your father."

My heart beats double time. "Oh my God, what's happened?" My throat is suddenly tight, forcing me to reach for it.

"He wanted to go for a drive, you see."

All kinds of scenarios run rampant through my head, and my eyes start to well with building tears. "Mum, please, tell me what's happened to him."

"Nothing's happened to him, darling."

"What?"

Jude frowns, withdrawing, his hands slowing in their strokes across my thighs.

"Your father's fine. Oh dear, I realise how that all sounded now."

I exhale in a rush of urgent breath, and Jude visibly relaxes too, shaking his head in exasperation. "Mum, you had me so worried."

"Oh, silly me."

"So why would I be upset if Dad went for a drive?"

"Because he went for a drive to Oxfordshire. And he brought me along too."

I jerk so hard, I could have been electrocuted. "What?"

"What?" Jude mouths.

"I said don't be mad!" Mum cries, and it all falls into place. *Oh. My. God.* "You're here?" I screech.

"Oh, Amelia, it's rather fancy, isn't it?"

"Wait," I say, abrupt, as Jude moves back, obviously concluding I'm not a risk to myself anymore. His face. Christ, he looks like he's seen a ghost. "Where, Mum? Where *exactly* are you?"

"In the lobby."

"They're in the lobby," I say, despite knowing he heard because his eyes widen slightly. "Don't move." I hang up. "They're in the lobby. My parents are in the lobby." I'm going to kill them.

Jude's cheeks expand, and his eyes fall to his open jeans, where his dick is shrinking before my eyes. "Jesus," he mumbles, fixing himself. "I thought I'd have a little more time to prepare for this." He takes my arm and helps me off the counter.

"I'll go," I say, while Jude swipes up my top and slips it over my head. I feed my arms through and grab my leggings, hopping on one leg as I feed my other foot through. "I'll tell them you're out on business."

He turns his eyes onto me, not impressed. "I'm a grown man, Amelia. I'm not hiding from your parents." Leaning in, he reaches for my elbow and steadies me so I can get my other foot in and pull my leggings up. "It's not ideal, but here we are."

"Jude, please, I beg you." I bunch his T-shirt in my fists and immediately regret it. "Fuck."

"Will you stop fucking hurting yourself?" He snatches my hand up and checks it, shaking his head. "You need to have this looked at—it should be healing by now."

"I don't think our relationship is ready for my father yet."

"You mean strong enough? What the bloody hell is that supposed to mean?"

"No, I don't mean that. I mean, I . . ." What *do* I mean? "It's . . ."

Jude smiles at my stammer, kissing my cheek. "I can handle your father."

I snort. "Your bravery is commendable."

"I'm not avoiding them, Amelia, and since they've taken it upon themselves to pay us a surprise visit, I will accommodate them and show your father that you're in good hands." He cups my boobs and gives them a cheeky squeeze.

"That's not funny."

"Stop stressing."

"You don't know my father."

"Well, I'm about to. Get your trainers on."

I jut my bottom lip out, and Jude curses, lifting me onto the counter and getting them on himself. "Your lack of cooperation is only delaying the inevitable."

"I'm happy to delay it."

"I thought you sorted things out with your father."

"I did, but that means nothing, and it certainly doesn't mean his brain-to-mouth filter is fixed."

Jude lifts me from the counter, takes my hand, and starts leading the way. "I've told you; I have wide shoulders."

He said that when we went to meet my friends, and then he stormed away from the table to calm himself down when Charley said something out of place. My father doesn't see his faults. And if he does, it takes him a while, but he never admits he's wrong. He just waits for me to visit and make him tea, which is code for *We're okay until you piss me off again soon.*

My apprehension grows with each step we take down to the lobby, my eyes darting, looking for them.

"I said, stop stressing," Jude orders quietly.

"I can't help it. Just take everything he says with a pinch of salt, okay?" Jude's about to get a strong dose of my family, and I'm sure I'm about to cringe to London and back.

"It's no big deal."

"What if he insults you?" I ask. "He doesn't mean to; it's just he has no self-awareness sometimes."

"I can't believe how worked up you're getting."

"I don't want him to put you off," I say, surprising myself *and* Jude.

He stops halfway down the stairs and faces me, his eyes level with mine from where he's standing on the step below. "And there we have it." His smile is fond. "Amelia, my brilliant, gorgeous girlfriend, there is nothing in this world that could put me off you."

My heart melts to nothing. "There's nothing that could put me off you either," I reply.

"I truly hope you mean that."

"I do." I push my mouth to his. "I love you."

"I love you more. We get this big dramatic meet over with, we finish what we started upstairs, and then we're booking our getaway, okay?"

"Okay."

"Right."

"Are you sure?" I ask. "My father is a *lot*."

"And my love for you is a lot *a lot*, so the balance of *a lot* is in my favour." Stroking my cheek, he comes close, nose to nose. "Are you going to argue with me?" I shake my head, making our noses rub. "Good. Let's go meet the parents."

He claims my hand, and I watch as he takes in air, obviously bracing himself, and then leads me down the curved stairs. "Oh God," I whisper, when I see my mother sitting on one of the chesterfield couches in the lobby, my dad pacing in front of the window. Jude squeezes my hand tighter and nudges me with his shoulder, and I look up at him.

"I've got you," he says, raking a hand through his mussed-up hair, prompting me to do the same. I must look like a sack of potatoes, all crinkled and flushed.

"Amelia!" Mum sings, hurrying up from the couch.

Jude releases my hand, allowing me to hug my mother. "I can't believe he's done this," I whisper in her ear, and she laughs, loud and uneasy. "Mum, this is Jude." I open up the way for her. "Jude, my mum, Jenn."

"Well, it's lovely to finally meet you officially." She gives me wide, excited eyes when Jude dips and kisses her on each cheek.

"What a pleasure," he says softly.

"And this is my dad, Dennis." I lock eyes with my father and mentally beg him to rein himself in and control his impulses. "Dad, this is Jude."

"Wonderful to meet you, Mr. Lazenby." Jude extends his hand, and Dad does a terrible job of smiling. It's tight. Forced. It doesn't bode well and begs the question of why he even came. It's exactly what I feared. He's not had enough time to get used to this.

My father doesn't correct Jude or tell him to call him Dennis. "Likewise," he says, making his shake quick, then pulling away and holding his hands behind his back. A horrific silence falls, and I shift uncomfortably, scratching through my head for something to say.

"Perhaps we'd be more comfortable in the Library Bar," Jude suggests, motioning the way.

"Oh, yes." I point across the lobby. "The Library Bar."

"You say that like there's more than one bar," Dad muses, gazing around again.

"There is." I motion to the other end of the lobby. "The Piano Bar is through there, and there's another in the club across the grounds."

"So there's three bars?" Dad asks.

"Four if you include the wine and champagne cellar." Jude leads on, leaving me to follow with my parents, still praying this is over with fast. "Can I get you a drink?" Jude hands the cocktail menu to my mother as he directs Dad to a table in the corner by the fireplace.

"Oh, there's a cocktail called the Amelia!" Mum sings, delighted. "I'll have one of those."

"It's new. Inspired by your daughter."

Mum's hand slaps onto her chest. "Oh, Dennis, did you hear that?"

"I heard," he says, lowering to a chair. "It's a very extravagant place you have here, Mr. Harrison."

Mr. Harrison? Give me strength.

"Please, call me Jude." Jude looks at me discreetly, and I send a million silent apologies to him. I bet he's regretting this. "Drink?"

"I'll have a tonic water, please."

"Coming up." Jude doesn't wave for service but rather goes to the bar to order with Clinton. He probably needs a break from them already.

I turn my eyes onto Dad, who does a damn fine job of avoiding my accusing glare. "What is this?" I ask, sending Mum into an instant fluster. "Showing up unannounced. What on earth were you expecting to find, Dad? Me chained in a cold, dank cellar mid-brainwash by the beast?"

"Now, now." Mum smiles like an idiot. "He seems very lovely."

"He is," I say, eyes back on my father. "*Very* lovely."

"He owns all this?" Dad motions to *all this*.

"Yes."

"And this appeals to you?"

"What?"

"All this extravagance and money. It appeals to you?"

"What's your point?"

"Well, you've always been so set on your independence, but I don't see much independence being had when the man in your life is stinking rich."

"Money means nothing to me."

"And yet you want to be successful and make lots of it."

I recoil, injured, and Mum reaches for my knee, rubbing as if trying to hold me down in my chair before I bounce off around the room in a temper. I can't be dealing with this. I preferred him when he was a pigheaded old fool one hundred percent of the time rather than giving me glimmers of hope that he might pull his dinosaur head out of his arse and accept my choices.

"Do you think my desire for success hangs on making piles of money, Dad?" I ask, sitting forward in my chair. "Because it doesn't. What success means to me is achievement. It means happiness and fulfilment. Self-worth." I stand up. "And to prove to my prehistoric father that I'm bloody capable of running his precious family business with my younger brother." I'm done. This was a terrible idea. I don't know what I was thinking to hope he might change. He's immovable. "You can see yourself out." I dip and kiss my mum, feeling her clutch beggingly at my hand.

"Oh, don't go, Amelia," she implores. "Please, we've come all this way."

"Just to shine his disapproval all over me. I'm not interested." I pivot and go to Jude, who's watching from the bar silently. "This was a waste of time," I say, taking his hand. "We're leaving."

"But it's my bar."

I pause for thought. He's right. I go back to my dad. "You can leave."

"You're throwing me out?"

"Yes, I'm throwing you out."

Poor old man looks like he's had a wet fish slapped around his face. "But I'm your father."

"Unfortunately, yes." The moment the words leave my mouth, I feel dreadful guilt, especially when his face falls. God damn it. I hate seeing him look so injured, no matter how clueless he is. So I turn and leave as originally planned, stalking past Jude, whose head turns, following me out of the bar. "Come," I order over my shoulder. I hear him snort, forcing me to look back. Rolling his eyes, Jude picks up

Mum's cocktail and Dad's tonic water and delivers them to the table, like Dad deserves his hospitality. Then he strides over to me and takes my hand, pulling me out of the bar. But I know he's not taking me away from here.

"I'm not letting you leave at odds with your father," he says once he's got me in the lobby, making me withdraw. "If he doesn't accept me, that's fine, but you don't get to walk away."

I stare at him like a sulky little girl, but all I can think about is Jude's parents. How he hasn't got them anymore. "There's no reasoning with him."

"There's more to this than plain disapproval, Amelia."

"How do you know?"

"Because there's no way on this earth that any father could not be proud of their daughter if she was you."

"I don't understand."

Jude doesn't get a chance to enlighten me. Dad appears behind him, looking sheepish. "Could I have my daughter for a moment?" he asks, quite politely, given the circumstances. But I note, and I know Jude does too, that he uses a possessive determiner rather than my name.

My daughter.

And suddenly, I'm not sure I need enlightenment.

Jude nods and practically hands me over to Dad. It's a conscious move. He's telling him he's not taking me away from him. *Oh, Dad.*

"Shall we walk?" Dad stuffs his hands in his pockets as Jude makes his way back to my mother in the Library Bar.

"Let's walk," I agree, smiling when he cocks his arm for me to link.

"You lead the way since all this is familiar to you." Dad raises a cheeky eyebrow. I roll my eyes and walk us out the front and around the side. My attention is set on the maze, but I soon divert to the Kitchen Garden when I remember what I've done in that maze.

It's silent for a while, but it's not uncomfortable. I know he's trying to unravel what he wants to say, and I'm truly interested in what that may be. Whatever it is, Jude seems to have figured it out very quickly. I, however, have been clueless—and frustrated—for years.

"I am proud of you, Amelia," he eventually says as we're walking through the cabbages. "Here, sit." Dad points to a bench nestled between the carrots and parsnips, and we lower.

Dad takes my hand. "Ouch!" I hiss, making him drop it.

"Damn it, I forgot about that."

"I can switch sides."

"You should have it checked, Amelia—surely it should be healing by now. And this bandage should be off; it needs air."

"I'm sure it's fine." I move to his other side and give him my uninjured hand. He smiles, taking it and bringing it to his lips, kissing it.

"I'm proud of you."

"Okay," I say slowly. Unsure.

Dad frowns, looking off across the various vegetable beds, back to unravelling. "I don't want to lose you," he blurts, surprising me.

"What?"

His shoulders drop. He sighs. Breathes in. Faces me. And he smiles, almost embarrassed. "I suppose I stupidly thought curbing your ambitions would keep you close."

"Oh, Dad," I breathe.

"Nick was a safe bet," he goes on, looking a little ashamed. "I like the boy, yes, but I liked that he desperately wanted a family."

"You knew that?"

He's back to sheepish. "He mentioned it one of the first times we met."

"Are you joking?" He's been holding out on Nick because he thought he'd get me chained to the kitchen sink and pushing out babies, therefore keeping me close by?

"I'm not," he sighs. "All this ambition of yours, your dreams, what if they take you away from me?" He squeezes my hand, and all frustration for my father leaves my body, making it shrink.

"You foolish old man." He's done the exact opposite by cutting me out of the family business and pushing me away.

"Or not so foolish. Now you've met this Harrison bloke, you're in another county."

"But it's not ambition that has brought me here, Dad."

"Then what is it?" His eyebrows rise in interest.

This is it. No more skirting around it to save feelings. "Love, Dad. I love him."

"I feared as much."

I laugh at the irony. "I feared as much too."

"You did?"

"Yes, because it was unexpected and, obviously, it crept up on me at the trickiest time."

He hums, amused. "Nick."

"Nick," I confirm. "But more you, Dad. I don't want to hurt Nick's feelings, of course, but I've always been more concerned about you."

"You have?"

"Yes, because I can't dump you, can I?"

He chuckles, and it's the sweetest sound. "No. No, you can't."

"And I wouldn't want to."

"Oh, my girl." He hooks his arm over my neck and tugs me into him for a hug. I feel his lips on the back of my head. "You'll never know how blessed I feel to have you."

"I feel blessed too. Most of the time." He nudges me, and I smile. "I have no plans to leave London."

"You don't?" he asks, sounding hopeful as he releases me.

"No, I don't."

"What about Harrison?"

"Will you please call him by his actual name?"

"Jude," he grunts. "I'm sure he expects you to move here."

"It's new," I say. "We've not talked about long-term, Dad. I'm just going with this."

"But you love him?"

"Deeply," I admit.

"So you *might* move to Oxfordshire?"

"I don't know." I laugh. "And you're talking like it's another country. I'd be across a couple of county borders."

His shoulders drop. "It felt like miles getting here."

"Is that why you came? To see how long it took to get to your daughter?"

He cocks me a sideways smile. "I know I'm a pain in your arse, Amelia. I know I drive you to distraction. But the thought of another man being more important to you than me doesn't make me feel very good."

God love him. "No man will be as important as you, because you're my dad."

"That's sweet. And this . . . Jude. Does he support your career?"

"He does."

"I see." His nose wrinkles. "Nick stopped by earlier." Looking at me, he squeezes my hand. "I get it now. I understand."

"Understand what?"

"Well, he hardly lights up the world, does he?" He huffs to himself. "But he was predictable and reliable, and I know it's awful for me to admit this, but he licked my arse so much, I knew he would never dare take you away."

"That really is terrible."

"I know." He turns to me, smiling and cupping my cheek. "You'll always be my little girl first."

"I will."

"Good." He nods, assertive. "Then I suppose you ought to take me back into this outrageous mansion and I ought to show a bit of grace to the king in his castle."

"Just one more thing." I stop him from getting up. "Promise me you won't mention Jude to Nick, okay? That has to come from me."

"I promise," he says, dropping a kiss on my cheek. "And promise me you'll get that hand checked."

"Promise."

Settled, I smile wide as Dad helps me up and walks me back to Arlington Hall. I never for a moment considered there could be a deeper reason for his prehistoric stance towards my ambitions. Turns out, my old man is scared.

"Be nice, now, okay?" I order gently when we make it back to the Library Bar.

"Yes, yes."

Mum and Jude are talking quietly, my man looking so insanely handsome as he smiles at whatever Mum is saying. When she spots us, she sits up, hopeful, and Jude cranes his neck a little to see, standing as we near.

Dad offers his hand, and Jude takes it, flicking his eyes to me. "You'll look after her." It's definitely a demand.

"Without question."

"Respect her."

"Endlessly."

Dad eyes me briefly. "Support her career."

I laugh mildly and Jude smiles. "Always."

"Love her."

"Until I die, sir."

"Oh, well, that's a statement and a half."

Mum looks like she might faint, her wide eyes jumping between Dad and Jude.

"I mean every word." Jude looks at me. Not them. Just me. I tilt my head, and he tilts his.

"Then welcome to the family." Dad drops Jude's hand and opens his arms, and I nearly fall flat on my face in shock. I'm certain Mum would too if she weren't sitting.

"Thanks." Jude welcomes his olive branch, accepting the man hug. I'm speechless.

"And you can call me Dennis."

Mum's eyes are welling. My world just got a whole lot better.

"Well, since you're here," Jude says. "Would you like to eat?"

"Yes." Mum's up like a shot, answering for them both. "We'd love to, wouldn't we, Dennis?"

"Sure. Why not."

"We might have to settle for the Piano Bar." Jude comes to me, slipping his arm around my shoulders. "The Orangery tends to get booked up in advance, and it would be cheeky of me to kick some guests off the reservations list."

"You managed to get a table rather sharpish when you lured me here to seduce me," I mumble under my breath, for only Jude to hear.

He doesn't say a word, but his lips twitch in amusement as he leads us to the Piano Bar, my parents all but swooning over Arlington Hall. We sit at a table in the far corner, and Jude hands menus over to each of them. It's then I remember we've already ordered our lunch.

"It's in my apartment, probably cold by now," Jude says quietly. "Just reorder." He goes to the bar, and I lower next to my dad.

"So this is the Piano Bar," he muses, scanning the menu.

"This is the Piano Bar." I relax for the first time in a while and take in the wonder of my mum and dad sitting with me.

In Arlington Hall.

After meeting my new boyfriend.

And, better, accepting him.

I feel like a weight's been lifted.

An hour later, I'm in my element listening to the easy conversation. Jude knows all about the family business and my grandparents, and he and Dad have found a common interest in rugby, of all things. Dad's talked with keen interest.

"Jude's brother plays for England." I speak up, noticing that Jude, once again, hasn't mentioned it himself.

"What?" Dad's flabbergasted. "What's your brother's name? Wait. Wait a minute. Harrison! Well, would you believe it?" Dad looks at Mum and laughs. "Jude's brother plays for the England rugby team."

"Well, that's impressive. So tell us about the rest of your family," Mum says.

The atmosphere distinctly shifts, and I watch Jude discreetly as I nibble on a halloumi chip. "Well, there's Rhys, as you know—he's my littlest little brother. Then there's Casey, my biggest littlest brother. He's a chef."

"Oh, where?"

"Private mostly. Yachts, dining experiences, that kind of thing. He won't hang around the same place for long. I think the longest he's ever stayed put was when he went to France and completed his degree in French culinary in his early twenties."

"A chef, a sportsman, and a successful hotelier." Mum looks at me, eyes wide, impressed. "Your parents must be so proud."

I bite down on my lip, seeing Jude shifting in his chair. "Sadly, my parents are no longer with us."

"Oh. Oh, that is a shame."

"I'm sorry," Dad says. "Were you very close?"

Jude looks out the corner of his eye to me. "Yes. My mother particularly, after she lost my father."

I study Jude as I pick at the last few halloumi chips on my plate, seeing him withdrawing from the conversation. He lost his father too. I recall him mentioning with perfect clarity that he found it hard talking about his dad. Hard or angering? He can't be mad at his dad for dying. I would never tell him so, but it seems so unfair for Jude to place blame for the loss of his mother.

Jude drops his napkin on his half-eaten plate. "How about I show you the nightclub that's named after her?"

He avoids my questioning look, standing, and keen to discover more of Arlington Hall, both my parents stand too, finishing their drinks as they do.

"Wonderful," Mum says as Jude walks them out and I follow. "Oh, I wish your grandma was here to see this."

"It's a shock enough that you are," I counter sardonically.

"But it all worked out in the end, didn't it?" She looks over her shoulder to me, her grin impish.

"Yes, I suppose so." I watch Jude point out various things to Dad as we walk.

"The golf course is out the back there," Jude tells him as we wander through one of the glass corridors. "Eighteen holes."

"A golf course!" Dad looks back at me. "Why in the heck would you buy me lessons somewhere else if Jude has eighteen holes?"

I give Jude a tired look when he chuckles. "You're grumbling about me dating a man who lives in another county because it's too far, but you're happy to travel for golf?"

"I don't know where she gets her sarcasm from," Dad muses, making Jude smile mildly. "It certainly isn't me."

"You're welcome on the course anytime."

"You know, I might take you up on that offer."

"I had no idea how serious this was, Amelia," Mum says quietly. "I'm so happy for you. But you really do need to be honest with Nick."

The thought doesn't thrill me at all. "I just need to find the right time and the right words. I can't just text him."

"I understand. And does Jude know about him?"

"Oh, he knows." I laugh, but not in humour. Mum casts me a sideways, curious look. "Never mind." I link arms with her. "Wait until you see Evelyn's."

We walk through the lobby, and Mum stops at the portrait. "Oh my, is this her, Jude? Your mother?"

"Yes, that's her. Evelyn Harrison," Jude says, observing his mother for a beat. "She passed away shortly after this portrait was painted."

"Do you mind telling me how she died?"

Oh Jesus. I throw Jude an apologetic look that he catches, shaking his head lightly. "I think it's what the romantics call a broken heart." He's visibly swallowing hard.

"And your father?"

"Shall we?" Jude asks, completely ignoring Mum's not-so-subtle pressing of the cause of his father's death.

"Oh, yes, of course. I need the bathroom." Mum looks around. "Do you mind?"

"Just through there on the right." Jude points the way. "We'll wait for you here."

Mum leaves, Dad wanders across to a nearby coffee table, instantly happy to see the *Financial Times* on it, and Jude acts like he's not just shut my mum down. Not that she should be asking such personal, sensitive questions, but still. Because I know what I know, the questions I thought were explained suddenly feel open again.

"What?" Jude asks when he catches me observing him.

"Did you and your father get along?"

"Yes, like a house on fire." He slips an arm around my shoulder.

So he's just mad at him for dying? "I'm struggling to unders—"

"This is nice," he says, squeezing me tighter. "Me, you, your parents."

My parents. Because I have parents. And Jude does not. Empathy suddenly won't allow me to push him. And I would be wholly insensitive if I demanded more information. If there's even more to know. Is there more to know? I just get the feeling there's more to it, more he's not telling me.

"It's really nice," I reply, pushing my wondering away for now. "So we're taking my parents clubbing?" I hold his hand where it's draped over my shoulder.

"Looks like it." Jude chuckles as Anouska walks through the glass doors. He spots her and releases me. "Give me a second." He goes to her, and she falls into stride beside him, both walking slowly, talking quietly.

I take the opportunity to search for Mum to make sure she's not gotten lost, finding her in the ladies', her phone held up in front of her. "You should see it!"

"Who are you talking to?" I ask.

Mum whirls around, looking guilty. "Oh, oh, um, no one."

"Is that Amelia?" Grandma's voice fills the room.

"Mother!" I scold her, pursing my lips and taking the phone from her hand, seeing Grandma's ear on the screen. "Grandma, you're on FaceTime."

"Oh?" She appears, her face close. "Ah, how lovely to see you, Grand Girl."

"And you," I reply, giving Mum a pointed look.

"I wanted to show your grandma around."

"Another time. You've just met him." I go back to Grandma. "Mum will see you tomorrow."

I hang up and collect my mother, steering her back to the lobby before she can go AWOL again. "Will you be normal?"

"I'm just so excited! Do you know the last time I had a cocktail in the afternoon?"

I look at her, observing. "Are you drunk?"

"Maybe just a little."

I walk her through to the lobby and find my father, watching him for a few moments, seeing him swaying. "Oh God," I breathe.

I release Mum and let Dad take over, both of them wandering off as Jude joins me again. "They're tipsy. They didn't even get tipsy at Clark's wedding."

"It's nice." Jude slips his arm around my shoulders. "They're enjoying themselves."

I watch them a few paces ahead, arms linked, steadying each other. "Thank you for doing this."

"Well, I'd rather have you in bed, licking champagne off your body, but needs must." He eyes me cheekily. "Has your ex been in touch any more?"

I shake my head.

"Aren't you worried your dad will tell him about me?"

I stop him walking, my head hurting. "Why the concern about Nick all of a sudden?"

"I'm not concerned." His voice is soft as he takes my hands. "Can you give me the heads-up when you intend to tell him?"

"What? Why?"

"So I can be prepared."

"Like I was prepared for Katherine?" I ask, failing to remove the sarcasm from my tone.

The rolling jaw's back. I'm a master at spiking it, which is a joke in itself. "Let's not be petty."

"You don't need to worry about retaliation from Nick."

Jude scoffs. "I'm not worried about retaliation."

"Then why the big deal?"

"It's no big deal."

I stand back on a small smile. "Are you worried he'll convince me to go back to him?"

"Really, Amelia? I just want us to communicate, and I know it won't be nice for you. I want to support you."

"Wow."

"Shut up." He frames my face with his hands and smacks a kiss on my lips. "Let's take your parents clubbing."

I laugh loudly, freeing myself of Jude's clutches as my phone rings. "It's Clark. Mind?"

"Sure." Jude takes the opportunity to make his own call, wandering off a few paces.

"Hey," I say when I've answered. "Are you back?"

"Just pulling out of Heathrow."

"Was it amazing?"

"Stunning. Where are you?"

"At Arlington Hall."

"Of course."

"With Mum and Dad."

"What?"

I look at Jude. He's frowning down at his mobile. "Yeah, they showed up. Dad's become all passive, given Jude the dad talk, and everything seems . . . well, lovely, actually."

"The dad talk?"

"Did you know he only liked Nick because he was wet?"

Clark laughs hard. "He admitted that?"

"Yes, he admitted it. He also confessed that he doesn't want to lose me to another man." Jude's frown is stretching by the second.

"God love that old goat. So you had lunch?"

"Yes, and now we're taking them clubbing." Mum and Dad round the corner towards Evelyn's.

"Come again?"

"They've had a few cocktails each. We're taking them to Evelyn's."

"I'm on my way."

"What?"

"I need to see this. I'm diverting up the M40. See you soon." Clark hangs up, and I make my way to Jude, who is still frowning, his head tilting as he moves his phone around, checking the screen at different angles. "What's up?"

He clears the screen quite speedily. "Nothing."

"Then why do you look like something is up?"

"Nothing's up." He waves a hand flippantly. "Just some irritating supplier issues that I shouldn't be dealing with on a Saturday." His hand finds mine. "Sorry, I was distracted."

"It's fine. I thought something was wrong."

"Ready?"

"You get the pleasure of my brother and sister-in-law too."

"What?"

"Clark's just arrived back at Heathrow from his honeymoon. He doesn't want to miss the opportunity of seeing our drunk parents clubbing."

"Yay. A family reunion."

I elbow him in the side, making his torso fold, and let him lead us into Evelyn's.

It was a joke. My clubbing references. Except Mum and Dad are God knows how many cocktails deep now, and both are on the dance floor in Evelyn's getting their groove on to Joris Voorn and Nathan Nicholson. I'm fucking staggered.

"What the fuck?" Clark breathes, finding us at the bar, his eyes on our parents on the floor.

"Yeah, what the fuck?" Rachel mimics, seeming mesmerised by the sight.

"They're having fun." Jude offers a hand to Rachel. "Jude Harrison."

Rachel cocks me a sideways smile. "I've heard lots about you. I'm Rachel."

"Congratulations."

Rachel's hand instantly goes to her stomach as she shoots me a shocked look. "I can't believe you told him."

"I didn't." My lips straighten. "He was talking about your recent vows."

"Oh."

"You're pregnant?" Jude says.

"Shhhh," we all hiss, checking the whereabouts of our parents. We're safe; they're in a full-blown dance trance.

"Well, congratulations on that too," Jude says, before putting his mouth to my ear. "Sounds disgusting."

I laugh and nudge him. "Stop it."

"Thanks." Clark shakes Jude's hand. "Nice to see you again. When I'm vertical and not bent backwards over a bar with my throat in your clench."

Jude visibly cringes. "Again, my apologies. What can I get you to drink?"

"Water. I'm driving, and she's expecting." Clark turns back towards the floor. "I can't believe what I'm seeing."

"Me either." I join him, observing our parents. "In fact, today has been a constant string of what-the-fuck moments." And like a sick omen, right on cue, Katherine walks into the club. "What the fuck?" I breathe, watching as she scans the space.

"I'll deal with this." Jude passes us fast, urgent, and goes to Katherine, guiding her back out of the club.

"Who's that?" Rachel asks.

"No one." I knock my drink back, my eyes burning from staring at the entrance as I half-heartedly listen to Clark and Rachel tell me about their honeymoon.

"And then I had a full-body massage which involved a very happy ending, and, bonus, Rach could watch."

I blink and look at my brother. "What the fuck?"

"Yeah, you're right, the *what the fuck*s just keep coming today, don't they?" Clark points to the entrance. "Who is she?"

"Jude's ex," I say quietly. "And you think Nick's finding it hard to let go."

"Oh, shit."

"She spews venom like a premenstrual spitting cobra."

"Go. I can tell you want to."

"I want to but don't." I can feel my feet lifting, readying to take me there, but my head, the sensible part, is warning against it. "Fuck it." I pass Clark my half-empty glass. "Back in a minute."

I pace across the club and push my way out the doors to the outside area, where a few people are smoking. Jude's on the far side, Katherine opposite him, arms folded, looking as indignant as a woman could look. "I swear," Jude hisses, "if I find out you had anything to do with it, I'll ruin you, do you hear me?"

Katherine laughs. It's condescending as fuck. "You seem to be forgetting one small detail, Jude," she counters, leaning in. But then she spots me and backs off again. "Ah, here she is, the *girlfriend*." Her eyes drop down my sports top and leggings. "You're hardly dressed for the occasion."

"And what's the occasion?" I ask.

"He's getting to know the parents." Katherine smiles. "This really is serious." She turns her steely eyes onto Jude again. "But how well are they getting to know you, Jude?"

"What does that mean?" I ask, approaching.

"Jude's never been serious with women."

"That's because none of them were Amelia," he snaps. "Including you." He puts his arm around me and leads me away. "Fuck off home to your husband, Katherine, and leave me the hell alone."

Then he places a kiss in my hair, and I can't help but think he's pacifying me. "What did she mean, how well are they getting to know you?"

"She means what she says. Katherine has some warped notion that no one knows me better than her."

"Because you were engaged," I murmur.

Jude stops me, putting himself in front of me, holding the tops of my arms. "Stop it," he warns. "Stop letting her get under your skin."

I sigh. "You need to tell her to leave."

"I know," he says. "But like you do with Nick, I have to choose my moment."

God damn him. "Nick's not making you miserable."

Jude laughs, pinching the bridge of his nose, seeming to take in air and patience. Does he disagree?

"What?" I ask.

"Nothing." His chest expands, his breath deep. "Come on, it's been a lovely afternoon and evening. Let's not spoil it now." He collects me and walks us back inside.

"She denied scratching my car, didn't she?"

"Yes," he says, flat and clipped. "I think I might need to find a room for your parents tonight." And just like that, the conversation is over. I exhale, fucked off with myself for feeling so irritated. "And tell me we can book our break tomorrow."

"We can book our break tomorrow," I confirm quietly, feeling a bit deflated. My mum and dad are still lost in the music, and probably their tenth cocktail now.

"Hey." Jude nudges me in the side. "Snap out of it. Everything will be okay."

I force a smile, and it's an effort.

Because something doesn't feel right, and I can't put my finger on what.

Chapter 21

Mum and Dad woke up with sore heads on Sunday, but a lavish breakfast got them back on track. Poor Jude was hit with more of the Lazenbys when Mum insisted on repaying him for his hospitality and invited him for one of her famous Sunday roasts. Which, of course, meant he got to meet Grandma and Grandpa too. So that's it. He's met my entire family. And, I admit, when we left my parents and headed back to my place, I was a little worried Jude would try to worm his way out of this relationship we've unexpectedly got ourselves into. He didn't. Instead, he took me to bed and whispered sweet nothings in my ear as he made love to me. Then the next morning, he made me a coffee with the new kettle he brought for me on Saturday while I was at the gym. Then he drove me to work. Kissed me long and softly before he let me get out of the car. It was the best start to my day, but that's where my good day ended.

My Monday rapidly went downhill.

Gary was out of the office all day in client meetings, so I couldn't talk to him about Jude. A client, Mr. Coldfoot, emailed to tell me he's moving to the South of France and, therefore, moving his money too, putting a tidy hole in my portfolio, and a Zoom call at ten with Mr. Jarvis that was only allocated an hour turned into two hours, fucking up the rest of my day's schedule and meetings. I've been chasing time ever since, run off my feet, but I haven't achieved much. In fact, thanks to Mr. Coldfoot moving to France, I've gone backwards.

At three o'clock, I drop my mobile to my desk on a sigh and go to get myself some needed caffeine. I watch the coffee trickle out of the machine slowly and add some cold water when it's done, drinking it on my way back to my desk. Three more hours to get through. Just three. I push my way back into my office and nearly throw up what I've just drunk when I see someone sitting on the opposite side of my desk.

"Nick?" I breathe, as he looks back at me. "What are you doing here?" My feet refuse to take me to my desk, keeping me by the open door.

He smiles and stands. "I had a meeting."

"What?" I look back into the corridor, seeing it empty. "With whom?"

"Sue."

My blood runs cold, everything telling me I'm not going to like what's coming next. He's blocking the way to my desk. "Sue?"

"About the new position that's come up."

"New position?"

"So how have you been?" He lowers back to the chair, getting comfortable, while I stand like a statue trying to process the bombshell he's just landed on me. I round my desk and sit, grateful for the huge piece of wood now serving as a barrier between us.

"New position?" I repeat, not wanting to get into idle chitchat.

"You didn't know LB&B are hiring?"

"No, I didn't know." What the fucking hell is going on? My eyes drop to my mobile on my desk. I'm itching to swipe it up and call Gary to find out. And, maybe, to tell him they can't hire Nick. "And since you're here, I'm assuming you're thinking of going for it."

"I would have mentioned it had you called me like you said you would."

I look up sharply, not appreciating his sarcasm. "I've been busy."

"I gathered. The interview went great, by the way."

I laugh under my breath in disbelief as my thoughts scatter all over my desk. No. This can't be happening. "I thought you were happy where you are."

Gazing around my office, he nods to himself. "I think LB&B might be a better fit for me."

But definitely not for me. "I have a three fifteen call."

"Oh, right, sure." Nick stands, tucking the chair in neatly before fastening his jacket. "I'll let you get on."

"Thanks."

"Maybe we could grab a coffee sometime so you can give me a few pointers."

"A few pointers on what?"

"Life at LB&B."

He sounds certain he'll get the job. I need to make sure he doesn't. What the hell is he playing at? This is borderline stalking. *Tell him about Jude!* Except I don't. Instead, I turn my eyes onto my computer and randomly move the mouse around the screen.

"Good to see you," Nick says, eventually leaving.

I stare at the door, at a loss.

I'm mentally drained by the time six o'clock rolls round, my mind turning in circles over Nick's surprise visit. Anger has taken pole position now. Sue wasn't available to talk to, and Gary hasn't answered my calls, but when I do get to speak to either of them, I will be pleading with them not to take Nick on. And don't even get me started on how I will explain this to Jude. Hopefully I won't have to.

I drag myself out of my office to meet him, finding him waiting at the end of the street, his arse resting on a post, and God, he's a sight for sore eyes and a shot of energy into my tired bones.

Concern makes his smile falter, his shoulders falling. "You really look like you need that holiday."

I stop before him, heavy. "It's been a shitty day," I say, drained. "I don't know if I'll keep my eyes open for much longer."

Jude pouts, unable to hide his disappointment. "Let's do dinner in the city." He slips an arm around my shoulders and pulls me close, practically holding me up as we walk. "Do you think you can stay awake for that?"

"Yes, I'm starving." *Because I missed lunch, thank you very much, Mr. Jarvis.*

"What's close by?" he asks. "I'll stay at your place tonight."

"There's a few restaurants in a courtyard down the street."

"Sounds good."

We settle on a casual pub and order a chicken burger and chunky chips each. I need stodge. "Not quite Michelin star, is it?" I muse, dunking a chip in some mayo and popping it in my mouth. "So what did you get up to today?"

"I had someone come out and take a look at your car," he says, and I wince. "It needed respraying."

"It's been done already?" I ask, surprised.

"He did it on site. Then I got a lecture from Anouska because the smell wafted around to the front of the hotel and polluted the traditional countryside stench of cow shit." His face bunches, and I laugh. "And what made your day so challenging?"

I groan. I absolutely don't want to talk about my work. Or Nick. "I've had a bellyful."

"Okay, let's talk about Florence. When can I take you? Tomorrow?"

I nearly choke on my chip. "Tomorrow? I can't go tomorrow; I have my meeting with Tilda on Wednesday. What's the rush?"

Jude peeks up through his lashes as he pushes the coleslaw around his plate. "No rush," he says quietly, straining a smile.

My chewing slows, another chip halfway to my pot of mayo. "Is there something wrong?" I've caught him many times these past few days lost in thought, like there's something on his mind.

"No, nothing." Another strained smile. "I'm tired, that's all."

I don't believe him. Dropping my chip to my plate, I brush my hands off. There's more to it, and it's not helping the lingering something inside me that's wondering if I'm reading into nothings and making them somethings. "I don—" Someone in my peripheral vision catches my eye, making me do a double take and snap my mouth shut. *Fuck.* My eyes quickly dart to the table, my shock obvious.

And Jude doesn't miss it. "What's up?" he asks.

Fuck, fuck, fuck. "My ex just walked in." It just falls out of my mouth, like my brain won't take time to weigh up the consequences of such a catastrophic word vomit. What the hell is Nick doing here?

Jude cranes his neck, every inch of him tensing. Oh Jesus, this could be messy. Nick's emotional, and Jude's got a vicious temper.

Mortified, knowing Nick's seen me, I brave looking up. His eyes are batting between me and Jude. My unease grows. Shit, I don't know how to handle this.

"Fuck," Jude exhales, as Nick approaches, his face a picture of disbelief.

"Nick." Standing from my chair is an effort. My legs shake, adrenaline pumping as my body braces for a showdown.

"Jude, this is Nick Phillips," I say quietly, once again at a loss. "Nick, this is Jude Harrison." So I introduce them? *Oh God, this is fucking awful.*

"Jude Harrison?" Nick says, not with hatred as I'd expect, but in question. I tilt my head. And then Nick mildly inhales, taking a step back.

"Yes, Jude Harrison." Jude rises, clearly wanting a presence and, God, does he have one, the passive-aggressive possessiveness rising with him. Reaching for his arm, I touch him, trying to interrupt the potential imminent eruption. "That's me," Jude grates, his eyes suddenly wild. "Nick *Phillips?*"

I want to crawl under the table and hide, but as I look between the men, something feels . . . off. Jude's as stiff as a board, his eyes the darkest I've ever seen them. It's standard Jude in the face of rivalry, but it feels like there's more. I glance at Nick again. There's no hurt in his expression. It's more shock, which is confusing because he found out I was seeing someone before, and this was not his reaction. Except then, he didn't know who I was seeing. Now, he does. And Jude is an imposing man.

Jude finds it in himself to back up and lose the crazy radiating from every fibre of his being, flicking me a wary look. My cautious gaze returns to Nick. He does the same, peeking out the corner of his eye at me before quickly looking away.

"Do you know each other?" I ask, the question falling past my lips impulsively.

"No."

"No."

I retreat and laugh under my breath. "Are you sure?" There was definitely a sense of realisation in Nick when I introduced Jude.

"We're leaving." Jude takes my elbow.

"We've not finished eating."

"I'm not hungry."

So he's lost his appetite now? Jude swipes up my bag and tries to walk me out, but Nick moves, blocking us.

"Get out of my way," Jude grates, his expression deadly.

"Amelia." Nick comes towards me, prompting Jude to step in his way, and all I can do is stand like a useless idiot, my mind twisting, trying to figure out what the hell is going on here. "He's not—"

"Move," Jude snaps, shoving Nick aside and pulling me along behind him.

I hiss, feeling his squeeze of my hand, at the mercy of his strength and determination. "Jude, you're hurting me."

He immediately eases his hold but not his pace, and when we make it outside, I'm guided to his Ferrari, my cautious attention on his profile. He looks like he could burst. "Jude, will you tell me what the hell just happened?"

"Nothing."

"Nothing?"

He opens the door, puts me in the seat, slams it, and I release a disbelieving puff of air. I don't know why I let him just remove me from the pub. Maybe because I needed to escape the god-awful tension. Except I've not escaped. In fact, I feel like I've stepped out of the pan and into the fire. Or maybe I hoped leaving would get me answers faster. Do they know each other?

Jude gets in and starts the car, pulling away fast. I frown at my lap when Yeah But No's "Run Run Run" plays, frowning harder when Jude turns the volume up, making it impossible to talk and be heard. His driving is a little manic, his persona fraught. I constantly glance across to him, getting more worried each time I note his ticking jaw and eyes like lasers on the road. Does he think there's nothing to talk about?

Reaching for the controls, I turn the music down. "What did he mean?"

"What?" he snaps, his knuckles around the wheel turning white.

"What Nick didn't get to finish because you dragged me away. What did he mean?"

"I didn't hear what he said. Where's your phone?"

"What?"

"Your phone, Amelia. Where is it?"

"In my bag."

"Give it to me."

"Why?"

He slams the ball of his palm into the wheel. "Just give me your damn phone!"

"Not until you tell me why, Jude!"

He huffs and reaches across for my bag, and I watch in astonishment as he helps himself, rummaging through and pulling it out. "What's your code?"

"I'm not telling you my fucking code, Jude." I try to swipe it back, but he's too fast for me. "Tell me what the hell you're doing. What are you trying to prove?"

"There are nearly ten million people in London, Amelia. Thousands of pubs. I find it really fucking hard to believe your ex would just happen to turn up in the pub we're having dinner in." He turns dark eyes my way as I push back in my seat, not liking what he's suggesting. "What's your code?"

"My birthday," I say quietly.

Jude opens my phone and splits his attention between the road and his working thumbs, and when I see his jaw tighten further, I know what's coming. "He's fucking tracking you."

I stare at Jude's profile, speechless, my head bending, my stomach turning.

"Does Nick know your PIN?"

I swallow and nod when Jude looks at me for an answer, my reality falling heavily.

"And when might he have had the opportunity to access your phone?"

I sink into my seat, dread cloaking me. "Today." I can feel Jude's questioning eyes turn onto me as he pulls up at a red light. It can't have been before today; otherwise Nick would have undoubtedly turned up at Arlington Hall any of the times I was there. "I left my phone on my desk when I went to get a coffee. Nick was in my office when I got back." I can't look at Jude, can't face the rage I know is there. And there will be more to come.

"What was he doing at your work?"

"He was interviewing for a position." I sound as nervous as I feel.

Jude laughs, and it is full of disbelief. "And you didn't think to mention that?"

"No, actually, I didn't." I brave facing him. "Are you going to tell me what the fuck happened back there?"

Jude's jaw twitches with the force of his gritted teeth.

"I'll take that as a no." I unclip my seat belt and take the handle to get out but get precisely nowhere.

"Forget it." Jude reaches across me, yanks the door closed, and reclips my belt before pulling away from the lights fast. He places my phone in my lap. "You need to stop sharing your location."

My fingers are already working the screen before he's finished, and I throw the phone back into my bag, propping my elbow on the window and staring out, the atmosphere excruciating. My question unanswered.

◆ ◆ ◆

When Jude pulls up outside Arlington Hall, he gets out and rounds the car, opening the door for me. How very gentlemanly of him. And ridiculous. He still looks fucking livid, and I know I feel it.

I am *not* going into Arlington Hall until he talks. "What happened in the pub?" I demand, my voice strong.

"What happened?" Jude laughs with no amusement whatsoever.

"You couldn't have gotten me out of there faster."

"Your ex showed up. Of course I left. I can think of a million things I want to do with you, Amelia, and dining with your ex isn't one of them. I left because I was afraid of what I'd do if I didn't."

"What, like hit him?" Why am I asking that? This is Jude Harrison. Of course he wants to hit Nick.

"He tracked you to a bar, Amelia. He hijacked *my* dinner with *my* girlfriend, and you're wondering why I'm fucking fuming?"

"That was a lot of possessive determiners," I snap like an absolute idiot, snatching my bag from his hand and stomping into Arlington Hall. Am I being paranoid? Overthinking? After all, Nick's the fucking snake in this situation. I can't believe he intended on tracking me. What the hell is with that? And what was Nick going to say?

"Oh, well, there's a surprise," Jude murmurs as he follows me, forcing my feet to a stop halfway up the stairs. "She's not trying to leave."

Swinging around, I nail him with an incensed glare. "That can be arranged."

Two palms rise in surrender, his inhale long. "I'm sorry."

His apology lacks any sincerity, pissing me off more. "Maybe I *should* go." I take one step back down the stairs and meet his chest, and I'm over his shoulder before I can even *think* to protest.

"We need to let off some steam," he mutters, making me laugh dementedly as he carries me up the stairs.

"You want to have sex?"

"No, I want to fuck you."

"Why?" I hiss. "Feeling threatened?"

His growl is deep and deadly as he carts me up to his apartment, dumping me on my feet just inside the double doors of his private lobby. He steps back, putting a metre of space between us. "Take your clothes off," he orders.

My mouth drops open, my disgust rampant, but will my feet move? No. They're cemented to the carpet, Jude's blazing gaze keeping me in place. Lust mixes with my outrage, and I watch his chest expand as he shoves his jacket off.

"Do it." He unfastens the buttons of his shirt one by one, revealing his gorgeous chest, sending me further into bedlam.

"No."

His working hands stop, his shirt hanging open.

And he takes another step away.

Bullets of energy come at me, my feet shifting, desire at risk of dominating me.

"Go then," he whispers, pulling a hand through his hair. "If you really want to leave, fucking go, Amelia."

"Fuck you," I hiss, stepping forward, grabbing his shirt, and yanking his mouth onto mine, needing an outlet for my frustration. I kiss him like I hate him, hard, forcefully, biting his lip, his tongue.

And he takes it all, hissing when I fist his hair, sucking in air when I bite him. We stagger around the small lobby until his back slams into a wall. I eat him alive, and he spins us, thrusting his hips into mine, trapping me with his body.

The weight of my thoughts leaves me.

Fire.

Fighting.

And now, we make up.

Jude bends me over the circular table between the two sets of double doors and shoves my dress up. My laboured, desperate breathing drenches the space, my head craning to see him behind me yanking his trousers open. He sneers at me, bringing his palm down on my bare cheek, the sting real.

"Fuck you," I grate through my teeth, earning myself another whack on the other cheek. "Fuck you!" I smack the wood with both palms, my teeth clenching to sustain the pain I'm causing myself.

"And fuck you, Amelia." He pounds into me on a loud bellow. *Bang.* "Fuck you for fucking up my plans." *Bang.* "Fuck you for stamping all over my fucking heart." *Bang.* "Fuck you for taking up every tiny part of my mind." *Bang.* "Fuck you for showing me peace." *Bang.* "And fuck you for making me fall in love with you."

I scream, hitting the wood as Jude hammers into me, fucking me without mercy, and I'm here for it. The relief is needed, my head empty, my body accepting.

"Tell me you fucking love me," he yells, pounding on, his skin slapping against my arse, jolting me forward every time. "Tell me!"

I can't talk, can only focus on keeping my legs steady. He's lost it, and for some fucked-up reason, I'm happy to sustain his brute force. I'm glad I'm his outlet.

The strength in my arms fails me, and I lower to my front, my cheek on the wood, and close my eyes, drifting away, listening to him yelling his pleasure as I quietly enjoy mine. Every advance pushes us a little bit closer, the buildup a crawl to release. The points on my hips where his fingers are hooked are numb, my calves stretching, every muscle screaming at me.

"Tell me," Jude repeats, over and over. "Tell me, Amelia. Fucking tell me."

"I love you," I whisper into my darkness, opening my eyes and staring at the picture on the wall, a beautiful landscape painting of Arlington Hall. The colours are wishy-washy. The detail sketchy. Maybe because of my foggy vision, or maybe because of the artist's style. I can't tell. "I love you," I breathe, jolting, a tidal wave of pleasure ripping through me, forcing me to push myself up by my palms and tense harder, the intensity almost unbearable. "Fucking hell, Jude," I yell, my voice shaky.

Looking over my shoulder, I just catch the smoke of his eyes, the strain in his jaw, the twitch of his torso, before he smashes home one last time and gasps, holding himself deep, reviving my orgasm, the swelling of him inside me pushing against all my walls, taking off the sensitive edge. Sweat trails from his temples, his hair darkening as a result, and wet patches litter his white shirt.

Spent.

He's still shaking. I'm breathless.

Exhausted, I lower my front to the wood again, my body rolling as Jude peels his fingertips from my hips, letting blood flow there. I wince.

"Sorry," he whispers, reaching for my zip and pulling it down, exposing my back. His lips meet my nape and kiss their way down my spine. "I love you, Amelia," he says quietly. "It's as hard for me to deal with as it is for you."

I don't reply; I'm unable to muster the words.

And not because I'm out of breath.

So I reach back and slip my hand in his hair as he kisses my ear.

"Let's go away tomorrow."

I shake my head. I have my meeting with Tilda Spector, he knows this.

"Please," he says, nuzzling my face. "We need some time to ourselves."

Is he saying all these triggers will be eliminated if we leave England?

"I can't just up and leave."

"It's important."

"So's my career."

"I'm not saying it isn't," he whispers in my ear. "Wednesday, then. I'm just asking for a few days. We can leave after your meeting."

Something isn't right. *Jude* isn't right. Every word he roared as he fucked me in ownership is circling my mind on a loop.

My unease is rapidly growing.

And the question remains: What was Nick going to say before Jude hauled me out of that pub?

He's not . . .

What?

And why the urgency to get me out of the country?

Chapter 22

He's asleep, on his back, but his head on the pillow is facing my way, giving me the wonderful view of his peaceful beauty. Except I sense the turmoil inside him. Feel it in myself. The uncertainty is messing with my head. My emotions feel like a yo-yo, up and down, high and low. He's euphoric. He's disastrous. I'm so torn, unsure if I can sustain the force of Jude's swinging moods.

Slipping out of bed quietly, I pull on his shirt and pad on bare feet to the lounge to find my bag, expecting to see endless missed calls from Nick. There are none. It only fuels the mayhem inside. Increases the questions.

In despair, I call the girls, tucking myself in the corner of the couch. "Hey," I say quietly when they both answer, Abbie on her sofa, Charley in darkness.

"I'm in bed," Charley whispers. "Is everything okay?"

"No," I admit, trying so hard to stop my voice from cracking. "Nick was at the pub Jude and I ate at this evening."

"Oh no," Abbie breathes.

"He turned up at my office today too. He's applied for a job at the company."

"What the fuck?"

"He knew what pub I was in because he got into my phone and shared my location."

"Wait." A load of rustles and knocks come from Charley before a light pops on. She's in her kitchen now, her wild hair wilder. "Are you serious?"

I nod. "Jude completely lost his shit."

"Fuck, did he hit him?" Abbie casts aside the bag of crisps she's munching her way through.

"No." I sigh. "He manhandled me out before it came to that, but there was something not right."

"How so?" Abbie asks.

"I got the feeling they knew each other."

"What?" they both whisper.

"I don't know. It was tense." I sink farther down into the couch. "Nick was saying something but couldn't finish because Jude shoved him out of the way."

"Saying what?"

"He said, *He's not . . .*" Both girls raise their brows. Both are finishing that sentence like I am. *He's not . . . who you think he is.* "My new car got vandalised too. Someone scratched *gold-digging bitch* into the paintwork."

Abbie gasps, outraged. "Who would do that?"

"I think Jude suspects Katherine."

"Her husband needs to put that woman in a cage." Charley's head is shaking.

"What's Jude going to do about it?" Abbie asks. "Just let her carry on terrorizing you?"

My poor brain isn't up for this kind of mindfuck today. "I'm not worried about Katherine. I'm more concerned about what happened with Nick."

"Have you asked Jude?"

"I've tried."

"Then ask Nick," Charley says.

I tilt my head, not relishing the thought. But maybe she's right. And for the sake of my sanity . . . "Do you think I should?"

"God, yes."

I sit up straight. Yes. Yes, I should. Because now my mind is taking every moment since I've been with Jude and overthinking it. Like the night last week when Nick showed up at the restaurant we were at when Jude met my friends. He wasn't tracking me; Lloyd told him we would be there. And now I'm wondering if Jude left the table for a whole different reason. Did he see Nick before me? Does he know Nick? "I'm going to call him now. Thanks for listening to my woes."

"Let us know, okay?"

I nod and hang up, bracing myself to call Nick. I chicken out four times before I eventually brave dialling him. It goes straight to voicemail, and I contemplate leaving him a message. But . . . no. I need to talk to him. Actually, I need to talk to him face-to-face.

Now.

I go back to the bedroom and quietly get dressed, watching Jude sleeping peacefully as I do. He doesn't stir. After collecting my things, I slip out of his apartment quietly, constantly questioning if I'm doing the right thing. Whether I'm being paranoid. If I'm making somethings out of nothings. Regardless, I need to tell Nick to back off, and I will. He's taken things too far. Tracking me, the interview at my work.

Way too far. It ends now.

Anouska is in the lobby when I make it there, saving me the trouble of finding her. If she can't help me, I'm going nowhere. "Hey, Jude's asleep, and I don't want to wake him. I don't suppose you would know where he put my keys after the repairs were made on my car?"

"I have them, give me a second," she says, smiling as she pops through a door, then reappears a moment later.

"Thank you." I give her praying hands.

"Is everything alright?" Her head tilts, the questions in her eyes rampant. "I saw you get back earlier."

I force a smile. So she felt the tension too? Saw the explosions. "Everything's great." I don't hang around, pivoting on my heels and walking out of Arlington Hall. "See you later," I call, hurrying past Stan, whose smile falters as I go.

"Miss Lazenby," he says in question. "Do you need any assistance?"

"Not today, Stan." I walk the line of prestigious cars and head round the back to the staff car park, aiming my fob at my Jaguar. Not taking a moment to admire the newly repaired and polished paintwork, I hop in. Jude's request not to drive these roads in the dark taps at the corner of my mind. It's hard to ignore it, but I start the engine and reverse out of the space, knocking it into drive and pulling away. I hardly make it twenty feet before I'm braking, Anouska appearing and waving for me to stop.

"Shit," I curse, letting down my window.

"There's a man at the gates saying he's here to see you." She puts the phone to her ear again, listening. "Nick Phillips. Do you know him?"

My heart crawls into my throat and chokes me. "Yes, I know him." How? How did he know where to find me, or that Jude Harrison—a man he's just been introduced to—owns Arlington Hall? My unease is making me feel nauseated, especially when I suddenly recall something else. Nick knew of Arlington Hall. When I mentioned my spa day with the girls at that painful birthday dinner all those weeks ago, he recognised the name. And come to think of it, he was a little weird. None of this helps my wariness. I don't know what to do, my head spinning.

"Amelia?" Anouska calls quietly.

"Umm." I shake my head, trying to find some sense.

"He's blocking the way," she goes on. "What should I tell Nelson to do?"

"Tell him to let Nick know I'll call him."

Anouska, a full frown in place, goes back to her phone, relaying my instructions. Listens. "He's refusing to leave."

My eyes clench, along with my hands around the wheel, and I hiss at the sharp pain that radiates through my palm. "Let him through," I say quietly, reluctantly. "I'll deal with it." My mind's racing with questions. "Can you ask Stan to direct him to this car park?"

"Sure."

"Thanks, Anouska." I reverse back into the space and take a moment to wonder how the fuck I'm going to handle this and what the fuck Nick is going to say, as I stare out the windscreen, my heart beating wildly.

Nick's white Audi S4 rolls around the corner slowly, and the swooshing, sickly feeling inside grows. I get out of the Jaguar, looking around as I wander over to where he's rolled to a stop. I need to keep this contained. Whatever this is. And I'm praying Jude doesn't wake up and come find me.

Apprehension feels like a vise around my throat. "Nick," I say, stopping on the opposite side of his car to him. "You were tracking me." He must know I know, assuming he got a notification when I stopped sharing my location with him. "And now you're not, so how did you know where to find me?"

"Nice car," he says, with no sentiment at all, as he shuts his door, nodding to my Jaguar.

I ignore his insincere comment. "How do you know Jude?" I fold my arms over my chest, my instinct to protect myself overwhelming me, which only makes me more anxious. Something deep and unstoppable is telling me I'm about to feel even sicker. "That's why you're here, isn't it?" I ask. "To tell me how you know him." What the hell is he going to hit me with? And can I take it?

Nick makes his way around the car to join me on this side, observing the protective barrier I've got in place. I keep my arms folded. "I love you, Amelia," he says quietly.

Oh, Jesus, stop. "Nick, no." He didn't come here to tell me that again.

His lips press together. "I want you back. Please, we can work this out."

"Nick," I snap. "How do you know Jude?"

He moves closer, but I make sure the space remains, stepping back. "How do *you* know him?"

"I'm seeing him—you know that." *In love with him.*

"He's not interested in you, Amelia."

The pressure in my head is becoming too much, my patience hanging on by a thread. "Why would you say that?" I ask, my voice surprisingly even. "To hurt me?"

"I just know."

"Tell me," I grate.

"Come back," he implores. "Please, come home with me. I can make you happy, Amelia."

"Tell me!" I yell, losing my shit.

"Amelia!" Jude's distant bellow of my name has me whirling around, my trepidation rocketing. He's jogging this way, his feet bare, his hands midway through pulling a T-shirt down his torso. The button fly of his jeans is only half fastened. All signs he was in a rush. Jude's alarm is screamingly obvious, his worried gaze batting back and forth between me and Nick as he hurries over.

I raise a hand, halting him in his tracks before he makes it to me. "Don't come near me," I warn, needing space. Needing information. Keeping my hand held up as a pathetic barrier, I give my attention back to Nick. "Tell me how you know him," I order.

"It doesn't matter. He doesn't want you, Amelia. I love you."

"Shut the fuck up," Jude seethes.

But Nick goes on, unperturbed. "Please, come home with me."

"I'm warning you." The deadly edge to Jude's voice is potent.

But it doesn't deter Nick. "We can sort this out," he presses. "I can make you happy, Amelia."

"Shut up," Jude hisses.

"We can wait until you're ready for marriage," he goes on, as if Jude's not there. "And babies. I'll wait as long as you want."

"She's fucking mine!" Jude's roar echoes in the dusky sky. "Do you hear me?"

I startle, my shocked gaze bouncing back and forth between the men. And I still have fuck all information to tell me what I'm dealing with.

Drained of patience, I go to Jude, livid, and bunch his T-shirt in my balled fists, yanking his face down to mine, ignoring the pain in my hand. My eyes are stinging, my heart hurting it's beating so fast. "Tell me how you know him," I order, my jaw ticking, my eyes rooted to his, searching for the answer I need. "Tell me, Jude."

A thunderstorm of emotions rolls through his gaze, his stare infinitely stuck to mine. "I love you," he whispers, his voice cracking. He pries my hands from his chest and guides my arms around his waist, making me hug him. "I didn't expect to fall in love with you." His hands come up and hold my face, desperation leaking from him. "I just wanted to take you away, talk to you, explain."

"Explain what?" I ask quietly, dread keeping me still, letting him touch and feel me.

"I wanted to tell you."

It sounds like both men have things to tell me, but both are reluctant. "For God's s—"

Suddenly, Jude's mouth is on mine, swallowing my words, his kiss desperate and starved, and I'm momentarily caught up in the pure emotion he's pouring into me.

"Jude," I say, taking his wrists and pulling his hands away from my face, his mouth from mine. "What did you want to tell me?"

He stares at me, a lost man, as my pounding heart turns in my chest. I hold my breath, bracing for impact.

"I love you," he whispers.

"Jude, please, talk to me."

I look over my shoulder at Nick, fighting Jude when he tries to pull me back around. "Will one of you tell me what the hell is happening?"

"He doesn't love you," Nick says, his face sharp and disgusted. "It's all a fucking game to him. He's not who you think he is."

I inhale. There are those words I feared.

"I love her," Jude growls, passing me, going for Nick, his body strung.

"Jude!"

The crack of his fist meeting Nick's jaw sends shivers down my spine and puts Nick on his arse. One punch. "I fucking love her," he seethes, bending over Nick's sprawled body, shaking. "Don't tell me how I feel."

"He's been using you." Nick's eyes are on Jude as he spits blood on the gravel. "You're nothing but a pawn to him. A weapon."

I step back. "What?"

"No." Jude abandons Nick and rushes to me. "Don't listen to him."

"He wanted to hurt me," Nick mumbles on, his sneer wicked. "So he made the woman *I* love fall for him."

"Shut up!" Jude yells.

My stomach drops as I push Jude's hands away from me, moving back. "Is it true?" I ask him, knowing before he can answer that it is. All the signs are there. *I didn't expect to fall in love with you.* "Oh my God." *You're the biggest surprise in this situation.* What about the bet?

"Amelia, I'm begging you, please," Jude whispers. "Just let me explain."

"Then explain!" I yell, staring at his pathetic form, his arms limp by his sides, his face a picture of sorrow. It makes me sick.

"I gave his family some inaccurate financial advice." Nick pushes his way to his feet.

"You fucking robbed him," Jude grates, an inferno blazing in his eyes. He looks like he's going to burst with the pressure. And then he does. "He was on the verge of losing everything!" He goes for Nick again, rabid, pulling his fist back, and I watch, horrified, but Jude lowers his arm and comes back to me. "Nick fucked everything up, Amelia," he says, feeling at my face. "Everything."

"You wanted revenge?" The floodgates of my mind open, too much information and too many realizations hitting me. "You used me to get revenge?"

Jude looks away, ashamed.

"Oh Jesus," I croak, feeling at my throat. It's closing up on me. "The bet. Katherine said I was a bet."

His face twists. "She knew about Nick and what he did to my family."

"Because you were engaged to her at the time." My voice is so quiet. So defeated.

"I didn't want her to know who you were. I knew she'd tell you." He closes his eyes briefly, taking in air to spit out his truths. "She wasn't supposed to be at the restaurant with me that night. She invited herself along and noticed I was distracted." He grabs a breath. "I went along with the bet because that's what I fucking do, Amelia."

He likes the chase. The game. He made me just like any other girl he's bet on.

I'm going to throw up. "You sick bastard," I whisper, panic falling into me fast, tears stinging the backs of my eyes. *Do not let him see you cry.* "And you?" I turn my fury onto Nick. "Stay away from me."

I've got to get out of here.

I walk in circles, my brain failing to give me instructions. The Jaguar. It's not mine. But it's my only option.

"Amelia, wait," Jude says, fretful, as I pace towards the car.

My head's going to explode. I yank the door open and drop to the seat, but I don't get it closed before Jude's blocking it. "Leave me alone," I yell, fighting against him, trying to close the door, but his strength is far superior to mine.

"No, you have to listen to me."

His words tip me over the edge I've been balancing on, and I fly out of the car like a mad bitch, shoving him away. "It's all a fucking lie!" I scream, losing control of my temper. It's better than crying on him. "I hate you, Jude. I fucking hate you." He has the nerve to look hurt. So I shove him again. "Never come near me again." I know my face spells the hate I feel. "Ever."

I drop into the seat and pull away, forcing myself not to put my foot down and speed off. My heart squeezes, every second of my time with Jude parading through my head as I drive.

Torturing me.

And the tears pour down my cheeks, hitting my lap in fat drops.

I surrendered.

And now I'm destroyed.

Chapter 23

Abbie's face drops like a rock when she opens the door and sees the state of me, the tears still relentlessly falling. "Oh fuck." Her arms envelop me, hugging me as I sob.

"It was all a fucking lie," I say through my tears, the humiliation and hurt blending. "I was just part of a sick game."

"What?" she breathes, pulling back and looking at me, rubbing my eyes. It's pointless, more tears replacing the ones she's wiped away on my cheeks. "The bet?"

"No." Revenge is so much worse than being a bet. "He was using me to get back at Nick."

Eyes like saucers, she stares at me in shock, waiting for me to go on.

"Nick gave Jude's family bad financial advice years ago."

"Are you kidding me?"

I shake my head, so fucking mortified. "I feel so stupid."

Abbie ushers me inside and takes me to the couch, sitting me down and filling my hand with a glass of wine. "So you spoke to Nick?"

I take a sip, snivelling. "I was leaving Arlington Hall to go see him, but he showed up there."

"He came to you," she says, surprised, lowering next to me. "Where was Jude?"

"Asleep. Nick wouldn't talk, just kept going round in circles, telling me to give him a chance, that Jude didn't want me. Then Jude found us, and the shit hit the fan." I put my wine on the coffee table and bury my head in my hands, another wave of tears falling. "Being a bet seems attractive now. Being used to hurt someone?" I laugh cynically, thinking what a great fucking job Jude did. Not only did he seduce me, but he actually made me love him.

My phone rings, and I move away from it, wary.

"It's your brother," she says, frowning. "Isn't it a bit late for him to be calling you?"

"Not if Nick's let him know what's just happened."

"Oh," she breathes, putting both hands between her knees as I reach for my mobile, braving answering it.

"What the hell is going on?" Clark blurts, sounding half asleep. "Are you okay?"

"I'm fine."

"I've just had Nick on the phone talking a load of I don't know fucking what."

"I'll call you tomorrow," I say, without the energy to go through this again. "I'm at Abbie's."

"Not Jude's?"

"No."

A short pause. "Why?"

"Because I'm no longer seeing him." Seeing him? Dating him? In love with him?

My heart twists.

"And what's Nick got to do with this? Are you back with him?"

"No. God, no." I'm seriously off men for life. "I'll call you tomorrow, okay? I'm fine, I'm at Abbie's, I'm no longer seeing Jude Harrison, and I'm not back with Nick." I never want to see either man again.

Clark sighs. "Okay. Right, yes, okay. Get some sleep." He hangs up first, and I fall into Abbie's side, staring ahead at the TV. Sleep? I doubt that'll happen.

"Let me change this for you," she says, taking my hand and turning it over, revealing blood spots on the bandage.

"It's not healing." I give myself a moment to acknowledge the throb.

"It could be infected. You should get it checked."

Everyone's told me the same thing. Get it checked. And I haven't. I've been too sidetracked. Too distracted. "I will." I need to look after myself. My hand will eventually heal. But my heart? "I don't know if I'll get over this," I say quietly, wincing at the flashbacks parading through my mind. All Jude.

Abbie hushes me, hugging me. "I've told you before, you are stronger than you think."

Then why do I feel so utterly broken?

Chapter 24

I have no idea how many missed calls I've had from Nick. Or how many I've rejected. His messages are being deleted immediately. Same goes for Jude. I don't want to see or speak to either of them.

I meet Clark for breakfast the next morning and tell him everything. I don't relish it, but I need him to lay off the questioning and have my back when my parents inevitably grill me. I can't let them see how affected I am. It won't make sense to them, since I was only briefly involved with the force that is Jude Harrison. But they met him. And they loved him. Everything was so fucking perfect; I should have known the universe would fuck me over.

"Well, fuck," Clark says, brushing his hands free of breadcrumbs. "So Nick gave him some shitty financial advice and—"

"His dad," I correct him. "Nick gave Jude's dad some shitty advice."

"His dad," Clark repeats. "So Jude has a gripe and he's used you, the woman Nick loves, to get back at him? Seems a bit over the top, doesn't it?"

I hum, annoyed with how much space this is taking up in my head. "Look, Jude wanted to hurt Nick and he succeeded. The end."

"But he dragged you away from Nick when he found you in the pub. Why would he do that if he wanted Nick to be hurt? To be hurt he'd have to know Jude was seeing you."

I stare at Clark, not liking where he's going with this.

He leans closer. "Maybe because Jude really did fall for you and didn't know how to tell you."

"Are you actually defending him?"

"I'm just—"

"Well, don't. I'm done."

His hands come up, defensive.

And now, back to the breakup diet of work and wine. Except I'm on a different breakup. "Look, I have a meeting with Tilda Spector tomorrow that I need to prep for, and I want to get to the gym." My work brain is switched back on. Distraction. I stand and drop a kiss on his cheek.

"Okay," he murmurs, here but not here.

"Hey," I say, smacking his shoulder. "Stop overthinking it. I'm over it, so you should be too."

He laughs. "Sure. Over it. Fuck me, Amelia, you were spending every spare minute with him. That's never happened in the history of my sister. Mum and Dad met him. Jesus, Dad even softened. You loved him."

I flinch. "I didn't know who he was, Clark," I say quietly, smiling, using every ounce of my energy to do so. "He's a liar. A womaniser. A fucking arsehole. I hate him." I kiss his head and leave, slipping my earbuds in and shuffling my favourite tracks. Moby's "Why Does My Heart Feel So Bad?" comes on, and I move through the crowds on the pavement, listening.

Until I can't listen anymore.

I yank out my earbuds, my chest tight, and pick up my pace.

It dislodges the tears, and they fall once again.

I reject yet another call from Jude as I walk across the lobby to the elevators. "Amelia," Gary says, joining me as I hit the button. "Sorry I didn't return your call yesterday. Everything okay?"

"Did you know Nick was interviewing?"

"Ah, yes, I meant to let you know about that."

"Seriously, Gary? It just slipped your mind?" I feel at my forehead, exasperated. "You have to let the partners know he can't work here."

"Look, Amelia, I know he's your ex—"

"He's practically stalking me."

Gary recoils. "Oh?"

"He helped himself to my phone while he was here yesterday and started tracking my movements." That's pretty much all I can say.

"Stalking you?"

"Yes, Gary. And if he continues, I'll have no option but to report him." I'm not fucking around anymore, walking on eggshells to save someone else's feelings to my own detriment. I'm done.

With a heavy frown, Gary nods slowly. "Okay. Let me speak to the partners."

"Thank you," I breathe.

"No problem. Now let's pick up where we left off on Jude Harrison."

Don't flinch! "Where was it left off?" I ask, peeking at my phone when it rings again. I slam my thumb down on the red icon and switch my mobile to silent.

"You didn't want me to tell Leighton you'd met with him."

"Oh, yes." *Fuck, fuck, fuck.*

"He's going to have to know." Gary laughs. "As soon as a client signs, a memo gets circulated. You know that."

I'm so relieved Leighton interrupted my impromptu meeting with Gary and stalled me telling him about my relationship or I'd feel like even more of a fool. "I know that," I murmur. Problem is, now I have to break the news that Jude Harrison won't be a client at all.

"So are you telling him or am I?"

"Telling who?"

Gary frowns around a half smile. "Are you okay?"

"Yes, yes, I'm fine." I step into the elevator, Gary following. *Get it together!* "My meeting with Tilda Spector is tomorrow. My head is full."

"You must let me know how that goes."

"I will."

"So . . . Leighton?"

Fuck, how the hell am I going to tell Gary that Harrison isn't going to be a client? "I'll let you know," I say, smiling. Dying.

Gary gives his phone his attention, blessing me with a break and an opportunity to pull my shit together. And, luckily, he stays engrossed all the way to our floor. I dip out, calling a goodbye, and slide into my office, shutting the door. Breathing.

And coughing when I see a bunch of peonies in the middle of my desk. I creep towards them like they might leap off and attack me, my eyes scanning for the card. No card.

Lowering to my chair, I stare at them, getting angrier by the second. If I was completely heartless, I'd pluck every bloom off the stem and crush them with my bare hands. *Fuck you, Jude Harrison.* Except the compassion in me refuses to allow it. And that's only because I know these flowers were Evelyn Harrison's favourites. How screwed up is that?

I pick up the bouquet and put them on the floor behind my chair so I don't have to look at them, answering my desk phone when it rings. "Amelia Lazenby."

"I have Tilda Spector for you," the receptionist says.

"Thanks." I get my game face on and rest back in my chair as she's put through. "Hi, Tilda," I say, injecting a ton of enthusiasm into my voice. "Good to hear from you."

"Amelia."

I still in my chair as Jude's voice washes over my skin. I don't need to ask how he got past reception. Is there nothing Anouska won't do for him?

"Please, just hear me out. Give me a chance."

A chance to fuck me over again? No. That would be perfect for him, wouldn't it? The biggest and most successful fuck-you to Nick. I slam the phone down and stand from my chair, heading for the kitchen to get a coffee, feeling all the emotions I'm fighting to keep restrained creeping back up my throat. My mobile vibrates in my hand. Him. I shake my head, silently begging him to leave me alone. Let me lick my wounds in private. Let me at least *try* to get over him.

Gary's in the boardroom with Leighton when I pass, and both men look up at me. I force a smile but frown when Gary waves me in. Pushing the door open, I hang on to the handle and the doorframe.

"You two look cozy," I say in jest, rejecting another call from Jude. Gary clears his throat. "Leighton, would you mind?"

"Sure," he says, jumping up from his seat and making a hasty exit, forcing me to move aside to let him pass. He doesn't look at me. It's odd.

"Should I close the door?" I ask.

Gary nods, so I do, my curiosity raging. Something's wrong. Gary's acting awkward, and I'm quite sure I don't like it.

"Are you sleeping with Jude Harrison?" he asks. No foreplay. *Bam. Fuck.*

My world stops spinning as my boss studies me, obviously watching for my knee-jerk reaction.

"What?" I breathe.

"Are you sleeping with Mr. Harrison?"

Oh God, oh God, oh God. "I . . ."

"Shit, Amelia," Gary says around his extended gasp, the look of disappointment on his face painful. "What the hell are you thinking?"

"It's not like that, Gary," I rush to explain, as he drops to a chair heavily. "Jude . . . Mr. Harrison sprang it on me." I shake my head to myself when Gary's eyes widen. "I mean the financial-planning bit, not himself." Oh God, could I make a bigger mess of this? I rub my forehead. "I was seeing Mr. Harrison," I say. "Briefly. Not anymore."

"You realise what this looks like?"

"Yes, I do. *Did.* Mr. Harrison mentioned his current planner was leaving, so he wanted to move his interests elsewhere."

"So you didn't sleep with him to secure his business?"

"What? No! Jesus, Gary, come on. You know me."

"I know what this looks like, Amelia, and I don't like it. Leighton secured a meeting with Harrison, and the next thing he's cancelled and rearranged with you." He stands, palms pointing to the ceiling. "Are you saying that isn't the case?"

"No, it's not." Fucking hell, how am I going to explain? "I started seeing Mr. Harrison after the convention."

"But his wealth wasn't on your mind?"

I gape at him, indignant. "No, Gary, his wealth was the furthest from mind. In actual fact, I'd met Mr. Harrison before, but I had no clue who he was until the conference." I cannot believe I'm having to explain myself out of this. *Fuck you, Leighton, and fuck you, Jude Fuckboy Harrison.* But I can't very well tell Gary that Jude only arranged a meeting with Leighton Steers to warn him off me. Or can I? I rub my forehead again. "Gary, I had every intention of telling you that I couldn't take on Jude Harrison as a client because of my personal relationship with him."

He gets up and starts walking slowly up and down the conference room. "But you didn't."

I point to the door. "You were called away because of an emergency news flash, and then you were in meetings, and . . ." I laugh. Jesus. "Well, I'm no longer seeing Mr. Harrison, and I expect he'll find alternative arrangements for his millions."

Gary flinches at the mention of millions. I'm just making this worse. But then something comes to me. "Wait. How did you know I was seeing him?"

"You know I can't divulge that, Amelia."

I laugh under my breath. "Of course." Anger is rising. Leighton. *The fuckhead.* "Look, Gary, I pride myself on my integrity." I dig deep to remain calm. "You have to believe me; I would never do that."

He slows his pace and looks out of the corner of his eye. "I really don't want to take this to the board."

"Then don't. They never have to know."

He looks up at the ceiling, sighing. "I told them about Harrison, Amelia. They know he was here to meet you."

"Fuck," I hiss, losing control for a split second and hitting the table. I immediately apologise for it, taking some deep breaths.

"Look, leave it with me." He pulls his glasses off and rubs his eyes. "You'd better get back to work."

I nod and stand, my mind bending, leaving Gary in the conference room. I'm raging. And the control I was fighting to keep escapes me, my unstable emotions letting me down. I stalk to Leighton's office and burst in on him. "You fucking snake," I hiss.

He does a terrible job of hiding his smirk, sitting back in his chair casually. "I'm sorry, what?"

"You know what." I walk towards his desk, my fists bunched. "How did you know I was seeing Jude Harrison?"

"Oh, you're seeing him?"

"Was," I reiterate. "Briefly."

"Oh, you broke up?"

"How did you know?"

"I don't know what you're talking about."

"Sure." I place my palm on his desk and lean over it. My move seems to increase his amusement, therefore increase my fury. God, I'd love to smash his face into the wood. "You're a sad, desperate creep, Leighton Steers."

"Ouchy," he says, pouting.

"Go fuck yourself."

"Ouchy, ouchy."

I push myself up and leave before I follow through on my desire to cause him physical pain, my emotions needing an outlet desperately.

"Is someone on their period?" he calls, making my heels skid to a stop.

"Fuc—" My mouth snaps shut.

My period.

My stomach turns when my heart drops into it, my mind frantically working through the dates. I'm suddenly cold. So fucking cold. "Off," I whisper.

"And good to see you got your fancy new car repaired."

I exhale sharply, staring forward, another bombshell getting me. I look over my shoulder at him. "You?"

"Me, what?" he muses, kicking his leg up on his knee, reclining back.

Gold digger. But, crazily, I have something more important to deal with than Leighton and my vandalised car.

My period.

"I hope you're happy," I say, picking up my heavy feet and walking back to my office. I get to my desk, pulling my calendar up, and count back to my last period. Twice. Three times. "Shit," I breathe, counting again, hoping by some miracle I've miscalculated by a week. "No, no, no."

I'm a week late.

I grab my handbag and pull my makeup bag out, searching for my pills. My hands land on a pen.

I've got you. Jude xxx

Swallowing down the lump in my throat, I toss it aside and find my pills, counting through the empty holes in the foil. "No," I whisper when I discover two more pills than I should have. I drop the packet on my desk and stare at them.

This can't be happening.

Chapter 25

They're not, but paranoia—and maybe the anxiety too—is making me feel like everyone in the pharmacy is looking at me. I smile tightly at the lady as she places the box on the counter. "Thank you."

"Anything else I can help you with?"

I look at my bandaged hand, and then extend it towards her. "I cut it nearly two weeks ago. It's not healing very well."

"Did you visit a hospital?" she asks, taking my hand gingerly and feeling the skin around the bandage.

"Yes. It was stitched up."

"You should make an appointment with your doctor. It's hot to the touch, maybe infected."

"Right. Okay."

"The pregnancy test is twelve ninety-nine."

I tap my card and stuff the box in my bag before my payment's authorised, picking up Clark's call as I'm hurrying out. My heart is still in my stomach, my tummy still churning, my anxious shakes not improving.

"Hey," I say, breaking free from the stifling space and dragging in air. I take a moment under a tree to switch my heels for my trainers. "What's up?"

"It's been bugging me," he says, his breathing a little laboured. He's walking to the Tube.

"What's bugging you?"

"Nick. He doesn't strike me as the kind of planner who'd fuck up so monumentally. Because it would have to be monumental to spike such an act of revenge, right?"

My hand wedged into the tree trunk, I bend a leg in turn and get my trainers on, my phone held to my ear by my shoulder. "I haven't really thought about it." *I'm busy having a meltdown of epic proportions and nursing a broken heart.*

"I did a bit of digging."

"Why? I want to forget it ever happened." And deal with this . . . issue. And yet I haven't really paid much thought to how I'm going to deal with it. *If* I need to deal with it. Oh, please let me *not* have to deal with this.

"Did you know Nick changed his name?" Clark asks.

"What?"

"He worked at Flagstar when the bank went tits-up ten years ago."

I laugh, getting my bag back on my shoulder. "No, that can't be right. I'd know something like that."

"I'm telling you, Amelia. I'm looking at a picture of him when he was, I don't know, early twenties maybe. It's definitely him, but it says his name is Nicolas Green, not Phillips."

"Nicolas Green?" I ask, my face bunching. "Why would he change his name?"

"I don't know."

My mind takes me back to the bar, the standoff between Nick and Jude after I stupidly introduced them. But I quickly pull myself back into line, adamant I won't waste any more thinking space on them. "Look, Clark, I want nothing to do with either of them, so you can stop wasting your time on an undercover investigation."

"You're not curious?"

"No, I'm too busy in a crisis."

"What?"

"Nothing." I pick up my feet. "I won't make it to Mum and Dad's this evening."

"Again? What's going on?"

"Nothing, Clark. I just found out the man I was seeing was using me, so forgive me if I'm feeling a little wounded and unsociable." I sigh, wishing I hadn't said that. But what's the alternative? Telling him I think I've been even more stupid and got myself pregnant? A bench a few feet away catches my eye, and my tired bones relent to its lure. My arse hits the wood, and I take a moment to try and breathe steady for the first time since . . .

I don't know when. Maybe it was before I met Jude. Everything feels blurred and distorted.

"I said I'd pop round Charley's. I'll call you tomorrow, okay?" I drop my phone to my lap and watch the world go by for a while, wondering if I'm mentally stalling what needs to be done. Probably. "How did you let this happen, Amelia?" I ask myself, smiling at an old boy walking a spaniel when he gives me questioning eyes. I put my bag onto my lap and look at the box inside. Am I?

I text Charley.

Are you home?

Yes. Abbie's here too.

I stand and head for the Tube.

Chapter 26

The front door swings open and Lloyd's face drops. "Oh fuck, what's happened?" he breathes. "Charley!"

I thought I'd got a hold of myself, but the second Charley appears, the dam cracks again and emotion pours out of me rapidly. It might be the familiar face. I don't know.

"I'll leave you three to it," Lloyd says, claiming the kids and making a sharp exit, just as Abbie appears. That makes me cry harder. Charley hauls me into her chest, squeezing me, and Abbie's hand pats at my back. My sobs accelerate, becoming louder, my body more out of control.

"Amelia?" Abbie says gently, as Charley guides me to the kitchen and puts me on a stool. Abbie runs to the fridge, pours wine for everyone, and when she slides it across the island to me, I cry harder.

"Oh fucking hell." Abbie leans back on her stool, swigging her own wine with wide eyes, bracing herself.

A tissue is pushed into my hand, and I use the other to pull out the box from my bag and put it on the island. Both women stare down at it for much longer than they really need to. Both of their reactions are delayed. Both their round eyes shoot up. Both their gasps fill the kitchen. And then both of them slap palms over their mouths.

Shocked.

So shocked.

"Who?" Charley asks.

I can't even say his name, more tears coming, my throat getting thicker. "J—"

"Oh my fuck." Charley drops to a stool heavily and fills her glass. "And you're sure?"

I shake my head, pushing the box farther forward. "I didn't want to be alone when it's confirmed beyond all doubt that I'm a reckless dickhead."

Abbie coughs over an inappropriate huff of laughter, and Charley smiles softly. "Come on," she says, sliding the box off the marble and taking my hand. Abbie takes the other, and my two best friends walk me to the bathroom to do the dreaded test.

"Have you thought about what you'll do?" Abbie asks as Charley gets a test out of the box. I shake my head, my eyes lasers on Charley's working hands. I can't think past the fact that I have been so fucking dumb, on *every* level. And as if to remind me exactly how dumb, my mobile rings in my hand. I look down at the screen. My insides twist.

"Fuck off," I whisper, throwing my iPhone into the sink, needing rid of it.

Taking a deep breath, I hold my hand out. "Let's get it over with."

They sit on the edge of the tub while I pull my dress up, my knickers down, and lower, holding the stick between my legs as I pee.

Pee and pray.

Pee and pray.

Please, please, please.

I place the stick on the edge of the sink and sort myself out, washing my hands and starting to pace the small bathroom, up and down, up and down.

"I need a drink," Abbie says, taking the stick. "Come on. We'll be more comfortable in the kitchen."

Following her out after collecting my phone, I continue to pray. The girls work their way through another glass as I pace some more, around and around the island, looking at Charley every few seconds as she keeps an eye on the time. She eventually nods.

"Who's looking?" Abbie asks, keeping her distance, all of us staring at the small stick on the island that could potentially change my life forever.

"I can't," I admit, stepping farther away.

"Me either." Abbie looks at Charley, who visibly takes a breath and some bravery before walking determinedly to the island and swiping it up. My heart thuds relentlessly. She turns it over. I hold my breath, feeling Abbie's hand wrap around mine and squeeze. Charley swallows. I think I'm on the verge of a heart attack, my gaze searching her face for any clue as to what she's thinking.

I can't read her. It's driving me wild.

"Charley?" I whisper.

She turns it towards me, not that I can see the result from this far away. "Positive," she says quietly. Reluctantly. "You're pregnant."

I exhale, my torso folding, and my legs turn to jelly in an instant.

"Sit down," Abbie says, ushering me to a stool, where I flop onto the seat. I stare forward, my mind now deciding to give me a little refresher on the past few weeks, when I've been wrapped up in a whirlwind of passion and feelings. Jude's face relentlessly flashes through my mind. All his expressions, his charm, his smirks, his heat.

And finally, his desperation.

And the tears come again.

I bury my face in my palms and cry like a child, loud, body-shaking, desperate sobs. How could I have let this happen? How could I have been so completely irresponsible?

I'm quickly engulfed in my friends' arms, their soothing whispers and hushes quietly detectable past my sobs. This changes everything. I can't run and hide from Jude Harrison now. My vow to never see him again has been dashed, and it's my own stupid fault. Staying away was my saving grace. Not having to see him. I could move on, try to find myself again, work hard to put him behind me.

Except I never really lost myself.

If anything, I loved myself more when he was a part of my life. A part of *me*.

Which made forgetting him impossible even before this new bombshell. "What am I going to do?" I whisper for the sake of it. I'm not asking what I'm actually going to do; that's a non-question. More how I will cope. And I don't mean with a baby. I mean now I can't eliminate Jude Harrison from my future. Maybe I'm jumping the gun. He might run for the hills.

Sounds disgusting.

"Fuck." I roughly wipe my face and slam my fist down on the island. "Fuck!" My hand screams in pain, and I turn it over, seeing more spots of blood on the dressing. I've had enough of this fucking dressing. I take the edge and yank it off, gritting my teeth as I do. The wound is jagged and ugly. Weeping. It needs air. And definitely a doctor to look at it.

Tossing the bloodied bandage aside, I stand up and march to the patio doors, pulling them open and standing outside, flexing my hand. *I* need air. I can't breathe. "Fuck, fuck, fuck!" I grab my hair and yank, punishing myself, then march back into the kitchen. Abbie and Charley haven't moved, their faces alarmed. "Fuck," I say over a choked sob, crumbling again, the anger and helplessness getting all mixed up and confused. I'm not sure what I should feel.

"Sit down," Abbie says, pushing me to a stool. "Christ, Amelia."

"Are you going to tell him?" Charley asks, refilling her glass again.

Am I? I can't think. I don't know what to do. "I need to get my own head around this," I say quietly, wondering if I ever will. "I can't even think about what comes next."

"Well, a baby comes next, so you'd better think fast." Abbie laughs lightly, but it fades when Charley and I look at her tiredly. "Sorry."

We're disturbed when the front door closes, and Lloyd appears in the kitchen doorway, seeming a little wary. "Someone for you," he says, looking at me.

"Who?" I ask, dread creeping in, my body becoming hard, ready to take him on.

Lloyd moves aside and reveals Clark. *Oh God.* I deflate, so fucking relieved. "What are you doing here?"

"To check you're actually here and not lying to me."

"Are you serious?"

"Yes, I'm serious. You were weird on the phone. And you've been crying."

"I'm hot off the back of a breakup, Clark."

He looks between Charley and Abbie, who are both unusually quiet and awkward. And Clark doesn't miss it. "What's going on?"

He really doesn't want to know. But it turns out I don't need to tell him. He spots the test on the island and reaches for it, and his gaze slowly moves from the positive window to me. "Fuck," he breathes.

And I cry again, confirming what he doesn't need confirming. Clark finds it in himself to come to me, clumsily rubbing my shoulders. "It's a mess," I say.

"Does he know?"

"I only just found out myself."

"Are you going to tell him?" All eyes fall to my phone when it starts dancing around the island, Jude's name illuminating the screen. I laugh at the irony, hitting the reject button. "I'll take that as a no."

"I need to think," I say, wedging my elbows on the marble and resting my head in my hands, carrying the weight. I can't think. My head is all over the place, nothing making sense.

"Come to my place," Clark says, turning me on the stool to face him. "I'll tell Mum and Dad that Rach isn't feeling good. Have some dinner with us. Rach is sorting through some of the photos people have sent from the wedding. You can help. It'll take your mind off things." He gives me a sad face and wipes my eyes for me, and I nod, although I doubt there is anything in the world with the power to take my mind off this.

And I can't very well bury my head in the sand forever.

Chapter 27

We're five minutes into our journey—and five more missed calls from Jude—when Rachel answers Clark's call after the third attempt. "Finally," he breathes.

"Sorry," she says. "I was hanging some washing out. What's up?"

"Change of plan. I've got Amelia with me. She's coming to ours for a bite."

"What's happened?"

I smile to myself. Of course she'd ask that. "I'll explain over dinner," he replies, reaching for my hand and patting it.

"But I'm already at your parents'. Your mum's cooked, and she wants to see all these pictures."

"You said you were hanging washing out."

"For your mother, because she's hard at it over the stove."

Clark glances across the car to me, cringing, as he puts the phone on mute. "What do you want to do?"

"It's fine," I say, waving off his concern. "I'll come too." Truth is, I need a hug from my mum. She can't know, but I need a hug. And to be surrounded by what's familiar in a world I don't know right now.

Clark unmutes his phone. "See you there, honey." He takes a right and reroutes to our parents'. "So the plan is to say nothing?" he asks.

"Nothing," I confirm, pulling out the test and looking at the result, as if to remind myself of the mess I'm in. "Not until I know how I'm handling this." I swallow and settle back, looking out the window at the streets passing, my eyes glazed. There's so much to think about, and I have zero brain space at the moment. I need my mum's home-cooked food and the usual calming chaos of my family around me.

"Okay. Well, you just take your time."

My eyes drop to my phone in my lap when it rings again. Jude. I turn it to silent and go back to watching the world go by. "Will Grandma and Grandpa be there?" I ask, keeping my attention out the window.

"They're always there."

"I know. I was just checking."

"And if anyone asks about Jude?"

Hearing his name out loud makes me flinch. "He's working."

"Right."

Twenty minutes and endless loops of my thoughts later, we pull up outside Mum and Dad's. Clark squeezes my arm as I take a deep breath, getting out of the car and walking on numb legs up the pathway.

Grandma and Grandpa are not in their usual spots when I walk into the lounge. It throws me. Frowning, I wander through to the dining room, finding them at the table. Grandpa's swapped his paper for a pile of pictures, and Grandma has swapped her knitting needles for a pair of scissors.

"You look different," she says as I dip and kiss her cheek.

Different? In turmoil? Heartbroken? *Pregnant?* "I'm the same."

Grandpa ushers me over and looks me up and down. "She's right. You're blotchy."

"I'm fine, Grandpa," I say, rubbing his shoulder. "What are you doing?"

"I got all the pictures people sent me printed off," Rachel says, wandering in from the kitchen. She recoils when she clocks my face. Shit, *am* I blotchy? I shake my head mildly, making her look at

Clark, who also shakes his head, taking her arm and leading her into the hallway.

Grandpa looks at the pictures in front of him, scratching his bald head and removing his glasses. "How many are there?"

"Hundreds." Grandma indicates the endless piles. "Are we putting them in an album?"

"Kids don't have albums these days." Grandpa points to an iPhone on the table. "They have camera rolls."

I smile and follow Clark and Rachel. I know immediately when Rach gives me a smile loaded with sympathy she can't hide that Clark's told her. "You know," I whisper when she pulls me in for a hug.

"We're here for you." I'm squeezed tightly. "What on earth's happened?"

"I'll come back to you on that one." I kiss her cheek and go find Mum. "Hey," I say, hugging her from behind where she's standing at the sink in an apron and some rubber gloves.

She stills for a moment, laughing lightly, before forcing me to release her when she turns. She takes me in from top to toe, and it takes everything in me and more to stop my lip wobbling.

"What's happened?" she asks quietly, removing her rubber gloves.

"Nothing's happened."

"Oh, please, Amelia. Are you forgetting who you're talking to?" She takes my hand and leads me to the laundry room. "Explain what these are."

A massive bunch of peonies is sitting on the worktop over the dryer. "Did he come to the florist again?" I ask.

"He looked terrible," she whispers. "What's happened?"

"I'm not seeing him anymore."

"But why?" she cries. "We had a lovely weekend with you both, Amelia. You and Jude, you just looked so happy together, and your father hasn't shut up about him since!"

Everything inside wilts. Isn't it just typical that my father would change the habit of a lifetime now? "It didn't work out," I say, approaching the flowers.

"There's no card. I removed it."

"Why?"

"Well, I didn't want your father reading it."

"Why?"

"Well, in case this is a storm in a teacup."

"In case I work it out with him?"

Mum pouts. "Will you?"

I laugh, and there's an edge of sarcasm. "No, Mum, trust me. We won't be working it out." *But he's the father of your impending grandbaby, so I can't tell you why and make you hate him as much as I do.* "He shouldn't have come to the florist." That's tactical.

Mum pulls the card from the pocket of her apron and hands it over, her lips pursed. "He sounded terribly sorry for whatever's happened." The questions swirl in her eyes.

"Mum," I breathe, taking her hand. "Please, let's forget about him."

"But, my darling, I saw a sparkle in your eyes I've never seen before." She comes closer. "That's got to mean something. And he was so handsome and charming and refined."

And a liar and a cheat and a vengeful, immoral bastard.

"It's over," I reiterate, the words fighting past the lump in my throat. Any contact I must have with him going forward will be transactional. "And, honestly, I'm fine, so please stop worrying." *Save your worry for when I drop the baby bomb.* "I'm starving. What's for dinner?"

I go back into the kitchen and check the pot on the stove, lifting the lid. "Mm," I hum when the steam rises and a waft of rich gravy hits my nose. "Casserole?"

"Beef."

"Amelia," Dad sings, coming in from the garden. "Did you see the flowers Jude sent for you?"

"Yeah, Dad. I saw them."

He looks around. "Where is he?"

Oh my God. I look at Mum, who shifts, awkward, her eyes begging me not to tell him. "Jude and I split up," I say, aiming for assertive, but I know I sound as defeated as I feel. Mum deflates, and I give her sorry eyes. There's no point delaying the inevitable.

"What?" Confusion invades every inch of Dad's face.

"It didn't work out."

"Didn't work out? How ridiculous. We spent most of the weekend with you both. I've never seen you smile so much. And . . . and . . . and I like him!"

Guilt flares, for a reason I never imagined. "I know you did, Dad. I'm sorry." This is bizarre. And fucking painful.

"This doesn't make any sense." Dad looks between us, wounded as he drops to a chair. "I don't mean to be judgy, darling, but what are you thinking?"

Judgy. We'll see how judgy he gets when I tell him he's going to be a granddad *and* I'm not with the baby's father.

"He loves you."

"He doesn't love me, Dad," I assure him. I was just a pawn to him, and suddenly everything we shared is null and void. Meaningless. He wanted me to fall in love with him, and I did. Job done. I'm not going back so Jude Harrison can prolong Nick's punishment. "I need some air," I say, leaving them in the kitchen whispering angrily to each other, and heading out the front. I sit on a wall and take a moment to myself, trying not to fall victim to my memories again. Impossible.

How the hell did I end up here?

My attention is caught when I see a car pull into the cul-de-sac. Nick's car. "Is he for real?" I whisper, standing from the dwarf wall. The anger is reignited as I wander to the end of the path to meet him on the pavement. Has he come to make me feel even stupider? Does he expect me to fall into his arms, sob and apologise?

"You need to leave," I say, my tone defensive and hostile. "You can't just keep turning up at my parents' house, Nick." Is he hoping for an ally in Dad?

"I thought . . ."

Oh my God, he does. He thinks there's a chance? After everything? I laugh under my breath and turn, walking back to the house, hoping that simple reaction tells him what he needs to know with no further energy drained. But then something comes to me, and I stop.

"Why did you change your name?" I ask, facing him.

The wave of surprise that crosses his face can't be hidden. "What?"

"Your name."

"Is that what he told you?" He stands taller in some kind of pathetic display of strength. It's defensive. And really fucking suspicious.

"No, it's what Clark told me." Wide eyes stare back at me, and I tilt my head, suddenly interested. "Why did you change your name, Nick?"

"My mum remarried after my dad died," he says, his words rushed.

"Wait. Your dad died?"

"Yes, my dad died."

"And you didn't think to tell me that?" We were together for five years!

"I *did* tell you that."

I laugh. "Nick, don't you think that's information I would remember? So Frank's your stepfather? You took your stepfather's name?"

"Yes." He shrugs, but I know there's way more to it, just by how shady he's behaving.

"Just like that, you took on another man's name?"

"Mum wanted me to have the same name as her."

"I call bullshit."

"I'm telling you the truth, Amelia."

"You wouldn't know the truth if it slapped you around the face, Nick."

"Look, I don't know what to tell you. I didn't have the best relationship with my father. He expected a lot from me. I didn't cope well with the pressure, and after he died, I wanted to be my own man, be recognised as me, not as my father's son."

"So you forgot he ever existed? Didn't think to mention to me that your dad died and you changed your name?"

"I must have told you, Amelia."

"You never told me." I don't need to rack my brain. He did *not* tell me. "I don't even know who you are." I feel like I've lived in the dark the whole time I was with Nick. Been deceived, made a fool of way before I met Jude Harrison. "Stay away from me, stay away from my family, and stay away from my work." I'm one stride away from the front door when it swings open, my brother appearing.

"There you are." Clark exhales, relieved to find me. "I was worried. Do you feel okay? Sick? Because Rach is getting terrible morning sickness, and she thought you might be too."

I stare at him. Just stare.

"You're pregnant?" Nick blurts from behind me.

"Oh fuck." Clark tilts his head slightly to look past me and confirm who's here.

"Pregnant?"

I'm frozen, my brain failing me. *Think.*

"Pregnant?" Nick says again, his voice getting louder, closer. "You're fucking pregnant?"

"Who's pregnant?" Mum appears behind Clark, and my whole world just got a little bit messier.

I close my eyes briefly, at a loss. "Me."

"Oh my Christ," Mum breathes.

"Is it mine?" Nick asks, his expression everything I hate. Hope.

"Nick?" Dad joins Mum on the doorstep. "Is what yours?"

I stare at Clark in complete despair. Poor thing looks absolutely mortified, his eyes wide and full of apologies.

"Amelia's pregnant," Nick declares.

"What?" Dad coughs over his shock. "How ridiculous. She can't be."

"I'm pregnant." I say the words clearly for my dad to hear, looking back at Nick. "And it's not yours."

He jerks, like he's been shot. "Him?" he gasps in disbelief.

I don't need to answer. This is horrific. Utterly horrific. And not because of Nick; I couldn't give two shits about him. But my family?

"Amelia?" Dad sounds as lost as I feel.

"Okay, I think we need to give them some space," Clark declares, taking Mum and Dad and pushing them back into the house.

"Pregnant?" Dad cries. "She's pregnant? But how?"

"Oh, Dennis, come on. Do you really need an explanation?"

"Yes! She just told me she's split up with Jude, whom, by the way, is a cracking chap. Why is she splitting up with him if she's expecting his baby?"

"Jesus." Clark throws me so many apologetic looks as he herds my parents back into the house, slamming the door.

I stare at the wood, feeling Nick's presence, unable to face him. "He's a cracking chap?" he says over a laugh. "So you've obviously not told your parents that he was using you."

"No, Nick, I've not told them. I've got other things on my mind right now."

"Of course. Jesus, Amelia. I don't believe you." He laughs. "How could you do this to me?"

"You?" I ask, stunned, sounding shrieky. "How could *I* do this to *you?*"

"What the fucking hell are you talking about?"

Honestly, I don't know. But I'm mad, and I fucking hate everyone right now. I'm fighting to keep myself from toppling over, I'm shaking so much. "I'm the fucking victim, Nick. Me. Jude Harrison used me because of whatever shitty financial advice *you* gave his family years ago, so don't stand there being *oh woe is me.*"

He backs down quickly, his mouth snapping shut. "I'm sorry, okay. I'm just dealing with a lot here."

I laugh out loud, and then back up when he comes closer, his face imploring. *Oh no.* "This can still work," he says, taking my shoulders, holding my useless form before him. "We can start again. Me and you."

I stare at him, flummoxed. "You'd still have me with another man's baby?"

He looks down at my stomach. "Well, there are solutions for these kinds of problems."

"Solutions?" And I'm a problem? My baby is a problem?

"Yeah, you know . . ." He shrugs. "I mean, I'm sure your dad will lend us the money to go private."

"Private," I murmur. "For an abortion."

"Yeah. Only the best care for you, Amelia. You know that. It'll be a new start. I can hop onboard with your brother at Lazenby Finance; you can, I don't know, do your thing at LB&B for a while." He smiles. "At least we know you're fertile for when we try."

What the hell am I listening to? "I'm not having an abortion, Nick."

His face falls. "What?"

"You heard me."

"But you have to, Amelia. I can't raise another man's child."

"Are you fucking insane? Have you missed the past few months? I don't love you, Nick. I have never loved you."

"But what will I do?" he asks. "What about me?"

"What about you?"

"I was supposed to get into Lazenby Finance, Amelia!" he yells, exploding, making me flinch. "It was supposed to be mine." He takes a breath, blinking, as I step back, stunned. "Ours. It was supposed to be ours."

"It will never be yours."

"Because you ruined everything!" His cool is lost again, and for the first time, I feel like I'm looking at the real Nick. "Some rich prick shows you a bit of attention, and you drop your knickers in a heartbeat." He laughs, and it goes right through me. "And now look at the state of you. Fucking pregnant. How dumb could you be?"

Very dumb, apparently. Because I have no idea who this twisted, bitter arsehole is. "Is that why you're so desperate to get me back? Because you want the business?"

He huffs, waving a hand in the vicinity of my stomach. "Well, I don't want you now, do I? You've fucked it all up, Amelia. My future, your future, your family's business's future."

I should slap him. But I don't get a chance. Clark appears from nowhere, bunching Nick's shirt in his fists and thrusting him down the pathway. "You're out, Nick. Done for. You'll never be a part of this family or our business, so back the fuck off and stay away from my sister."

Nick staggers a few feet away, startled. "Your dad always wanted me to help you run Lazenby Finance, Clark. Perhaps because he saw more potential in me."

"You fucker."

"I would have been an asset! You would have been lucky to have me." He gives me a filthy look, one that could turn me to dust if I allowed it.

"Get the fuck out of here!" Clark bellows before collecting me and taking me inside.

"Dad wanted Nick to help you run the business?" I ask, an old, familiar pain back. Nick but not me?

"I never told you because I didn't want you to hate on Dad any more than you already did." He slams the front door, slightly out of breath. "I would have fought him, trust me."

I don't believe this. Was I going to have any say in how I lived my life and who with?

"She'll be a single mother!" Dad yells.

"Oh, shut up," my brother shouts, all out of patience, pacing to the kitchen, me following. "Amelia's right. You're a bloody dinosaur."

"Now, now, Clark," Grandpa says. "Let's not get excited."

"Tell *him* that!"

I wander into the kitchen, and everyone shuts up, looking at me. "I'm okay, by the way," I say, the words strained and broken. I'm far from okay. "In case any of you were wondering." I collect my bag and throw it over my shoulder. "I'll be going now so you can all carry on arguing about my life."

"Amelia, for Christ's sake, pregnant!" Dad's hands go into his hair. "Who will support you?"

"I'll support myself," I snap. "And were you ever going to tell me that you were planning on giving Nick what should have been mine?"

Dad looks stung. "It was the natural progression."

"It was bullshit, Dad!"

My anger refuses to allow the tears to break free as I storm out of my parents' house. "Amelia, wait," Dad yells, coming after me. "Amelia, I'm sorry."

Even that one rare word from my father doesn't stop me, and I keep hold of my emotions until I reach the end of the road.

Then I cry like a baby all the way to Abbie's, distraught. The blows just keep on coming, and I don't know how much more I can take.

Charley's there when I fall through the door in tears, and they both dedicate the rest of the evening to feeding me, watering me, showering me, and tucking me up in bed. Charley spoons me, and Abbie spoons Charley, all of us cuddled up on the bed as I sob myself to sleep and my best friends comfort me.

My world falling apart around me.

Chapter 28

My head isn't in the game today. I've had three Zoom calls with clients, and I can hardly recall what was said, what I need to action, what I advised. No flowers have arrived today. Just a few more texts.

I'm sorry.

I know I don't deserve your grace.

I'm begging you, Amelia. I need to see you.

Let me explain.

I don't want to see him ever again. Problem is, I have to tell him I'm pregnant *and* far sooner than I hoped. But I need time to build my defences. Make sure I'm immune to him. Be strong in the face of my weakness. But now that Nick knows, news of my situation will spread like wildfire. I'm going to see Jude tonight. I'll tell him, make it clear I expect nothing, and leave.

Sounds disgusting.

I reach for the pen and click it a few times, reading the words on the edge. Reading his lie. I drop it in the bin next to my desk, looking up when Gary walks in. I can tell by his face that he doesn't come bearing good news. He doesn't sit. "The senior partners have requested a meeting next Monday," he says regretfully. "HR will be present, and you can bring a witness of your choice if you wish."

"Sounds official," I murmur, making his lips press into a straight line.

"I'm sorry, Amelia. I tried to fight your corner, but they feel there are some unanswered questions." I wonder where Sue sits on that front. "On the plus side," he goes on, "you have your meeting with Spector today, right?"

I nod, feeling a little bit more fight leave me. And more hatred for Jude rise. He is literally ruining my life piece by piece. My eyes drop to my stomach, guilt flaring. *I don't mean that,* I think, as if it might hear me. I have to pull it together for my meeting. It could be what saves me. "I have a doctor's appointment after my meeting." I hold up my hand, and Gary winces. "I think it's infected."

"Okay. Let me know how things go with Tilda, and good luck at the doctor's too."

I smile with effort and knuckle down, refining my subtle pitch, struggling so hard to concentrate with so many mammoth question marks hanging over my life. Even if I do make the deal with Spector work, the fact of the matter is, I'm pregnant, and as sad as it is, that puts me at a massive disadvantage in the workplace.

When one o'clock hits, I leave the office for my lunch with Tilda, answering my phone on my way to the elevator. "Amelia Lazenby," I say.

"Miss Lazenby, good afternoon, my name is Harriett Jenkins. I'm personal assistant to Mrs. Spector."

"Oh, hi."

"I'm afraid she can't make your lunch."

I come to a stop at the elevator, the small piece of optimism I had left draining away. "Oh. Well, that's no problem, we can rearrange." I reach for the call button and hit it. Pret it is for lunch, then. The doors open, but I hold off stepping inside, afraid I'll lose my signal. "When would work for Mrs. Spector?"

"I don't believe there's cause to rearrange."

"I'm sorry, I don't understand."

"The lunch was to discuss a possible acquisition of clients, and Mrs. Spector has now moved those clients."

"She's already found a new adviser?"

"That's correct."

"But . . ." I look down the corridor, finding Leighton Steers standing outside his office, casual, his hands in his pockets, his shoulder resting on the wood.

A smirk on his face.

"I see," I whisper. I can't believe this. Did he seduce her? *I thought she was smart.* I laugh on the inside, hysterically. Because I thought I was smart too.

"But Mrs. Spector did want me to pass on her gratitude and wish you all the best for the future."

"That's very kind."

Leighton pushes his shoulder off the doorframe and backs into his office.

"Goodbye." Hanging up, I stand, motionless, feeling completely lost.

Everything.

In tatters.

Chapter 29

I left the office, but I didn't go to Pret for lunch. I couldn't stomach a thing. I wandered the streets of London, losing track of time, walking aimlessly.

Lost.

I didn't return to work in the afternoon either. It felt quite pointless. I visited my doctor, who confirmed the wound is infected and prescribed some antibiotics. I also took the opportunity to share my recent news. Pregnant. The doctor smiled and congratulated me. She had me do another test to confirm it, recommended some vitamins, and told me I'd hear from the prenatal care team soon about a scan.

It was all a bit surreal.

Then I went to Abbie's, and when she got home, I cried on her again. For an hour straight. And she just held me, silent, letting me get it all out. Except the tears won't fucking stop coming. And the pain in my chest won't fuck off.

"I need to get away," I say, my words sounding as broken as I feel, as she hugs me more.

"You shouldn't be on your own."

"It's what I need right now." I pull away and smile through my tears. I have never felt pain like this. I feel like I'm grieving. "Will you help me find somewhere?"

She nods, but I can tell she's reluctant. I also know she'll be putting in a crisis call to Charley. I pull out my laptop and sit back, starting to scan my options, flicking through the various pages of places that are apparently the perfect getaway for someone who needs peace and tranquillity. A small villa in Sorrento by the old fishing village. Quiet. Warm. Far away.

"This," I say, scrolling through the pictures.

"I'm not sure," Abbie says, unenthusiastic.

"About Sorrento, or me going anywhere at all?"

"The latter." She shifts up close to me, looking at the screen. "The problem won't go away because you do, Amelia."

"I just need some breathing space." My mobile starts ringing, backing me up, but I don't check who's calling.

"You can't avoid him forever."

"I won't." I go back to the screen and scan the flight options, taking a breath and holding it as I click to confirm the booking.

To leave this evening.

"I'll speak to Jude before I go. I need to take the Jaguar back, anyway."

"You're being a bit hasty. Why do you have to go this minute?"

"Because I can't sit here any longer crying, thinking, wondering how I could have been so stupid and why the universe has been so cruel."

"I'll get wine." Abbie sighs, standing. I look up at her. "Shit, you can't even have wine." She lowers back to the couch.

"Shame, because I'd kill for a glass." I go back to my computer and start drafting my letter of resignation. And hold my breath again when I send it to Gary. Out of fight. "Done." I snap the lid of my laptop closed.

"Okay?" Abbie pats my knee.

"No," I admit, getting up. "I'm going home to shower and pack." I leave her with a kiss, feeling her worried eyes on me as I go.

◆ ◆ ◆

I feel so numb as I pull through the gates of Arlington Hall. Mum's been calling me, and despite my messaging her to tell her I'm okay, she persists. I finally relent and answer her call as I crawl up the driveway past the stream.

"I'm okay," I say, hearing the emotion in my voice, defying my words.

"Where are you, darling? We're all so worried. Abbie's called, Charley's called. And Jude. He's called too."

I watch the evening sun shimmering on the surface of the water. It's perfect. This whole place, perfect. But not. "I'm going away," I tell her. "Just for a few weeks to get my head together." I'm flying out from Birmingham. Birmingham via Oxfordshire to drop my Jaguar off and tell Jude Harrison he's going to be a father.

"Oh, Amelia, please come home. Your dad is worried sick. He thinks you're mad with him."

"I'm not mad with Dad," I assure her. "I'm mad with myself."

"You should be with your family."

"I should be with myself," I say, letting my thoughts spill out. I don't want to make her feel guilty. Or my dad. "I need to be with my thoughts, Mum. With my body, my emotions. Everything's shifted so fast and unexpectedly." Fuck, my voice is wobbling. No. Not now. Now, I need to be together. "I've got to give myself grace and time to adjust."

"Oh, Amelia Gracie. I don't like this. Promise me you'll call every day," she begs. "I don't want you to be on your own. You're never on your own."

"I'll call every day," I assure her. "I love you." I pull up outside the grand doors of Arlington Hall and park on the end of the row of stunning cars. "I've got to go. I'll be okay." I hang up and take a long, deep breath, then get out.

"Miss Lazenby," Stan says, hurrying over when he sees me pulling my luggage out of the boot. "Please, let me."

"I have a car arriving soon," I explain. "Would you mind putting my bags in when it gets here?" I check the message confirmation. "It's a grey BMW."

He frowns, confused. "Um, yes. Of course."

"Thank you, Stan."

My lungs are starting to burn with my focused breathing as I pass through the glass doors into the lobby and see Anouska pacing on her mobile. The second she spots me, her face falls and she abandons the call. "Amelia," she says, more in question. She looks so stressed, and I naturally wonder why. "It's lovely to see you."

I force a smile. "I'm here to see Jude."

"Of course. He's in his apartment."

I nod and take the stairs, pausing when she calls my name. Glancing back, I see her shifting uncomfortably.

"He's got company." She's painfully awkward, and I laugh under my breath, frozen where I stand, my feet unwilling to take me any farther. He has company. Brilliant. "I think I've made a mistake," I say, walking back down the stairs. I told myself it was the decent thing to do. To tell him he's going to be a dad. What the hell is wrong with me and my stupid fucking choices these days?

"What?" Anouska flanks me as I walk out of Arlington Hall. "You're leaving?"

"Yes, I'm leaving."

"Then why did you come?"

I skid to a stop and think. Breathe. Face her. "I came because I thought it was the right thing to do." I hold up my car keys. *His* car keys. "And to return the Jaguar." I drop the fob in her palm and point to Stan. "I have a car arriving shortly. I'll wait out here."

"Come into the Library Bar," she suggests, hopeful. "It's more comfortable."

"Honestly, I'd rather wait out here." Anouska will never appreciate how grateful I am she didn't let me go up to Jude's apartment and further my humiliation. I reach for her hand. "Thank you."

She deflates, exasperated. "I like you, Amelia. You're smart. Please don't let Katherine be the reason you abandon whatever it is you have with Jude."

"It's not Katherine," I assure her, and she tilts her head. I laugh a little. "I wish it was just Katherine." I have an opportunity in front of me, and I fucking hate myself for wanting to take it. "May I ask you something?"

"Of course."

"Katherine thought I was a bet."

"Thought?"

"Jude led her to believe I was just another woman in one of the games they play. He didn't want her to know that he was actually using me to get back at my ex."

"I'm sorry, I'm not following."

"Jude has a grudge with my ex. Something about bad financial advice."

Her eyes close as she sighs. "Amelia, I—"

"Sorry." I shake my head. I shouldn't be grilling Anouska, making her feel bad. But then I'm talking again, unable to stop myself. "How many women before me have they bet on?"

I see her body language shift very slightly, and she glances away. "I've worked for Jude since the doors of Arlington Hall opened," she says, sounding almost wistful. "His life and soul have gone into making this place what his mother envisaged. And he has. He's had flings here and there, but they've never lasted. He's never been serious with anyone, and, believe me, that wasn't only Katherine's doing." She shrugs, uncomfortable. "He was different with you. The black cloud that's hung over him for as long as I've known him lifted, Amelia. That's got to stand for something."

It stands for revenge. "It really doesn't matter anymore."

"And it's not because of Katherine?"

My head shakes. "I have to go." I pull my phone out to check my Uber app. It's fifteen minutes away. "Do you think someone can get my bags to the main gate? I feel like a walk."

"Sure." She waves Stan over. "I hope to see you again." Her arms come up, and I walk into them, hugging her, neglecting to tell Anouska that she likely *will* be seeing me again. When I drop off or pick up my child.

If Jude wants to see it.

"Thanks for everything." Releasing her, I collect my handbag, but I only make it a few paces.

I hear someone call, "Miss Lazenby!" and I stop, looking back. A man in whites is coming towards me, drying his hands on a tea towel. "I just had to apologise personally," he says. He must catch my frown. "Sorry, I'm Henry, the executive chef here at Arlington Hall."

"Oh, hi." I turn to face him. "Apologise for what?"

"I run a tight ship, Miss Lazenby. I was mortified when I heard what happened with the Eton Mess."

"Oh God." I smile softly. "Please, mistakes happen."

"Not on my watch. She should never have been allowed the opportunity to do that."

"Who shouldn't have been allowed the opportunity to do what?" I ask, confused, seeing Anouska move in closer, listening.

"What are you talking about, Henry?" she asks.

"Katherine," he goes on. "She was seen loitering around the kitchen on the evening Miss Lazenby had her allergic reaction to the Eton Mess, which, of course, has *never* had nuts in the recipe."

"Oh God," Anouska breathes, shaking her head, while I stare at Henry in disbelief.

"Did Jude know about this?" I don't know why I'm asking. A very clear flashback of Saturday night at Evelyn's has just hit me.

I swear, if I find out you had anything to do with it, I'll ruin you.

He wasn't talking about my vandalised car. I laugh to myself, looking past Henry and Anouska into Arlington Hall. I suppose he's in there now, ruining her.

Henry looks all kinds of uncomfortable as he shifts on the spot before me. "I took it to Mr. Harrison the moment it was confirmed."

"Which was when?"

"Sunday evening."

I nod, feeling surprisingly calm. "Thank you, Henry." I turn and start the walk to the gates, keeping my eyes forward, taking in as little of my surroundings as possible. The mad bitch is welcome to him. I have more important things to deal with, and since Jude and I are no more, I will assume I'm safe from Katherine.

More important things.

Looking up at the sky, I blink, forcing the building tears back. I never ever considered having kids. I definitely didn't consider being a single mum. I have no job now, no man.

But it could be worse.

I could have gone deeper.

I'm not sure how that's possible, to have gone deeper, but I have to keep telling myself . . .

It could be worse.

And the pain in my chest *will* subside.

One day.

Hopefully before I push a little human out of my vagina and have to get my shit together. Jesus Christ, I'm going to be a mum. Am I ready? No. But I wasn't ready for Jude Harrison, and he was one bombshell after another. This little thing inside me can't possibly hurt me as much as he did.

A small ironic huff of laughter breaks past the lump in my throat as I dip into my bag and get my phone. I pull up Jude's name. Click to type out a message. Take a breath.

Hey. I wish it hadn't turned out like this. I wish such a monumental moment in my life didn't feel so wrong. I want to tell you that I don't know how it happened, but I do. I was stupid and careless and for what it's worth, I'm sorry. I'm pregnant. I'm not telling you because I expect anything. I'm only telling you because it would be wrong if I didn't. I'm going away to try and get my head around it. If you want to discuss what happens going forward, I'll be back in a few weeks. Amelia.

I slow to a stop, laughing at myself for signing off with my name. Because chances are, I could be one of many. My thumb hovers over the send icon, my laughter dying. Then a splash of water hits the screen of my phone. "Shit," I sniff, wiping my eyes. *Send it.* I can't move my thumb.

Send it.

I try to force my thumb down, one part of my mind telling me to do it, another telling me to wait, and another telling me not to tell him at all. That he doesn't deserve my openness and honesty. And I don't know which part to listen to.

"Amelia!"

My name lingers in the air behind me, and my shoulders rise to soften the impact of his voice hitting my back.

Don't look!

"Amelia!"

Instructions flood my mind, but I can't follow any of them through. *Don't look. Walk away. Send the message. Don't send it.*

I dare to glance back, wincing immediately. He's not running, not even jogging, just walking with a determined pace. Half the buttons of his shirt are unfastened, his sleeves pushed up to his elbows roughly. Dark-blond hair kicks out from his nape, his facial hair on the longer side of tidy. And when he's close enough, I see one of his eyes is black. He's been in a fight?

Jude holds up a palm, as if halting me from walking away. I would, I'd run if I could, but my legs have lost all feeling. "You're here," he breathes, slowing to a stop a few feet away.

"I brought the car back." I can't look at him. Reminding myself of all the small things I fell for isn't what I need right now.

"The car's yours."

"I don't want it," I say quickly, pushing back my shoulders, facing him. "And I no longer need it."

His jaw tics, which pisses me off. He's annoyed? "Your brother came to see me." He points to his blackened eye.

"Clark?" *Fuck, did he tell Jude?* "I . . ."

"I deserve more." He takes one step closer. "Anouska said you have luggage." Another step.

"I'm going away."

"Where?" One more step.

"That's none of your business, Jude."

Fire blazes in his gaze. "So you came here to return the car?" Another step. "That's it?"

"I would've brought the keys up to your apartment, but I was told you had company."

"Amelia."

"Were you sleeping with her?" My eyes fall down his half-buttoned shirt.

"No," he grates, coming at me.

I hold a hand up, warning him back. "Katherine put the nuts in my dessert. Why didn't you tell me?"

"I didn't want to worry you."

"Be worried that your ex-fiancée tried to kill me?" I laugh, and it's cold. "What the hell does she have over you, Jude? What's so big that you can't tell her to fuck off, even after she's hurt me?"

He blinks, shying away, and that tells me all I need to know. Katherine will never be gone. "She's out of my life, Amelia. I've told her."

"Then why the fuck is she still here?"

"Please, Amelia." He braves moving closer. "I'm fucking lost."

I back up, and he stops, his entire upper body rolling.

"Don't do this, please."

"Do what?" I ask. "Walk away from a man whose sole intention was to seduce me as payback to a man who pissed him off?"

He looks like he could explode, and that just riles me more. He has no right to be angry. He should be on his fucking knees begging for my forgiveness. Not that it would make any difference. I'm done. Which begs the question of why I'm still here.

"Pissed me off?" Jude asks through his teeth.

Something behind him catches my eye, and when I see what, my jaw muscles are instantly sore from tensing so hard. He turns to see what's got my attention. "Fuck off, Katherine," he says calmly, making her head retract in surprise.

I blink, just as Katherine's husband emerges from the double doors, taking in the scene. He looks at his wife. Then at me.

Katherine doesn't take one bit of notice of him. No. Her attention is on me. The problem. "It's for the best," she says. "You don't fit in around here."

"This isn't about you, Katherine." I'm calm. "It's so much more relevant than you."

She coughs over her indignation, looking at Jude. For backup? She doesn't get it, so returns her attention to me. "You thought you could turn him against me by having your car vandalised and blaming me?"

"I know it wasn't you." I hold Jude's gaze. "It was Leighton Steers. He found out I was sleeping with Jude. Thought I was playing dirty to win business and get ahead of him."

Jude flinches, and Katherine huffs. "Do you believe me now?" she says, going at Jude, taking his arms.

Jude stares at her blankly as she gazes at him with hope. "Rob." He takes Katherine's arm and walks her back to her husband. "Keep her the hell away from me."

I watch, stunned, as Katherine fights Jude's hold, yelling at him, and Rob observes, not a scrap of emotion on his face. "Jude, I th—"

"I said, fuck off!" His bellow echoes around the grounds of Arlington Hall, his body shaking from the force inflicted on his strung body.

"Are you forgetting what I know?" she yells. "Do you want me to tell—"

"Go to hell, Katherine," Jude snaps, passing her to her husband before shoving a finger in his face. "I don't want her near me. I don't want her here, I don't want *you* here. Grow a fucking pair, Rob. This"— he waves a hand between them—"isn't fucking love." Turning, he comes back at me, and my feet start to walk me backwards.

Are you forgetting what I know? Do you want me to tell—
Leave.

I turn and walk, checking my Uber app, wilting when I see my car is still ten minutes away.

"Amelia." Jude's breath is laboured as he comes after me, his long legs eating up the distance between us. "Stop walking away." He lands in front of me, and in a blind panic, I spin and start pacing back towards Arlington Hall. I can't hold him off for ten minutes. I can't look at him. The confliction is fucking with my head. Hate him. Love him.

Katherine's wailing like a banshee, chasing Rob's heels as he walks away from her. He gets in his car, slamming the door, and she starts hammering on the glass, screaming endless insults at him. "You always knew you were the consolation prize. You knew! You can't bail now, you can't leave me!"

Rob reverses out of the space, but he doesn't get to drive off. Katherine puts herself at the front, blocking him, yelling for him to get out.

I stop abruptly and face Jude. "What does she have on you?"

"What?"

"What does she know, Jude? What is she holding against you that meant you wouldn't tell her to fuck off the moment she started meddling?"

"Nothing. She's just—"

"The night we ate out with my friends. When Nick showed up. You saw him, didn't you? That's why you left the table, so he wouldn't see you with me and expose your lies."

Jude's nostrils flare, a familiar shade of angry reaching his eyes. "I needed time to explain to you."

I'm doing it again. Hanging around to feel more stupid. No. I hurry into Arlington Hall, Jude tailing me. Anouska looks like she might pass out with stress as she guides some guests into the Library Bar, away from all the noise, her phone at her ear. "Just keep any guests at the gates for now," she says. "We have a little situation."

Me. I'm the situation. "Can I have my keys?" I ask in a rush. I'll happily leave right now.

"Amelia," Jude pleads softly.

His hand meets my elbow, and I roll it to remove his touch. "Anouska, please," I beg as her eyes bat between us. She eventually dips into her trouser pocket and pulls out the fob, probably concluding that me leaving will take the noise and commotion with me. "Thank you." I turn on my heels and walk straight back out, noticing that staff and guests are all hovering, observing, listening.

"Amelia, for fuck's sake, please, will you just stop?" Jude grabs my arm when I'm halfway down the row of cars, and I halt, inflating my lungs as he moves around me. I keep my eyes low.

Frozen.

Still in conflict.

Tell him. Don't.

Hate him. Don't.

"I love you." His words are so gentle. But they slam into me like a wrecking ball. It's a trigger. *Love?*

"I'm over you," I say, cool, braving looking at him. His anguish is potent, but I don't believe that either.

"Really?" he asks in disbelief. "You don't love me?"

"You've ruined my fucking life!" I let it all spill out of me. "You and your sick vendetta. Why me? You could have physically hurt Nick. Broken his nose, ruined his career, but instead you took me and made a joke out of me!"

"I don't regret it," he murmurs. "I don't regret a thing. Because I found you. I was going to tell you, Amelia. I wanted to take you away and explain."

"So that's why you were so desperate to whisk me away?" He wanted to appease me before someone else told me? "I can't be with you. Everything I thought we had was shat all over by your fucking lies. It means nothing anymore. *You* mean nothing. It was a fucking joke, Jude."

"A joke? Do you think I always tell women I love them for the fun of it?"

"You don't love me." I try to shout the words, but they end up croaky and pathetic.

"I do. I love you so fucking hard." He drops to his knees before me.

"What are you doing?"

"I'm begging you not to walk away."

"Jude, get up," I demand, hating the sight of him like this. On his knees. Submissive. Weak. Dipping, I reach for his forearms, trying to get him up. Mistake. Our skin touches, and everything around me tunnels into nothing but him. Us. How fucking amazing it was. The sex, the conversations, the feelings. *But it was a lie.* I'm in a world where I don't know what's real anymore.

"I love you," he says, pulling me down to my knees before him, swapping his hold of my hands for my face, getting closer, nose to nose. Tears fall, and I can't stop them. My barriers are being battered down. He kisses me, gently but desperate, swallowing my sobs. "I love you," he whispers across my mouth. "I love you, Amelia. I'll keep saying it until you believe me. I fucking love you."

I start to shake my head, the words refusing to leave me. I can't be with him. I will never trust him. I'll always question what the truth is. I can't live like that. And I can't forgive him for doing this to me.

Jude retreats and watches me pull his hands away from my face. "It's over," I whisper calmly.

"You promised me," he murmurs. "You promised you'll always listen to me when I talk. When I'm in front of you." He holds his hand out. "Take my hand when I give it to you. I'm in front of you now, Amelia. Begging you. Take my hand, *please.*"

I move back, and his hand drops. "That was before I knew who you were." A liar. A deceptive, heartless bastard.

"No."

I get up and walk away, everything hurting. I can't see properly; my legs are jelly.

"I won't let you go," he says, landing in front of me.

I push him aside. I just want to hurt him. I want him to feel how I feel. Broken. Lost. Confused and helpless. "I hate you more than I love you, Jude. And you made that happen. That's on you. So fucking deal with it. There's no going back."

He recoils, shocked, and watches me yank the door of the Jaguar open. I fall into the seat and reverse out of the space fast, forcing Jude to jump out of my path on a loud curse.

"Amelia!"

I hold the hysteria tight inside me as I drive to the gates, faster than I should. Nelson is there, my luggage by the gatehouse. I stop and throw it in the boot with his help, and as soon as I'm back in my car, I let the dam break. Emotion comes over me like a tidal wave, and I squeeze my eyes shut, trying to clear them of tears so I can see the road better. Knots riddle my stomach, my body convulsing with sobs. So much pain. So much regret. So much anger and resentment.

I don't know how I will ever get over this. I don't know if I will ever trust again. Make myself vulnerable. Allow myself to fall in love. I hit the steering wheel with the ball of my hand on a yell. And again. And again.

And again, and again, and again, shouting past my body-racking sobs.

Ruined.

The Jaguar fills with the sound of my phone ringing. "Shut up," I snap, glancing at the dash, seeing his name. I reject his call and frantically fiddle with the knobs, desperately trying to find some music to drown out my screaming head. *Any* music. "War of Hearts" by Ruelle bursts through the speakers. Not loud enough. I turn it to max, roughly wiping my nose, laughing sardonically at the fucking irony as I take a turn in the road.

I love you.

It wasn't a lie.

I think I'm in more trouble now than I was an hour ago.

"No!" Louder.

The road becomes blurry, my head banging, my fist constantly whacking the steering wheel.

The music cuts. My phone rings.

"Fuck off!" I yell, hitting the reject button on my wheel, making the music kick back in. *Louder.* Another turn in the road approaches, and I barely slow into it, feeling the wheels pull, struggling to stay on the road.

The music dies again.

My phone rings.

My lips twisting, I accept. "Fuck off!" I yell, slamming my palm into the wheel again.

"Amelia, listen to me."

I glance at my rearview mirror as another bend appears up ahead, seeing Jude's Ferrari in the distance, a black dot on the horizon.

"I need you to slow down."

"It was all a fucking lie," I sob.

"Amelia, slow down."

Why is he talking so calmly? "I fell in love with you," I mumble. "I fell so hard. I need this pain to fuck off. I need *you* to fuck off."

"And I fell in love with you too, Amelia," he says, so gently, the roar of his engine making him even quieter. "That part wasn't a lie."

"Stop it!" I check my mirror again as I take the next bend. "Stop lying to me!"

"Listen to me. Please, please, I'm begging you. Just pull over and listen to me."

"You expect my grace?" I ask, my words breaking.

"I don't expect it. I'm begging you for it. Your grace is one of the things I adore about you. I'm depending on it. That and your heart, Amelia. Please, pull over."

His Ferrari appears in the distance behind me again, small but there, just before I take a corner far faster than I should, snivelling, swiping at my brimming eyes angrily. "I'm not stopping for you. I don't want to hear what you have to say. I'm ov—"

"Fuck!" he roars, making me flinch, the sound of him punching the steering wheel clear down the line. "My dad killed himself, Amelia."

I stare at the road ahead, my body suddenly still.

"He killed himself, and he made sure it was me who found him."

"What?"

"He hung himself."

I cough over my sob.

"I've spent years hiding that truth from my family, Amelia. I lied to people, made sure there were no question marks over his death. I couldn't shatter my mother's perfect romantic notion of what she had with him. What they'd built. I shielded her from the truth, made sure the man she loved wasn't tarnished."

I stare ahead at the road.

"He nearly lost everything because of shit advice from an amateur cowboy adviser."

"Nick," I whisper.

"He couldn't face the shame and guilt." Jude's voice cracks, and he curses a few times before he continues. "Nick's father was on the board at the bank involved. He covered up his son's fuckup and took a massive retirement package before the institution was investigated for insider trading and gross misconduct. He died before he could be put in front of a judge, and Nick walked away scot-fucking-free. No repercussions. No consequences. He changed his name and got on with his fucking life, Amelia, while mine fell apart around me."

My arms brace against the wheel, the road blurry as I drive, on autopilot.

"Dad killed himself, and I had to make sure no one would know so his life insurance and policies would pay out. I had to lie to everyone— my mum, my brothers, the police. I had to cut his fucking body down from the rafters in the garage and unravel the sheets from around his neck. I had to get the pills he took for his angina. Make it look like a heart attack. It's made me so fucking heavy, Amelia. It's made me hateful and vengeful and tired. He left me to deal with everything. Mum was my purpose, and then he took her with him too. I hated him for that. I hated him for being such a fucking coward. I've been angry for so long, limping through life wondering if I'll ever feel normal and light again. I've been broken, pretending to be together, and every day a little bit more fell away, and it was that little bit tougher to put on an act." His voice lowers to a rough, pained whisper. "You've changed everything, baby. *Everything.* You've changed *me*. Please, pull over."

My mind is a mess, my stupid heart struggling to beat. "Why didn't you tell me?"

"I had every intention. You have to believe me. I just didn't know how. I didn't want you to think it was all a game, because it wasn't. You're the best thing that's ever happened to me. You're the hope I needed. I can't lose you, Amelia."

I blink, my mind trying to process everything he's urgently thrown at me.

"You made a mess of me," he whispers. "You. Made. A. Mess. Of. Me. But it's the best mess I've ever been in. With you. Finding you."

I sob, gripping the steering wheel harder. "You made a mess of me too."

"I know, baby. And you're the most beautiful mess."

I sniff back my tears, wiping my eyes.

"I love you." His voice is hardly together. "So fucking much, and if I can't fix this, fix *us*, then there's nothing for me except pointless praise and endless loneliness."

"I'm pregnant," I murmur, my throat so tight, making the words quiet.

"What?"

"I'm pregnant, and now I'm terrified everything you just said won't matter."

"Oh my God, never. Fucking hell, never, do you hear me?" His voice cracks. "You're pregnant?"

I nod, struggling to talk through the thickness in my throat. "It sounds disgusting, doesn't it?"

"Oh, baby, it sounds really fucking wonderful, actually."

I cough over my half-sob, half-broken laugh. "I love you."

"I love you t— Fuck!" Jude's curse is loud and urgent. "Baby, the next turn is sharp, you need to slow down."

I blink, my hands numb from the tightness of my grip on the wheel.

"Amelia, baby, please, slow down."

I can't find my feet. I can't see.

"Amelia!"

I lift a heavy foot off the accelerator, but not nearly soon enough. The bend is on me fast, and I turn the wheel sharply, feeling the wheels jump across the tarmac.

"Amelia!"

The bushes scrape along the side of the Jaguar, the tyres screeching as I fight with the wheel to get the car straight.

"Amelia!"

The sun hits the windshield, and I squint, a scream bubbling in my throat.

"Fuck, Amelia!"

My feet tread around frantically trying to find the brake.

"Amelia, no!"

I'm slammed back, my arse leaving the seat, and every muscle in my arms tenses, bracing against the wheel as I'm thrown around, my cries loud. Clouds of dust burst up before me, hampering my view.

And suddenly, the engine is quiet.

Everything is still.

Staring ahead, I watch as the plumes before me float down, and the countryside comes into view again. My gasp is loud and long, my heart rate registering, thumping, my chest pumping.

"Oh my God," I whisper, looking around the car as I unclip my belt, reaching for the handle and getting out. My legs wobble, my grip of the door holding me up.

"Amelia?" Jude yells, his voice coming through the car, just as the sound of a roaring engine invades the quiet.

Jude's Ferrari flies round the corner.

Too fast.

Way too fast.

And I'm in his path.

Time stops, my scream echoing as his curses spill through the speakers, and I just catch sight of his panicked face as he yanks the steering wheel to the right, making his body catapult across the car.

The gust of wind triggered by his speed and closeness as he sails past nearly takes me off my feet. "Jude!" I yell, watching in horror as his Ferrari glides sideways down the country road, the tyres screeching, before the force becomes too much and it flips. "No!" It spins in the air countless times, sparks flying, before it hits the ground again. "No, Jude!" The sound of concrete and metal scraping is deafening, as I cling to the side of my car, numb, helpless, watching in horror as his car continuously flips across the concrete, the whole scene unfolding in slow motion, until it lands on its roof and glides down the road. It eventually slows to an eerie stop, rocking, creaking, black, dense smoke billowing up to the sky.

"No," I whisper, my feet like bricks, refusing to take me to him. "Jude!"

Chapter 30

I come into my body on a jolt and a gasp. All I can see is blue flashing lights. All I can hear are panicked yells. Chaos everywhere. Firemen bark instructions at each other; paramedics talk calmly to me; the police run back and forth up the road. I look down my body. I'm sitting down. I'm cold. *So* cold. The rustle of something makes me frown, a flash of light making me squint. I'm wrapped in a foil sheet. What's happening? I look up and around at all the strange faces, but then I see someone I recognise breaking through the crowds. Something inside surges. My confusion quickly transforms into something else. Rage. I push the foil sheet off my shoulders and stand.

"Miss Lazenby?"

I look blankly at the man coming towards me.

"Please, you must sit, you're in shock."

I start pacing towards her, shaking, my blood boiling. I feel so out of control. I want to hurt her.

As soon as I make it to Katherine, I grab her, adrenaline consuming me, and throw her to the ground. And I don't stop there, dropping to my knees, letting it all spill out of me, my arms flailing, hitting her repeatedly, yelling as I do.

I feel unhinged. Crazy.

"Amelia!" Rob appears, pulling me off her, bellowing my name over and over, as I fight against his hold, not knowing much but knowing I want to cause her pain. I want to hurt her so badly.

"You will stay away from him!" I scream, the sound bloodcurdling.

"Amelia!"

"Stay away or I'll make sure the police come after you for attempted murder."

Katherine's face falls.

"Oh Jesus," Rob breathes from behind me, restraining me. "Amelia, calm the hell down."

"Do you understand me?"

"Yes, yes, she understands you," Rob answers for Katherine as she drags herself to her feet, looking dazed, shocked, a tidy scuff marring her cheek. Did I do that? "She understands," Rob says, releasing me, blocking my path to Katherine, hands up as he backs away.

I blink and look around, willing my mind to catch up with what's happening. Where am I? What's going on?

"That's enough." An officer grabs me and pulls my arms behind my back, and I fight with him too. "Miss Lazenby, calm down!"

My breathing is shot to bits, and I relent, my adrenaline drained. "Let me go," I yell, blinking back flashbacks, the sound of screaming tyres piercing my ears.

"Just calm down, okay? This isn't helping."

I heave, my body rolling, as I'm held in place, and another officer approaches Katherine, her face concerned.

"I'm fine," Katherine murmurs, her wary eyes on me.

"You have quite the mark here." The female officer motions to the scuff on Katherine's cheek. "This is assault. Would you like to press charges?"

"No, no, it's fine, just a misunderstanding." She covers the mark. "I'm leaving."

The officer nods, and the one holding me releases my arms slowly, as if bracing himself to catch me when I fly at Katherine. "Amelia," he says, using my first name as a paramedic moves in. "You need to be checked over."

I stare at the officer. He has a kind face. Soft features, an uneven beard. "What?"

"Come." The paramedic puts an arm around me, leading me towards an ambulance.

"Where are we going?"

"You're in shock." She sits me down.

Slow down, Amelia!

I wince, feeling the force of a car speeding past me. I blink, seeing Jude's face behind the wheel. Terror. "Jude," I whisper, looking around, my mind a mess. I see the blue flashing lights. The chaos registers again. "Where is he?"

I physically jolt, as if I could have just landed back in my own body. "Jude?" Panic surges, lifting me to my feet. My eyes dart, and when I see his car on its roof in the distance, I nearly cough up my stomach. "Jude!"

I get precisely two steps before the male officer blocks my path. "Please, Miss Lazenby, you must let them work."

"I need to see him." I try to get past, but he holds my upper arms, keeping my weak body in place. "I need to see him! Please," I beg on a whisper. "I have to see him." My fight leaves me when three firemen ease a body out of the Ferrari. "No." There's so much blood. He's limp, his arms dangling. "No, no, no, no, no!" I find a new strength, shoving the officer aside and running, my legs feeling like they're trying to get through quicksand.

"Amelia!"

I run. I run so fast, the vibrations of my pounding bare feet shaking my body, and when I make it to the Ferrari, another officer catches my running form and holds me in place. No amount of fighting him will get me out of his locked arms.

"Let me go!" I scream, seeing them lay Jude on the ground. "Oh my God." His face isn't visible past the blood. "What are you doing? Take him to the hospital!" My mind is unable to compute the mess of a man before me. "Is he breathing?" This is my fault. "Tell me he's breathing!"

I see a paramedic move in and rip his shirt open, revealing endless injuries and cuts.

"Someone get her out of here," she snaps.

"No!" I screech, fighting with the hands stopping me from getting to him. "Please, no, no, no."

The officer resorts to physically lifting me from my bare feet and carrying me away. "Amelia, you have to give them space."

"Please," I beg. "Please, please, please." I'm placed on my feet, but he doesn't let go of me.

"He's not breathing!" a paramedic yells, starting chest compressions.

My hands in my hair, I turn away, unable to watch as they try to resuscitate him. "No!" I look at the heavens through my tears and scream at the sky, a high-pitched, agony-filled cry.

Chapter 31

Bursts of dandelion fluff float in the air, the sunlight catching them, making me smile a little. Just a little. I feel my face muscles pull as I do, the strain almost too much. Staring at the headstone before me, I circle my stomach, a bunch of peonies in my grasp.

Jude would want me to do this. So I set about changing the flowers and refreshing the water, before dusting off the headstone and placing a fresh bottle of Chablis down.

I hadn't planned on staying long, but it's so quiet here, so peaceful and pretty. Odd thing to say about a graveyard, I know. I lower to the grass and start plucking blades, trying to remember all the things I wanted to say. Isn't it funny how you think constantly about something, unravel your words and feelings in your head, and then when it comes to the moment you have the chance to express it, you're blank.

I'm completely blank, but the words and feelings are still there somewhere. Perhaps the universe doesn't think I need to say anything. Maybe just one thing. "He loved you so much," I whisper.

And that's really all I need to say. So I leave the rest buried wherever it's hiding inside me and get up, making my way to my car, smiling down at my feet in the long grass. But I don't see *my* feet. I see a pair of beautiful emerald-green mules. Completely impractical. And totally Evelyn Harrison.

I get in and reach down to the passenger-side floor, pulling my bag up onto the seat. Something catches my eye, tucked away in the corner.

My heart turns a little as I stretch and pick up Jude's gold-rimmed Ray-Bans. Turning them over in my hand, I see him in my mind's eye. Every glorious, unbroken, smiling piece of him.

My swallow is lumpy as I stare out the windscreen, seeing him holding my hand, running, the rain pouring down on us. I'm forced to shake my head clear and blink to stop the tears falling.

Then I slip on the shades and start the Jaguar, rolling slowly out of the churchyard.

◆ ◆ ◆

The smell is familiar—one I wish weren't. I reach the door and brace myself to see him. Brace myself for the guilt. Pushing my way in, I'm taken aback when I see he's awake, even sitting up. The nurse is redressing one of his wounds.

She looks up and smiles mildly. "Look who's wide awake."

He's been in and out for days, stressed, in pain. They even had to sedate him yesterday because he was confused, thinking he needed to get up for work. I was told it was the high dosage of meds, which were absolutely necessary after his surgeries. A broken leg, five broken ribs, a punctured lung, ruptured spleen, countless cuts, and trauma to his neck and throat, which stopped him from being able to breathe alone. The tracheotomy, done by the side of the road while I watched in horror, saved his life. It's hard to believe he'll ever be okay again.

I unload my bag on the chair and check him over. And then he smiles at me, and for the first time in days, I believe everything really can be okay. I pull the chair closer and lower, taking his hand, being careful of the needle in the back.

"Hey," I whisper, seeing he's completely with it now. He just smiles again, his bare, bruised chest rising and falling as he breathes loudly.

"He'll struggle to talk for a while," the nurse says, tapping her throat.

The tube that was poking out from his throat is gone, a large dressing covering the incision. I wince.

"Doctor removed the tube now that the swelling in his neck and throat has subsided."

I feel emotion creep up on me, and I will it back. I just have to look at him, take him all in, appreciate him.

"Are you in pain?" I ask, rolling my eyes to myself. He nods with effort. "Okay, just blink. Once for yes, two for no, okay?"

A small smile tips his lips, and it's so fucking beautiful. Then he blinks once.

"I've got some more morphine here," the nurse says, changing the bag on his drip stand. "Shall we try some water?"

I raise my brows at Jude. He's still smiling. I don't know what he's finding so amusing. Look at the state of him. He blinks once. "Yes, he'd like some water." I look around and find a beaker cup. Picking it up by the handle, I assess the spout, showing Jude. He blinks twice, and I laugh a little, as does the nurse. It's so good to see him awake, even if he's utterly broken. And he won't take his eyes off me, as if he can't believe I'm here. "Drink," I order, putting the spout at his lips and tipping. Poor thing is too incapacitated to object. He drinks, and it's painful to watch him swallow.

"Just a little," the nurse says.

"Will he be able to eat?"

"Yes, but soft foods at first." She pulls her gloves off and pops them in the bin. "Just use the buzzer if you need me."

"Thank you." I move closer, stroking the top of his hand, keeping his eyes. "Do you remember anything?" I ask. He blinks once, and I deflate, wishing he didn't, if only because of how hideous and terrifying the whole horrid scene was. "Everything?"

Two blinks.

"You swerved to miss me." I flinch away from the memory. It's replayed in my head over and over, torturing me. Seeing his car upend and spin in midair, hearing the god-awful sounds of the metal bending and screaming.

Jude blinks once. He remembers that.

"You told me about your dad."

One more blink.

I'm almost scared to ask if he remembers what *I* told *him*. I sigh and run my eyes down the length of him. I should tell him exactly what he's recovering from now he's fully with it. "You have a broken leg," I say. "The bone in your thigh. I can't remember what it's called. The femur, I think." He smiles a little, as if that's something to celebrate. "You have five broken ribs and a ruptured spleen." My face bunches, and Jude remains looking mildly cheerful as I list his numerous injuries. "Impact on your throat by something blunt meant they had to do an emergency tracheotomy. Do you remember that?" I ask, moving closer. Two blinks, and I exhale my relief. "I'm sorry," I whisper. My eyes well and Jude starts to blink over and over, shaking his head too. "I should have stopped sooner."

More blinking, more shaking.

"I love you." I'm struggling to get my words out, my throat closing. "I don't care about how I came to love you, just that I do, and that you feel the same."

He nods, telling me what I need to know.

"And do you remember what I told you before the crash?"

His eyes drop to my tummy, and I inhale. One blink. And definitely a widening of his smile.

"I'm pregnant," I say anyway, my voice tight, my words shaky. His eyes lift to mine, the green dull but still beautiful. "Disgusting?" He blinks twice, and I laugh over a sob, moving in closer, getting my face as close to his neck as I can. "I promise I'll never walk away again." I feel him squeeze my hand. "I'll always listen when you talk." Another squeeze. "See you when you stand in front of me."

A knock at the door interrupts our moment and I peek up, seeing Casey and Rhys enter. They both pause on the threshold and take in the mess of their brother on the bed. My initial reaction is to yell at them for being so blissfully unaware of their brother's turmoil. I want to tell them what Jude's burdened himself with for years to protect them from the added pain and grief he's suffered.

But that's not my call, and as I glance at Jude, I see with perfect clarity that he never will. But it's no longer a burden.

"Well, look at the state of you," Casey murmurs, approaching the bed. "Jesus."

"He can't talk." I stand, smiling at Rhys.

"How are you holding up?" he asks, dipping and kissing my cheek.

"I'm okay." Pregnant but okay.

"What the hell happened?" Casey asks, frowning at the dressing on Jude's throat. I shift, the guilt coming on strong.

And Jude doesn't miss it. "I . . ." he rasps, scowling, lifting a heavy hand to his throat and feeling around the dressing.

"Don't talk," I say, and he exhales, tired.

And, of course, he completely ignores me. "I . . . had . . . a . . . sh . . . ock."

I blink my surprise as his brothers glance back and forth between us. "A shock?" Casey asks.

Jude stares at me, blinking once, out of breath. He wants me to tell them? He blinks again. "I'm pregnant," I murmur, eyes on Jude. He smiles. His brothers nearly choke.

"And you chose to tell him that while he was driving?" Casey asks, laughing. "Fucking hell, if you'd come to me first, Amelia, I would have told you straight you'd have to sit him down and put a strong drink in his hand first."

I press my lips together, mortified, while Jude's smile remains in place, his eyes more alive.

Rhys chuckles and goes to Jude, bending over his broken body. "This is a first," he muses. "Remember all those times you whipped the back of my legs with a wet towel when we were kids?"

"F . . . uck . . . offff."

"And now you're helpless."

Casey nudges Rhys in the side. "Do you remember when he tied us up and locked us in the garden shed when Mum made that gâteau? Told her we were playing rugby at the park and ate the fucking lot himself?"

"Yeah, I remember," Rhys mutters. "I still have scars from the cable ties he used."

Jude blinks twice, shaking his head, and the three boys continue to banter, teasing each other, chatting. Or blinking.

"So, congratulations," Casey says, laughing under his breath. Jude rolls his eyes with effort.

"I just need to make a few calls." I hold up my phone. "Will you stay with him until I'm back?"

"I'm not going anywhere," Casey says, making Jude tilt his head a little. "I've taken some leave."

"Me too," Rhys pipes in. "We can help look after you." He drags his gaze across Jude's broken body. "Jesus, Jude, how fucking fast were you going in that damn car?"

Fast. Because he was chasing me. I shy away from Jude's eyes when he looks at me, slipping out of the room, guilt crippling me. Why didn't I just stop?

I put myself on a chair in the corridor and text the girls before I check in with my parents. "He's come round."

"Oh, thank God," Dad breathes. "Jenn! Jude's awake."

Clark's suddenly on the other end of the phone. "Amelia?"

"Hey."

"Fuck, you sound knackered."

I pull a hand through my hair. It desperately needs washing. "I am."

"How's he doing?"

"They've removed the tube from his throat. He's struggling to talk."

"So it'll be a while until he can repay me for the black eye I gave him."

I laugh lightly. "Probably. Have you told Mum and Dad you're expecting yet?"

"I wanted to talk to you first."

"Why?"

"Well, what with Jude and—"

"Tell them," I order. "It's great news. And, Lord knows, we all need something to smile about." My phone beeps an incoming call, and I pull it away from my ear, seeing who's calling. "Listen, I have to go. Jude's going to be fine. Go tell them about the baby. I'll call later, okay?" I hang up and take a few moments to myself. I've been ignoring Gary's calls, unable to talk to anyone, really. I'm ready. "Hi."

"Amelia," he breathes. "You've quit?"

"Resigned," I say. "I can't work with people like Leighton Steers, Gary. He's too cutthroat for me." I don't need to put myself up for that kind of competition. It wasn't about work anymore.

"Jesus, Amelia. Leighton's been suspended with immediate effect."

"What? Why?"

"He was sleeping with Tilda Spector."

I laugh. "I had an inkling. God, I thought she was smart."

"You knew? You had an inkling and didn't say anything?"

"I was too busy sleeping with Mr. Harrison," I quip, and Gary laughs lightly.

"Come back, Amelia. The partnership's yours for the taking."

I stare at the door into Jude's room, taking a breath, bracing myself to say something I never dreamed I would. "I've got something more important to do, Gary." My voice is surprisingly strong as I stand, smiling to myself. "So thank you, but no thank you." I cut the call and push my way back into Jude's room, finding his brothers both huddled around the bed, crowding him. I know he'll hate that.

They look up when the door closes, their laughter fading. "I think he needs some rest," I say, smiling when their eyebrows rise. "You're a lot."

They both laugh. "Well, I never thought I'd see the day," Casey says, coming to me and kissing my cheek. "Thank you. We can stop worrying about him now."

I let them both at me, accepting it, because Jude's not being stifled anymore. "Thank you for coming."

"You should've called sooner," Rhys says. "That's not to guilt-trip you."

"I'm sorry, I didn't know where I was, what I was doing. And then I didn't have your numbers." I eventually had Anouska call Rhys's club; it was the only way I knew how to get hold of one of them.

"It's fine." Rhys hooks an arm around my neck and hauls me into him. "We're here now. Just call if you need us."

"Thanks."

"We'll be back tomorrow," Casey says, and they both leave, but not before giving their brother a little bit more fuss and a hug each.

I go to Jude once the door closes behind them, sitting on the edge of the bed. He lifts a hand for me to take. Squeezes a little. His eyes speak to me.

"I love you more," I say, lowering and kissing his dry lips. He frowns at the bandage on my other hand. "It was infected. The antibiotics are working already. Are you hungry?"

"No." His voice doesn't quite sound like his. "I'm . . . s . . . orry."

"Stop it."

"I should . . . have—"

I put my finger over his lips, tilting my head in warning. I can't even begin to imagine the burden of his secrets. How much pain he's suffered. No more pain. I look down his body and wince.

"Can you let it go?" I ask. "The anger you have for your father, can you let it go?" Because that's the root of his hurt. That his dad bailed on life—bailed on his family—because he couldn't face being anything less than the hero his wife and sons made him. Nick's inconsequential now. He doesn't matter. But Jude's peace with his dead father does matter.

"I started to . . . le . . . t it go when . . ." He squints, swallowing, and it's painful to watch. "I st . . . arted falling for . . . you."

I clench his hand. "Good, because we're going to be a bit busy in the not-too-distant future. I don't want you distracted by hate and anger."

His smile. It lights up my world, and I inch closer, scanning his face. "I've got you," I murmur. "Always."

He nods, using what little movement he has in his hands to encourage me onto the bed. I gingerly settle beside him, every muscle tense to stop myself leaning on him and hurting him. "Stay . . . the . . ."—he swallows, flinching—". . . night."

My smile is soft. "I'm staying forever, Jude Fuckboy Harrison."

Epilogue

The physiotherapy is never-ending. Four times a week with a physiotherapist, an hour at a time, and every other day on his own. Or not on his own. I help. I know he prefers our own private sessions. Today is with the physio, Eric, who's become a regular around these parts. We're eight months into Jude's rehab. He's still suffering, but he plays it down. He can't, however, hide his limp. Eric mentioned a few weeks ago that he might not ever lose it. I saw Jude's face, his annoyance and frustration. But it's only been two months since he stopped using a walking stick. He must give it time. Time and patience.

I pass through the lobby of Arlington Hall, back from my second walk of the day, a basket of apples hanging from the crook of my arm. Anouska's assisting a party of golfers, and I weave through the bags of clubs on my way to the kitchens. I place the basket down. "Here you go, Chef. Fresh from the orchard."

"Thanks, Amelia," he calls in between beating eggs in a bowl.

I head back towards the lobby, dodging the golf bags again, and enter the Library Bar. I smile at Clinton and pick up the two glasses of nonalcoholic Amelias. "Thank you." I wrap my lips around one of the straws and suck as I head for the spa.

"Amelia." Anouska spots me and hurries over, flanking me as I walk. "I didn't want to disturb Jude while he's in his session."

"What's up?"

"The Valentine's Day menu needs approving."

"Really? We've not even served the Christmas menu."

"You know Jude's efficient."

I laugh. "Yes, I know. So what's on it?"

Anouska hands me her iPad. "Every aphrodisiac known to man."

My mouth waters as I scan the set menu. "Sounds delicious." I smile. "I approve."

"Perfect. I'll let Chef know. And while I have you, housekeeping has asked how many guests you have this evening."

"I need four rooms. Three doubles and a family for Charley, Lloyd, and the kids."

"You got it."

"Oh, and Casey and Rhys. They're coming too." I see the happiness in Anouska's eyes. "It'll be the first time all three of them have been together on the anniversary of Evelyn's death."

She nods, not needing to say anything. "And have you thought any more about making your input around here permanent?" Her eyebrows rise, and I smile as I wander off. Everyone knows I'm not going back to finance. I'm too content helping around Arlington Hall. My hands instinctively go to my bump, my inhale deep, my exhale full of peace. I'm never leaving.

Jude's still in the gym when I get there, and I watch as Eric puts resistance against his shin as he tries to raise his leg, the strain on his face painful to see. "You've got this, baby," I whisper, mentally encouraging him. He must feel I'm here, always does, because he turns his attention away from Eric mid-exercise and chat, finding me. And the session is over. Eric helps him up and slaps his shoulder, throwing a towel into his bare chest.

Jude makes his way to the door, wiping his face. I know he feels the lingering ache in his leg more acutely straight after a session. His limp is particularly obvious today, but I don't mention it.

As soon as I'm within reach, he scoops me up and carries me across his arms out of the spa. I hold the straw of his drink at his lips as I sip my own and he bobs me up and down, as if gauging my weight. "I'd say another two pounds," he muses.

"Since yesterday?"

"Yep."

"Jesus, put me down."

"This is part of my rehab. Shut up." He turns and pushes his back into a door, slurping more of his Amelia as he negotiates my body through the opening and heads down the corridor to the studios.

"I approved the Valentine's Day menu."

"What's on it?"

"Sexy food."

He chuckles. "Did you book us a table?"

"No, because I don't know if we'll be able to find a babysitter for the night."

His smile is blazing as he helps himself to his drink again. "If we can't, we'll get room service." Turning again, he pushes his way into one of the studios.

A smiling Glenda greets us, her hippy-dippy aura drenching the room. "Children," she sings, opening her arms. "Welcome. Please, please, join the circle."

There's a gap on the other side of the room, in between two fellow pregnant women. Jude walks us round and places me down by the mat laid out, taking the drinks and putting them out of the way. "Sit," he says, helping me down to my arse. I wince and hold my breath as he lowers behind me, not because I'm uncomfortable, but because I know he is. I've given up nagging him. He wants to do this. In fact, this antenatal class that's been running weekly at Arlington Hall since he was discharged was entirely his doing. And, actually, very popular—hence the room's full. "I'm fine," he whispers, cradling me between his thighs. His hands come under my arms and rest on my huge pregnant belly, his chin on my shoulder.

I glance around, smiling at the smiles coming back at us. Rachel is dead opposite me, Clark behind her. I wave, and she waves right back.

Placing my hands over Jude's, I breathe in deep, feeling him doing the same. Glenda's energy is something else. You can't help but be serene when you're around her. "Are you sure I can't ask her to be our full-time baby coach?" Jude whispers in my ear.

I chuckle. "Are you afraid?"

"No," he says quickly. "The only thing I'm afraid of since I met you, baby, is your father. Speaking of which, when are they arriving?"

"Teatime."

"Can't wait."

I nudge him as Glenda starts circling her arms up into the air, her eyes closed, her chest expanding.

"Are you ready for your breathing exercises?" Jude asks.

"Always ready."

"Good. They'll come in handy when I can bang you again with all hard eight inches of me."

I chuckle. "Your seven inches did just fine this morning."

"My *eight* inches will do just fine again in about an hour's time, when I get you back upstairs."

I smile and lean back into him, holding his arms where they lie over my enormous belly.

"Close your eyes," Glenda says, all soothing and soft.

And I do. Zoning out. Enjoying the quiet. And the feel of Jude blanketing me and our bump.

"Ready?" Jude asks as he wanders out of the dressing room, fastening the buttons on his shirt. He smiles when he finds me standing in front of the floor-length mirror putting my earrings in. "God, you're fit as fuck."

I laugh as he crowds me from behind and mauls my neck, his palms stroking over my belly. "Charley, Lloyd, and the kids just arrived, and Abbie's running a bit late."

"Uh-huh," he mumbles on my throat. "Your parents?"

"Working their way through the cocktail menu in the Library Bar with Grandma and Grandpa."

"They did that the last time they were here. And the time before that. And the time before that."

"They can only manage four per visit, and even then I have to escort them to their rooms in case they take a drunken tumble."

"Let me look at you," he orders, turning me around and taking my hands, standing back so he can drink me in. I do the same. Beige trousers. White shirt, open at the collar. His hair a beautiful mess. *Gorgeous.* "Disgusting," he murmurs around a smile, his eyes on my enormous belly. My grin is so wide. "You know"—he pulls some of the stretchy black material of my dress—"I think we should have another."

"Fucking hell, Jude, do you want to let me squeeze this one out first?"

He beams from ear to ear. "I didn't think I could fancy you more." He hunkers down, and I can tell by his poorly hidden wince that it's uncomfortable. "Turns out I can."

"Good for you." I scrunch my nose and rub it with his. "Stop doing things that hurt your leg."

"My leg's fine." Cupping my face, he slams a kiss on my lips. "Let the weekend family shenanigans begin." Claiming my hand, he leads us out of the bedroom and past the birthing pool that's been sitting in the middle of the lounge for the past two weeks.

"Are your brothers here?" I ask, sliding a hand under my bump to hold it, the pressure getting to me these past few days. I permanently need to pee.

Jude checks his phone. "Just pulling in. Casey's got to fly out to Qatar early hours, but Rhys is staying the night. He's not got a game until next weekend."

"How's he been lately?" That sex tape, unbelievably, never showed up. But Rhys hasn't learned his lesson and is—in Jude's words—still putting it about. Jude looks back at me with raised brows. That's my answer. I don't know how a top athlete does it and still plays so well. "Active, then?" I ask.

"You know Rhys. He could charm the knickers off a nun."

Laughter erupts out of me. "Shit."

"What?"

I stop, forcing Jude to a stop too, his face a map of worried lines. "A bit of pee just came out." I drop his hand and hurry back through the bedroom to the bathroom, groaning when I lower to the seat, just that change of position moving me from not needing a wee at all to being desperate.

"Want one of these?" Jude waves a nappy from the doorway on a grin.

"Stop it," I grumble.

"Want some clean knickers?"

"Please."

He disappears and returns moments later with a pair, holding them at his nose. "Smell clean."

"Sicko," I tease, taking them and shimmying them on as Jude holds my elbow. "Okay, I'm ready. Don't make me laugh."

He chuckles, leading me back out.

This time, we make it down to the Library Bar without any accidents, although when my mother hugs me, I fear the force of it might squeeze some more pee out.

"Look at you," she gushes, holding tight.

Jude makes his way around everyone saying his hellos, finishing with Grandma. She's the biggest Jude fan of all. I smile over Mum's shoulder as she practically yanks him down to the chair next to her and sniffs him.

"Grandma," I yell. She does that every time—sniffs him before she glowers at me. She knew about Jude before she even knew about him.

"How are you feeling?" Mum asks, breaking away and handing me over to Dad.

"Heavy," I quip. "Hey, Dad."

"I've been thinking," he says as he hugs me around my giant stomach.

"Oh God."

"About names."

I peek at Clark and Rachel, who both give me looks to suggest they've had this already. "What about names?"

"You need something strong. Give the kid the best chance."

"Okay, Dad." I won't ask him for suggestions.

Jude comes to save me, bringing his brothers too, making all the introductions, since it's the first time my family and friends have had the pleasure of the other Harrison boys.

"Well," Charley says, joining me. "More mercy needed." She sticks her tongue in her cheek as she takes in Jude's brothers. "Was there something magical in the air whenever their mum and dad screwed?"

I choke on nothing, laughing. And another bit of pee escapes. "Fuck," I hiss.

"Pissed yourself?" Charley asks. "Get used to it. After two, you'll never want to laugh, cough, or sneeze ever again."

I indicate to Jude that I'm popping upstairs again, and he shakes his head, mouthing, "Again?"

I pout and leave, hurrying back up to our apartment, or going as fast as I can. I change, pop a spare pair of knickers in my purse, and go back down. Abbie's coming through the doors as I reach the bottom of the stairs, looking a bit flustered. "Hey," I say. "What's up?"

She looks to the ceiling. "Hightower is running late. Something about a work emergency."

"Oh, well, that's okay. At least you're here." I link arms with her and start walking us to the Library Bar. "Everything going okay with him?" They've been dating for record time.

Abbie smiles, but it's tight, telling me there's something. "Want to have lunch next week?" she asks.

Oh dear. Maybe not so well. "Sure, if I'm still here. Everything okay?"

She looks down at my belly, smiling. "Everything is fine," she says, not convincing me. "I still can't believe you've got this."

"Me either," I admit as we enter the bar. It's so lovely to see Jude with all my family together. It's even lovelier to see Jude smiling, especially on a day I know he has always dreaded. Peace. It's beautiful on him.

"Fucking hell," Abbie breathes, coming to an abrupt halt.

"What?" I do not like the shock on her face. "Abbie?"

"That man," she whispers.

I look to where she's staring. "Casey?"

"Oh my God, he has a name."

"That's Jude's brother."

"What?" she blurts, just as Casey looks this way. His face falls. I'm so fucking confused.

"You know him?"

Abbie spins and leaves the Library Bar, and I hurry after her. Or wobble after her. "Abbie, what's going on?"

She paces up and down, laughs out loud, then slaps a hand over her forehead. "That's him," she says. "The best fuck of my life."

I gasp, my mouth falling open. "Casey?" I hiss. "The man from Paris?"

"Jude's brother?" she says, high-pitched.

And then Casey appears, looking between us. "You know each other?" he asks, clearly as stunned as Abbie.

"Um, yeah," I say, just as Jude finds us too, obviously wondering what the hell is going on. "This is Abbie." I can't believe this. "Abbie, this is Casey." And now they know each other's names.

"Fuck," Jude breathes, his finger waving between them. "You two . . . Abbie's the girl . . . Paris?"

Neither Casey nor Abbie confirms it—they just stare at each other as everyone else piles out of the Library Bar, joining the reunion in the lobby, everyone murmuring their concern. "Everything okay?" Mum asks.

Just as Hightower walks in. "Oh Jesus," Abbie breathes.

"And this is Abbie's boyfriend," I declare on a sing of delight. It's the nerves. Must be. Casey steps back. Abbie wilts.

"Welcome, everyone!" I look at Jude, like, *What the hell do we do with this?*

He shrugs, as lost as me.

And some pee trickles out. "Fuck, I'm peeing myself again."

"Amelia!" Mum scorns me as I rootle through my bag and whip out my spare knickers.

But then a loud whoosh rings through the lobby, and I still, just as I feel a gush. Then hear a splash. "Oh," I breathe, peeking down at the puddle I'm standing in.

"Yeah, I don't think those knickers are gonna do the trick," Rhys says, as Jude rushes over.

"And here we go," he says, cool as can be.

"But we have another three weeks!"

"Something tells me we don't, baby." Scooping me up, he heads for the stairs.

"Rachel should be first!"

"You're bursting my eardrums, Amelia."

"We're not ready!"

Jude winces at my sound level, giving me adoring green eyes. "Baby, we are so fucking ready."

I puddle in his arms, my bottom lip sticking out. "We are?"

"For anything."

My lips push into his rough cheek, emotion taking me by surprise. "I love you," I mumble, my voice broken. I don't know whether it's the sudden movement, but my stomach clenches, the pressure below increases, and a very intense desire to push overcomes me. "Shit."

"What?"

"I think I need to push," I say, panicked, as Jude walks casually to the stairs with me in his arms.

"Already?" he asks, scanning my face.

"Don't sound surprised, kids," Grandma chirps. "Your dad fell right out of me into the loo."

"Oh my God," I breathe. Dad gasps his horror, and Clark and Grandpa cackle like old women.

"I definitely need to push," I blurt, the pressure bearing down.

"Breathe," Jude orders. "Come on, you've done this before."

"Have I?" I start to pant. "Did we have a baby already, and I missed it?"

He looks at me tiredly as he takes the stairs, apparently in no hurry at all. "In classes."

I start to pant. "The pool's not even full."

"We can fix that."

"I don't think there's time." My stomach tightens and a wave of unbearable pain washes over me. "Oh my God," I gasp, gritting my teeth, trying to keep up with the breathing. "Oh Jesus, Jude, it hurts." The pain's taken me by surprise, not because I naively thought I'd sail through this with none, but simply because of how fast it's come on.

He backs through all the doors to the apartment. "Do you want to sit, stand, walk?"

"I don't know," I admit as he lowers me to my feet. "Stand. No, walk." I hold my belly as Jude starts to fill the pool, calling Glenda as he does.

A long, strangled moan falls past my lips, my hand shooting out to grab the cabinet. Jude looks up from where he's kneeling by the pool. My eyes close, my hand waving his concern off. "Shit," he curses. "Glenda's not answering."

He abandons the pool and comes to me, hooking his arms through mine from behind, taking most of my weight. I'm grateful.

"I need to walk."

"Then let's walk," he murmurs, starting to step slowly, letting me set the pace. Three steps in, I have to stop again. "Another one?" he asks gently, and I nod jerkily, my cheeks ballooning. "Come on, baby, I've got you."

I release a racked sob, his words, *our* words, hitting me in the feels along with the contraction. "This isn't how I planned it," I cry. "It's supposed to be calm and serene and enjoyable." Everything feels like a total rush.

"Everyone is here, Amelia. The whole fucking family. *Both* sides. That's fucking amazing."

The pain passes, but the desire to push remains, the heaviness bearing down unreal. "Walk," I say, clinging to his arms as he starts to move us again, taking us round the lounge a few times until the pool is suitably full. He stops me by the side and puts my hands on his shoulders for support, then bends and takes the bottom of my dress, pulling it over my bump and head.

After removing my bra and knickers, he lifts me over the edge. "Warm enough?" he asks, holding my hand as I feel my way down. I nod and settle, the signs of another contraction on its way. I wave my arm, silently demanding his hand, closing my eyes, bracing myself. It's another intense one, the pain like nothing I've felt before.

"I'm not sure I'm built for this," I mumble, my head resting on the back of the pool, my eyes closed. I'm so tired already.

"What? Labour?" he asks, pulling my hair into a high ponytail.

"Yeah."

"You've got no choice. My kid's inside you. I need you to push it out."

I blindly reach back and smack him on the head. "It hurts."

"Try being involved in a high-speed RTA."

"Jude," I hiss, smacking him again. He chuckles. "You're so together."

"One of us has to be," he replies. I hear a ringing tone. He's trying Glenda again. And I can't tell you how relieved I am when I hear her chirpy voice answer. "Amelia's in labour," Jude tells her, still so fucking calm. I suspect inside is a different story, but I appreciate his effort. "Yeah, can you turn around and come back? I don't know, maybe every couple of minutes. I think she's been in labour longer than she thinks."

I frown and open an eye.

"She's been pissing herself all day."

I snarl, and he smiles, as I go back to breathing, feeling calmer. Until another wretched wave of pain comes out of nowhere and takes me out. "Oh. My. God," I scream, the sound dragging out for an eternity.

A loud knock breaks through my noise.

"Come in," Jude yells, and a second later, Abbie's by the pool.

"The best fuck," I mumble drowsily, sounding drunk. "It's Casey."

"No shit." Abbie shakes her head in exasperation. "But that's a crisis for another day. How are you doing?"

"In fucking agony," I grunt. "It's his fault." I point a limp finger at Jude. "I only came for a spa day." I frown to myself as Abbie folds over laughing and Jude snorts from behind me. "Fuck off, both of you."

"Okay, enough of the sass, thank you, missus," Jude says, serious.

"I'm a miss."

"Maybe one day I'd like to change that." He raises his brows, and I huff my revulsion.

"Sounds disgusting."

"Can I get you anything?" Abbie asks.

"A gag?" Jude says.

"Oh no," I gasp, feeling another one coming. "No, no, no." I slam my eyes shut and circle my belly with my arms, riding the excruciating pain. "I need to push!" I strain the words as I bear down, the urge overcoming me. "Arhhhhhhhh!"

"Fuck." Jude rips his shirt open.

"What are you doing?" I pant.

"Yes, what the hell are you doing?" Abbie asks, as he kicks his shoes off and dips to tug his feet out of his socks before wriggling out of his trousers.

"I'm getting in." He's in the pool before I can protest, not that I can anyway, another awful contraction claiming me and bending my body, ballooning my cheeks.

"Oh God, this is horrific," I wail, pushing down through the pain, feeling things moving down below. "I need to move."

"Move?" Jude asks. "To where?"

"I don't know, but I need to move." I start scrambling to my knees and fall onto my palms, rocking my hips from side to side. "Oh, that's good," I mumble. "Rub my back."

"Yes, princess," he says sardonically, but kneels behind me, both his hands rubbing wonderful circles on my lower back. I fall into a bit of a trance. In fact, I'm pretty sure I doze off as Jude massages me and I sway. "I never thought I'd ever have you on your hands and knees in front of me and *not* get a hard-on."

"Okay, I'll leave you two to it," Abbie says, as Jude laughs her out. "Call me if you need me."

"Your arse looks fucking amazing, baby."

I groan, rocking some more, my head swinging. "I need to move again." I'm restless, constantly anticipating and dreading the next wave of pain.

"Where to?"

"I don't know." I cling to him as he helps my upper body lift until I'm on my knees. "Like this," I say, flexing my neck as Jude gets in front of me, mirroring me. I blink my tired eyes and take a moment to look at him. All of him. His eyes, his nose, his gorgeous mouth, his wide shoulders, his perfectly formed chest and stomach. And I feel him, dragging my fingertips across his flesh, from his lower tummy, up to his nose.

"Are you trying to turn me on?" he asks softly, holding my waist.

"Are you turned on?"

"You always turn me on." Lowering his mouth to mine, he kisses me gently, and I sigh around it, content amid my pain.

"Does your leg hurt?"

He blinks twice.

"I love you," I mumble, feeling another coming. He must too, perhaps because I become rigid.

"Love you more," he whispers. "Are you happy here?"

I shake my head, and somehow he translates that to me telling him I want to be on my back. He clenches my hand, his eyes on my belly as it undulates. His wonder is such a sight.

"It's coming," I gasp, tensing, taking in air, getting ready for a push. My wide eyes meet Jude's, and he nods his encouragement. "I've got you," he whispers, and with that it hits me, and I yell at the ceiling, feeling everything in my body push down. "Come on, Amelia," he says, calm but loud. "Push, baby, push."

The heat, the pressure. It feels like my head is going to pop off my shoulders.

Jude moves to between my spread legs, his arms extended so I can still hold his hands. "Go on, Amelia," he cheers. "Keep going. I can see a head."

"What?"

"Push!"

I listen and keep going, pushing so hard, every muscle yelling. And I push more, and some more, all the while watching as Jude cheers me on, my breathing laboured, my shouts loud. But I keep going. And suddenly the pressure subsides, my lungs scream, and I drag in air. And then there's silence.

I gasp.

"Fuck, she's here," Jude whispers, moving calmly and efficiently, handling our baby like he's done this a million times.

"She?" I breathe, all pain gone and complete wonder finding me.

"She." He brushes his hand over her face, prompting the crying to start. "Oh, my darling girl," he whispers, dipping and kissing her forehead. And I'm a fucking goner, emotion joining my wonder, tears streaming down my cheeks. "Go to Mummy," he says, putting her on my chest before reaching for a towel and laying it over her back.

She settles, and I stare down at her. Amazed. And instantly in love. "Well, hi," I whisper, stroking the top of her head softly with a fingertip as Jude comes and sits next to me, hooking an arm around my shoulder, kissing my temple.

"Well done, baby," he says, his other hand across her back. "You did great."

He's a laugh. I don't know what I expected, but he just breezed through that like a bloody pro. Another milder wave of pain travels through me, and I hold my breath, feeling the placenta come away. "Oh God," I whisper, grimacing. "I can't believe you're in here with me."

He hushes me and sighs, and we both just sit in silence for a time, staring at her.

The three of us.

"It's a girl," I say, looking up at him. "We agreed if it was a boy, I'd name him. If it's a girl, you would."

Jude nods, eyes still on our baby. But he doesn't speak, not for a while.

So I do instead.

"Evelyn," I whisper.

Jude swallows, his eyes darting to mine. They're full of tears. "Really?"

"What else would it be?"

He coughs a little over a light sob, reaching for her cheek and stroking softly. "I didn't think love at first sight was a thing. And now it's happened to me twice," he says quietly. "Shit, she's just so fucking beautiful."

"She is." Like the most beautiful thing I've ever seen. And neither of us can stop staring at her. This little girl who's changed everything. Jude works his big finger into her hand, and watching her wrap her little fingers around it hits me hard in my heart. I look at Jude as he stares down at Evelyn. Wonder. That's beautiful on him too.

"Oh, we have a baby!" Glenda bursts in, killing the moment.

"A girl," I say calmly.

"Oh, how wonderful. Well done, Mum and Dad."

Mum? Weird. *Dad?* I look at Jude and grin.

"So fucking weird," he admits, shaking his head.

"Do you want to cut the cord, Dad?" Glenda asks, snipping the scissors.

Jude moves in, and I smile when I see him wince as he chops down. "Send the placenta to the kitchen."

"What?" I blurt.

Chuckling, he comes back to us and dots kisses between our heads. "I better go let everyone know." He rises, leaving us with Glenda as he dries off and secures a towel around his waist.

She wraps our girl up and helps me out of the pool, handing her back to me when I'm in a robe and comfortable on the couch.

Then everyone piles in. Literally, everyone. There are swoons coming at me from all directions. Abbie's awkward as hell, as is Casey, both of them at opposite ends of the room to each other. When Abbie catches my eye, she shakes her head in despair, while Hightower throws her constant questioning looks. Jesus, what a shock.

"I want another," Charley declares.

Lloyd snorts, gathering up Elijah and Ena. "Two works for me."

"Oh my, look at her." Mum swoops in, hearts in her eyes. "Oh, Dennis, look, just look at her."

I smile up at my dad. I've never seen him look so smitten. "Perfect." He goes to Jude and shakes his hand. "Congratulations. You've made me a very happy man."

"A happy granddad," Jude says.

"My God, I'm a granddad."

Jude comes to us, dipping. "Let me." He takes Evelyn from my arms. "I'll get her dressed. She's getting all embarrassed being naked in front of everyone."

I smile as I watch him wander off to the bedroom, our tiny girl held to his big naked chest. A natural.

"How was it?" Rach lowers down next to me, her own belly causing her mobility issues.

"Like hell and heaven wrapped up in one confusing mix of fucking agony and complete bliss."

"Cup of tea?" Grandma asks.

"I'd kill for one." I exhale, resting back. "Sorry for ruining the family dinner." I spot Abbie heading for the kitchen after Grandma.

"She's gone for wine," Charley says. We both watch as Casey follows her, both of us throwing curious looks at each other. I find Hightower. He's talking to Rhys. Being distracted?

"Go listen," I order on a whisper hiss, nudging Charley. "I want to know what's said."

"Stop it."

"Oh, please."

"No."

"What's going on?" Rach asks, looking between us.

"Nothing," we sing in unison.

"Spoilsport," I mutter, but my indignance is forgotten when Jude comes round the back of the couch, bringing his arms over me and lowering Evelyn back onto my lap. "Oh, she's dre—" I gasp, pushing my back into the couch, trying to get away from my brand-new daughter, like she's just turned into a monster. "What the hell?" I breathe, staring at her cute little romper.

Jude appears in front of me. On his knees. He smiles. "Well?" he asks. "Will you?"

My eyes drop back down to our baby girl, who has a question emblazoned across her romper.

WILL YOU MARRY DADDY?

"Oh God."

Jude produces a ring.

"Oh God!" I pick Evelyn up and cradle her to my chest, the tears brimming in my eyes. Everyone is smiling, all attention pointed this way. "You all knew?"

"Yes, they knew," Jude confirms. "I was going to take you to see Mum and Dad, but little missy here decided to come early. So here we are." He takes my chin, directing my face to his. "On my mother's memorial. And now our daughter's birthday."

"Jude," I whisper, tears trickling down my cheeks.

"That's not an answer." He shuffles closer, holding the ring out, his face so gorgeous and perfect and hopeful. "I dare you to say yes, Amelia Gracie Lazenby." His voice drops to a murmur. "I fucking dare you."

I choke over a sob, and he smiles, slipping the ring onto my finger before crowding me and kissing my tears away, moving down to my mouth. "I fucking dare," I whisper against his lips, breathing every bit of him into me, wondering how we went from staying the night to staying forever. With a baby girl too.

It's a stupid question.

Jude Harrison is how.

And accepting his indecent invitation, surrendering to him, was the best decision I've ever made.

ACKNOWLEDGMENTS

Thank you to Amazon Publishing for being so fantastic to work with, and a special shout-out to Lauren and Sasha. What a breeze you've been! And once again to my readers, because there will never be enough thank-yous for you.

I hope you enjoyed your stay at Arlington Hall.

Love,
JEM

ABOUT THE AUTHOR

Photo © 2019 Abby Cohen Photography

Jodi Ellen Malpas is the #1 *New York Times* and *Sunday Times* bestselling author of numerous series, including This Man, This Woman, One Night, and Unlawful Men, as well as the stand-alone novels *For You, Perfect Chaos,* and *Leave Me Breathless,* among many others. She is a self-professed daydreamer with a weak spot for alpha males. Her captivating storytelling and complex characters have earned her a dedicated following, and her ability to weave intense emotions with sizzling romance and heart-pounding drama ensures her stories resonate with readers globally. Jodi was born and raised in England, where she lives with her husband, boys, and Theo the Doberman. For more information, visit www.jodiellenmalpas.co.uk.